Signs of Paradox

Signs of Paradox

---

*Irony, Resentment, and
Other Mimetic Structures*

ERIC GANS

Stanford University Press
Stanford, California
1997

Stanford University Press
Stanford, California
© 1997 by the Board of Trustees of the Leland Stanford
Junior University
Printed in the United States of America

CIP data are at the end of the book

Published with the assistance of the Dean of
Humanities, University of California at Los Angeles

pour Monique
en souvenir de Binic

Acknowledgments

The minimalist perspective of originary thinking provides relief from the particularism of recent years. Humanity is one in its very capacity for self-mutilation. It is only because we are mimetic to the point of paradox that we invent, or discover, a transcendental guarantee for our differences.

The unique event in which the verticality of human language emerges from the horizontal world of appetite is a moment of liberation reenacted in every subsequent act of representation. We must *think* our uniqueness that until now only religion has articulated.

*

The present work was begun under a travel grant from the Albert and Elaine Borchard Foundation of Woodland Hills, California. I thank the foundation and its director, Dr. Willard Beling, for giving my wife and me the opportunity to live in the Château de la Bretesche during the autumn of 1992. I would also like to express my gratitude to Dean Pauline Yu of the UCLA Humanities Division for her generous personal gesture of support toward the publication of this volume.

I am also grateful to my present and former students at UCLA. I have learned much about humanity from their work, and more from their friendship.

Eric Gans
August 6, 1996

Contents

Signs of Paradox

Introduction:
Why Generative Anthropology?

The departmental structure of the university provides us with a preliminary model of human knowledge, as well as of human self-knowledge—anthropology in the broad sense. At UCLA, the College of Letters and Science, which houses the agencies of theoretical learning as opposed to the practical world of the professional schools, comprises four divisions: Humanities, Social Sciences, Life Sciences, Physical Sciences. The last two touch on the human importantly, but peripherally. We are certainly physical bodies, and living ones, but even our most striking anatomical and physiological differences from our fellow creatures require no special sciences of their own. The crucial separation is rather between the two domains of the specifically human, the social sciences and the humanities.

The principle of this separation is a matter of language. Social scientists cannot ignore the human use of signs. But language for them is just another human trait, one that fortuitously allows them to ask people their opinions directly, rather than having to deduce them from consumption or voting patterns. The humanities, on the other hand, are devoted to the study of texts. Even today, at UCLA as at most universities, the fine arts occupy a separate school from the humanities because music and art, cinema, even theater, are not fully textual, not centered on a privileged use of language that can be studied independently of a scene of performance.

The distinction between the humanities and the social sciences is not historically symmetrical. The study of privileged texts is older than writing; it is the origin of the written texts themselves. In contrast, although systematic economics goes back a century earlier and political science—or at any rate "political theory"—is at least as old as Plato, social science as a well-defined domain of knowledge is not much more than a century old. It could not define itself as a way of thinking before the emergence of the most characteristic social science of all, sociology.

The humanities have endured because their discovery procedure has continued to be productive: texts recreate in their readers an echo of the crisis of human origin. The social sciences, for their part, claim to unearth crises in the social order that can neither be discovered nor understood by textual means. Durkheim's pioneering studies dealt with suicide as a reflection of "anomie" in market society. The phenomenon of suicide is not a public issue; it affects but a small number of individuals. Yet for the sociologist, the suicide rate, detectable only by counterintuitive quantitative methods, reveals the current level of disorder in the society as a whole. Texts, even contemporary texts, exemplify preconceived ideas of social reality, whereas empirical methods modeled on those of biological science—whose prestige in the late nineteenth century reflected its new successes on the medical front—uncover its hidden truth.

Since Durkheim's day, the humanities and the social sciences have engaged in a tug-of-war over the human, the rope going now one way, now the other. A generation ago, the deconstructionists' aggressive textuality crossed the border into scientific territory; today, in the multicultural era, the structures of textuality itself have become documentary evidence for the analysis of power relations.

At the intersection of these two academic visions of the human we find not a branch of scholarship but religion, which grants the same privilege to the text as the humanist but claims to find in it the objective truth studied by the scientist. Equally opposed to those who believe in texts that do not correspond to reality and those who believe in a reality that does not correspond to texts, religion takes their correspondence to be transcendentally guaranteed. This is a position neither humanists nor scientists can accept; the first, because it imposes intolerable limits on reading, the second, because it imposes intolerable limits on empiricism.

The humanist's approach to the religious text is to read it as a fiction, keeping its reality-claim in brackets—"the Bible as literature." This reading purportedly universalizes the meaningfulness of the religious text by treating its symbolic structure independently of any particular system of belief. In contrast, to the social scientist, the religious text is not the expression of a universal symbolic truth but the symbolic expression of a particular truth. The text is understood within the ritual context of which it is a part as a "behavior" functioning to preserve a given social order.

For the humanist, the text reflects a universal subjective reality; for the scientist, a particular objective reality. These positions are incompatible in the everyday world, where we are obliged to distinguish between subjective and objective, particular and universal. But they coincide at the moment of human origin, when the emission of the sign creates the subjective from the objective, the transcendental from the immanent. Hence reflection on the origin of the human—originary thinking—has always been the central focus of religion, and of religion alone. Religious ritual and myth commemorate the origin, not of the cosmos, however cosmic their reference, but of humanity.

At the origin, language coincides with the human reality to which it refers because it undecidably generates this reality and is generated by it. The originary hypothesis that is the foundation of generative anthropology is the first rigorous theorization of this originary moment, the common basis of both the humanities and the social sciences.

It is not illegitimate to wonder whether the separate methods of these two domains of knowledge that intersect only at the hypothetical originary point are not best maintained apart. Does not their assimilation violate the primary human necessity of differentiation as explained by the originary hypothesis itself? On the one hand, there are texts, a term that in its extended sense includes all the noninstrumental elements of human culture; and on the other, there are "data" that inform us of the operation of the instrumentalities that mediate between ourselves and the physical world. One must read texts, and one must collect data, and clearly the same methods cannot apply in both cases. On the contrary, centuries of human endeavor have gone into perfecting the methods used in each. How can we presume to disregard their methodological separation to concentrate on an unknowable originary moment?

It will not surprise those familiar with generative anthropology to learn that the answer to so fundamental a question should be not given directly but deferred. The purpose of originary thinking is not to supplant other modes of thought, but to provide a common point of departure that persists as a link between them.

It is tempting to offer one's readers a "methodology"—a term whose apparent seriousness masks its conflation of a technique (method) with a theory that purportedly justifies that technique (-ology). Generative anthropology neither is nor has a methodology. It provides no formula for either reading texts or gathering data. The rule of thumb of originary thinking is as simple as the word "anthropology": to remain always attentive to the human, understood as the paradoxical generation of the transcendent from the immanent, the vertical from the horizontal. Or lest the term "paradox" pose a stumbling block to social scientists, for whom the aporia that fascinates the humanist is simply proof that one has formulated one's hypothesis incorrectly, they may note that what I discuss in the following chapter under the rubric of "mimetic paradox" was originally formulated as "mimetic *crisis*." Paradox is the counterpart in the sphere of representation of crisis in the sphere of reality. Both are projections of the originary event of the human upon the different axes of text and world—the projections that define and distinguish the humanities and the social sciences.

The deconstructionists who, like their New Critical ancestors, purport to find everything in the text, are incapable of theorizing the emergence of the textual within the world—the very emergence by whose paradoxical structure they define textuality. Nor can the mathematical sophistication of chaos theory and the like by means of which social scientists seek to quantify the notion of crisis take the place of an anthropology that understands language and other forms of representation as specifically human means of deferring specifically human crises. To understand human origin as the punctual event that invents and discovers both crisis and paradox, crisis as the realization of paradox, paradox as the solution to crisis, requires a theory of its own.

The degree to which the disciplines of the humanities and the social sciences alike are reified as "methodologies" depends on their distance from the central core of the human. We may affirm with full confidence that "in the last analysis" they are all branches of the nonmethodology that takes this central core as its subject matter. But we no longer have the luxury, either as individuals or as a community, of entertaining last analyses. On the contrary, generative anthropology is intended as an antidote to the eschatologies, religious and secular, that have hitherto monopolized the human center. So we must forever defer our statement of the ultimate purpose of originary thinking. The effect of the most fundamental form of thinking on our overall system of thought must remain undecidable. But this very undecidability—this unpredictable addition of new degrees of freedom to the system—fulfills the theory's purpose according to its own conception of human culture: the deferral of violence through representation.

*

Like humanity and its language, generative anthropology has its own genesis. René Girard's originary scene, ambivalently monogenetic and polygenetic, universal and particular, situates the human community on the periphery of a circle surrounding a sacred center.[1] What this scene lacks is the linguistic sign by means of which the peripheral humans could avoid violence by deferring their mimetic-appetitive appropriation of this center. Whence my formulation in *The Origin of Language* of the "originary hypothesis" that the sign originates as an "aborted gesture of appropriation."[2]

But it is not enough to claim that language must be a part of any scene of human origin; why need there be a scene of origin at all? The value of our answer to this fundamental question of anthropology is proportional to its parsimony. Since formulating the originary hypothesis, I have continued to work toward its minimization, most recently by subordinating the naturalistic model of the originary scene to the fundamental triangular model of mimesis (see Chapter 2).

It should suffice to argue that because language intrinsically requires self-consciousness, it cannot emerge unconsciously. But this a priori, even if accepted, does not suffice to permit us to construct a scene of origin. Another argument is that although all higher animals have communication systems, "languages" of a kind, none have anything resembling religious observances, with their uniquely human scenic event-structure that can most parsimoniously be derived from a single ancestral event. But the historical evidence can never be sufficient to justify the reconstruction of an originary "big bang" that is by definition incommensurable with this evidence. Backward extrapolation cannot offer a compelling reason for abandoning the standard (non)explanations of human origin.

The skepticism that greets the originary hypothesis is a healthy one.

An anthropology is more than an intellectual construction; it is a world-view. For a radically new anthropology to be accepted as true, it must offer a demonstrable ethical advantage to those who accept it. I claimed in *Originary Thinking* that return to the origin establishes the conditions for universal human dialogue. But this formulation still fails to indicate why we need a scene of origin as a basis for dialogue instead of the more commonplace and less controversial proposition that we are all members of the same species.

At first glance, the minimal condition of the dialogue in which generative anthropology consists is that we agree on the fact of an originary event, the articulation of which can then become the first object of this dialogue. The reconstruction of the originary event provides a minimal configuration within which all essential human categories may be situated.

But let us take one step farther. What I have called the heuristic function of the originary hypothesis may also be put in terms of dialogue: whether or not we agree that it took place, or even that it is meaningful to ask the question, the originary event provides us with a minimal subject of conversation. Whatever our skepticism about the event's historical reality, if we want to speak together as human beings, the principle of parsimony entails that this event is the minimal object on which we can exercise our respective imaginations. And if, as a result of our dialogue, we come to agree on anything that will help us to attain an increased understanding of human culture, the originary event is the most limited, least confining object of such agreement.

Why a scene rather than a "theory"? But the minimal anthropological "theory"—in Greek, an overview, a scenic perspective—is one derived from a single scene. Because the birth of the human coincides with the birth of the scenic, it cannot be conceived as a series of nonscenic changes of state. To speak of the human as "always already" constituted is not to deny its essential scenicity; on the contrary. The rejection of the metaphysical notion of pure self-presence is not a rejection of scenicity itself; it is an appeal for the restoration of the anthropological concreteness or "ostensivity" that metaphysics had sacrificed in its effort to liberate itself from the irrationality of religious commemoration.

But let us suppose that the originary hypothesis is false; that nothing like an event of origin ever occurred; that language, and along with it, religion, desire, and all the other unique traits of human self-consciousness emerged imperceptibly within hominid communication systems. Sacrificial ritual and its derivative structures then commemorate no specific event; they are all ideological operations serving to impose closure on open-ended forms of interaction. Since they are preceded by no real event, we should say rather that they *invent* closure, presence, and so on.

But if such an invention exists, then it must itself be traceable to an origin. When the thought-form of Western metaphysics appeared to be the problematic invention, Heidegger traced its origin back to Plato. But if the presence of metaphysics is only an intellectual version of the logocentrism already manifested in religious ritual, then we are entitled to know at what point this earlier violence was done to the eventless origin of language. If the event represented in ritual commemorates no real event, at least we cannot deny that it commemorates a representational event.

For to take the deconstructive position to its extreme turns it into its opposite. If indeed language from the very first is a trace supplementary to a lost presence, so that the event it pretends to commemorate does not precede it but is in effect coeval with it, as the Son is coeval with the Father in Trinitary theology—I think this is a fair summary of Derrida's position in *De la grammatologie*—then all the theory of writing, of the supplement, of deferral, is in effect a theory of the originary event. It suffices to understand the always-already not as an abstract model formulated in the framework of metaphysics, but as a concrete one realized in an ostensive context among beings who only learn to think about their death because thinking is a life-and-death operation.

Closed forms of thought are built around apocalyptic events that provide "final solutions" to all the problems within their universe. If we would rid ourselves of this sort of thinking, we must exchange the apocalyptic model of the event for an originary model. Events are openings, not closures. The only acceptable intellectual utopia is one whose story has a beginning but no end.

The theorists of the "always-already" refuse in the name of an abstract openness the very idea of anthropology. When they have deconstructed the categories of human thought down to their founding paradox, they think they have found our thinking's fatal weakness, when in fact they have arrived at the source of its strength. Thought acquires new degrees of freedom not by expelling paradox, but by reproducing its pattern of supplementation. Man will ever remain the paradoxical animal, not least because today the very name of "man" has become unsayable.

*

The present book is divided into two parts. The first contains originary analyses of such phenomena as being, thinking, irony, and the erotic; the second deals with violence (the *sparagmos*), evil, rhetoric, and the victimary element of postmodern culture. Each of the two develops a different innovation with respect to my previous expositions of generative anthropology.

The chronologically prior innovation, more personal but less fundamental, is that of the second part. As a result of my emphasis on the sign rather than on Girard's "emissary violence" as the point of departure for the human, I had deferred the full integration of the latter element into the originary scene of generative anthropology. The present work gives violence its due within the originary scene by reinterpreting as the sparagmos, the tearing apart of the central object by the members of the nascent human community, what I had previously described as its "peaceful division" in the protosacrificial feast that brings the originary event to a close. For, in accordance with the minimality of the hypothesis, the division of the object need not be wholly peaceful so long as the violence it entails remains contained within the limits of the communal order established by the originary sign. In this way, the Girardian version of the originary hypothesis is not so much refuted as included within that of generative anthropology.

The relationship of the questions of violence and evil to the culture of the postmodern era is mediated by the Holocaust as the defining historical event of this new era. This idea informs the ensuing discussions of the "Jewish question," victimary rhetoric, and the "minoritary" cultural system that is emerging in the United States and, no doubt, in the world as a whole.

The second, more fundamental, new element may also be understood, although in a very different way, as a "return to Girard": it is the renewed emphasis on the subject-mediator-object triangle of mimesis and mediated desire. This triangular structure was first elaborated in Girard's *Mensonge romantique et vérité romanesque* (1961).[3] Eleven years later, in *La violence et le sacré* (1972), the triangle of individual desire was extended into a circular public scene, structured by the opposition between (multiple) periphery and (unique) center. But with this anthropological turn, the hidden interaction of the subject-mediator relationship in internal mediation was de-emphasized in favor of the more dramatic subject-object, or persecutor-victim, relationship.

In the present work, I propose to ground originary anthropology yet more rigorously than before by constructing the originary scene of language from the mimetic triangle alone. The "triangular" version of the hypothesis is not a naturalistic description of a plausible scene of origin, but a minimal analysis of the emergence of the sign within the triangle of mimesis as a solution to the "mimetic crisis" between the subject and the mediator.

This analysis, as my title makes clear, is primarily concerned with paradox, the becoming-form of the human as an emergent dynamic structure that continually absorbs the nonformal into itself. The human is paradoxical because at every point it is both tempted and obliged to represent itself anew. The "vertical" word-thing distinction that is at its core is constantly deconstructed and constantly reconstructs itself. The dynamism of this process of intellectual homeostasis gives it a capacity for absorbing new information that makes it incomparably superior to any conceivable static structure such as animal signal systems, where the "sign" is, depending on perspective, either wholly continuous or wholly discontinuous with its object-world.

I do not pretend to have said the last word here on the formalization of paradox, which is unformalizable by definition. Readers will judge for themselves whether the analyses of the first part of this volume represent qualitative advances over previous formulations of such categories as irony, being, thought, signification, eros, the unconscious. With respect to the tradition of Western philosophy in general, I would especially call the reader's attention to Chapter 6, which proposes an anthropological hypothesis of the birth of metaphysics/semiotics: the Platonic concept or Idea as a shared peace-bringing "content," the first notion of what would later become Saussure's *signifié*.

PART ONE

Paradoxical Thinking

Mimetic Paradox and the Event of Human Origin

Generative anthropology, like all projects of fundamental reflection on the human, whether they be called myth, theology, or social science, is a bootstrapping operation that seeks to explain in human language the origin of human language. This apparent aporia has traditionally been masked by transcendental figures that we may now understand as projections of the originary scene of language. The historical "death" of these figures in the modern era has been taken by some as revealing the inconceivability of the operation itself. What is indeed revealed is its paradoxicality. But the paradoxical is not the unthinkable; on the contrary, without paradox, thinking would be impossible.

*

Paradox is the privileged road to understanding the human, because paradox reveals the seam—the umbilical hole—in the hierarchy of sign and referent that is the essence of human language. The foundational modern definitions of the sign fail to grasp its double essence as a relation both real and ideal, dualist and monist, "vertical" and "horizontal."

For Charles S. Peirce, the sign is defined as "determined by something else," that is, it stands in a horizontal relation to its referent.[1] The inadequacy of this relation is then supplemented by a hypothetical third term or "interpretant," along the lines of the "third man" of Greek philosophy who furnishes the ground of resemblance between a real man and the idea of a man. The sign-relation is explained through a movement of infinite regress, thereby deferring the horizontal encounter between sign and referent at the cost of the definitional rigor of the system. In distinguishing families of signs by their type of motivation, Peirce can make no place for the *arbitraire du signifiant* that distinguishes human language; the *arbitraire* is not a zero degree of motivation but a formal absolute—one that, like all absolutes, is not immune to deconstruction.

In contrast to Peirce, Saussure sees in the sign nothing but verticality. In giving to the bar that separates signifier from signified the—in his perspective primordial—anthropological function of paternal interdiction, Lacan implies the necessity of a generative-anthropological explanation for the emergence of the formal-vertical from the horizontal. The bar is a mystery; if the sign and what it refers to are identical areas on either side of a sheet of paper, one wonders not only what function can be served by turning the paper over, but how we ever got from the real world to the paper in the first place. By bracketing the referent of the sign and substituting its signified or concept, Saussure only defers the understanding of the horizontal relationship between sign and referent as two worldly things.

My solution to this aporia was published well over a decade ago in *The Origin of Language*. The terms in which it was expressed, as well as those in which it has been repeated and refined in my more recent books, have sometimes been misunderstood as formulating a new "myth of origin." No doubt I grasped the essence of the problem better than the strategy for articulating it. I offered a minimal hypothesis for the origin of language, of the human—of "man," as we said at the time. But depicting a scene of origin of language, as opposed to merely affirming language's essential scenicity, could not fail to give the appearance of an excess rather than a minimum of content. Which is all the more the case when the rival hypothesis is that no hypothesis is conceivable.

The "triangular" version of the originary hypothesis that I present here differs little in substance from that of *The Origin of Language*, but that difference makes it henceforth impossible to tax the hypothesis with naturalistic naïveté. Our fundamental anthropological intuition is far more sensitive to the mode of narrative presentation of the hypothesis than to its real content. The description of a collective scene of origin goes against the grain of a postmodern intellectual climate suspicious of centers of mimetic attraction. My early formulations of the originary hypothesis defied this fact of our intellectual life, as was no doubt necessary to permit something new to emerge. Our intuition of minimality is infallible, but only in the long run; in the immediate, one adds to the imaginative burden in order ultimately to subtract from it. Now that the subtraction has been made, the reader should find it easier to grasp the minimizing principle at work both here and in my earlier narrative reconstructions of the originary scene.

The crux of the origin of language is the emergence of the vertical sign-relation from the horizontal one of animal interaction. The originary hypothesis claims that this emergence is conceivable only as an event because the communication of the new sign-relation to its users gives them a conscious, directly manipulable access to the sign as a transcendent form of representation. One cannot be given access to the sign without knowing it, which does not mean knowing what this access is—what language is—in our terms.

The emergence of the sign is the product of the becoming-paradoxical of mimesis in a situation of "mimetic crisis," of imminent conflict among beings that animal means of differentiation can no longer protect against dedifferentiation. Our model of this transformation requires only one presupposition: that mimesis, having reached a certain level of intensity, becomes incompatible with prehuman forms of differentiation. There are of course many kinds of such differentiation; among the higher apes there is no question of hard-wired divisions of labor as among insects. Differentiation serves the purpose of maintaining a social order, of avoiding or restraining conflict. Pecking-order hierarchies limit conflict to one-on-one attempts to rise in the hierarchy. But it is only as the result of viewing animal hierarchies from the standpoint of human equalitarianism that we understand their essence as limitation. In terms of the evolution of animal social organization, animal hierarchies introduce new degrees of freedom by rechanneling the mimetic energy of intraspecific rivalry.

It suffices then to hypothesize that the indifferentiation of mimesis overcomes at some point the differentiating force of animal hierarchy. Since this hierarchy did exist, there was mimetic conflict to be controlled; since the hierarchy has ceased to function, the conflict can no longer be controlled by it. Hence a new system of control is necessary, one that can operate under the condition of a collective dedifferentiation. This system is language.

The linguistic sign as an aborted gesture of appropriation is detemporalized, cut off from the practical domain in which imitative action slips unnoticeably into violent rivalry. The sign points before it imitates; its horizontal, metonymic relation to its referent turns back on itself as verticality, metaphor.[2] As the object of representation, the central figure takes over the negative role of the mimetic obstacle. The goal of the imitated worldly activity has become its otherworldly model.

Mimesis

Imitation leaves its ontology unthematized; it knows only that since you are like me, I can do as you do. Mimesis thematizes its ontology. This great misunderstood concept of the metaphysical tradition was confined by Aristotle's *Poetics* to the esthetic domain for over two millennia until Girard gave it its due by revealing that human desire, and the human as such, obeys the paradoxical structure of mimesis.

Imitation of behavior among similar creatures is generally unproblematic. More precisely, I can imitate your actions unproblematically so long as they do not involve the appropriation of a scarce object that we both desire to possess. But the search for such objects is precisely the kind of behavior that makes imitation advantageous. The evolution of higher animals has been driven by the difficulty of obtaining appetitive satisfaction, particularly food. If I serve as your model in the hunt, all will go well until your imitation reaches the point of reproducing my appropriative gesture toward the same object. At this point imitation provokes rivalry; the mimetic model becomes an obstacle.

The becoming-obstacle of the model is not in itself uniquely human. At the most elementary level of imitation, when a swarm of animals gather around a source of nourishment, each one becomes sooner or later an obstacle for the others. But the energy and attention of members of the group are directed to the prey, not to each other. If they do enter into conflict, or even begin to devour each other, this remains incidental to the appropriative operation that ultimately benefits the swarm and the species to which it belongs. The mimetic obstacle is there, but it remains epiphenomenal with respect to the benefit conferred by imitation.

In animal imitation, the becoming-obstacle of the model remains an unpleasant side effect that must be countered by the very process of mimetic evolution that serves to increase it. Whereas the less fit among the multiple members of lower species can easily be sacrificed, higher animals, of greater individual value to their species, are worth preserving within a hierarchical order that prevents mimetic conflict, or limits it to one-on-one battles for supremacy. The "alpha" animal is the product of a higher level of mimetic tension than can exist within the leaderless swarm. His maintenance of order implies a degree of rivalry with his fellows. But this order is not threatened by the reinforcement of collective mimesis. Animal imitation is naturally self-controlling; the tensions of rivalry reach a semistable equilibrium in the dominance of the most robust individuals. The mimetic model stabilizes at higher evolutionary levels in greater order rather than less.

But the emergence of humanity demonstrates the limits of this correlation between imitation and order. The mutual reinforcement of collective imitation leads to the overthrow of the one-on-one mastery of the alpha animal and the formation of the equalitarian human community. Once the conflictive structure of mimesis reaches the point of overwhelming the constraints of animal hierarchy, it can only be controlled, or more precisely, deferred, by the formal hierarchy that is human language. The origin of language is describable as the establishment of this new hierarchy, through which the linguistic sign acquires its uniquely human verticality. The originary hypothesis addresses the mystery of the generation of the vertical from the horizontal, form from content, or, in the old dialectical vocabulary, "quality" from "quantity."

In our elucidation of this mystery, we must concentrate our attention on the inherent conflictuality or protoparadoxicality of prehuman mimesis, where we will find the horizontal correlative to the verticality of the sign. This in turn obliges us to analyze more closely than previously the central idea of the originary hypothesis: that the originary sign is an "aborted gesture of appropriation" transformed into a gesture of representation out of fear of the mimetic rivalry of the others.

The Triangular Hypothesis

In a plausible historical reconstruction of the originary scene, the mimetic "other" or model would be a plurality of individual others. The novelty of the present exposition of the hypothesis reflects the hitherto unexploited fact that the original Girardian triangle is already a sufficient, and more truly minimal, model of this scene. At the moment in which the appropriative gesture is initiated, the prehuman mimetic relation is simply imitative: the other is my model, but not yet my rival. I reach for the object on the model of my model's gesture. But at that moment, I realize the incompatibility of my gesture with his; two movements toward the same object cannot both be fulfilled. The other-model leads me to intend an act that would make him an other-rival.

Here we must stop to consider precisely what makes this situation intolerable. It is easy enough, in the collective version of the hypothesis, to introduce two naturalistic explanatory elements. One is the obvious one of a plurality of others; in a collective situation, a single individual wishing to appropriate the object of common interest risks provoking the hostility of the group. The second, less obvious, element is the preexistence of the animal hierarchy spoken of above. Freud's scenario of the murder of the father in *Totem and Taboo* may be rewritten in ethological terms: the alpha animal attempts to exercise his normal privilege in appropriating the object of common desire, but because of the increased level of mimesis and consequent dedifferentiation, the others no longer defer to him but imitate his appropriative gesture "out of turn," with the consequence that he must abort his own action, the others then following suit.[3]

There is no reason to doubt the plausibility of this scenario; but its naturalism is incompatible with minimalist rigor. This is more obvious in the case of animal hierarchy, but it applies to the plurality of others as well—and this despite the necessarily public nature of the event of origin. For the "public" can be modeled as easily by two people as by two hundred.

The problem is not that an alpha animal may not have existed, but that its empirical existence, even were we certain of it, cannot be substituted for an explanation of the breakdown of its dominant role. To account for the end of hierarchy by its inherent instability is merely to beg the question. Thus the alpha's existence does not serve as a true explanatory element, but as a relay or intermediary stage that avoids the crucial question of fixing the degree of freedom inherent in the specific operation of human mimesis.

Animal hierarchy arises in order to avert the conflict implicit in mimesis. But this intermediate stage between lower life-forms and the human only interests us insofar as it determines the minimal conditions of emergence of the latter. That reliance on animal hierarchy is inherently misleading is already apparent from the examination of Freud's model, despite its lack of ethological references. Freud envisioned the prehuman horde as a hierarchically organized group, the liberation or dehierarchization of which corresponded to the appearance of man. But we cannot understand the mimetically dedifferentiated state in which the originary scene takes place simply as a product of the unexplained dissolution of a previous hierarchy. It must be explained from within as the subject's state of undecidability between the mimetic other-mediator's two roles of model and rival. This statement of the problem makes clear that it is unnecessary to postulate a protohuman animal hierarchy; mimesis itself defines a hierarchy, however unstable, between subject-self and other-model, and this hierarchy is the basis upon which all others are founded.

Similarly, the triangular formulation of the hypothesis eliminates the need for the independent postulation of the plurality of others. The determining factor in the conversion of the appropriative gesture into a sign is not fear of the violence of the other(s), but the incompatibility of the two roles of subject and other in the mimetic process. This correction should not be taken as a sanitization of our bloody past. "Fear" and "violence" are not the clear-cut categories they appear to be. If fear of the violence of my mimetic model(s) is supposed to explain my failure to carry my appropriative gesture to completion, it hardly explains why I continue to perform the gesture under a new intention, or why I remain within the mimetic configuration rather than seeking to escape from it. The subject's attachment to the scene, whatever its dangers, demonstrates that mimesis rather than fear is the explanatory element; but in that case, the most economical explanation is the one that presupposes nothing beyond the triangular mimetic configuration.

*

Reduced to the mimetic triangle purged of all naturalistic elements, the originary hypothesis may be formulated as follows: the sign originates as the solution to the "paradoxical state" or "pragmatic paradox" engendered when the mimetic relation to the other-mediator requires the impossible task of maintaining the latter as model while imitating his appropriative action toward a unique object. Put in geometric terms, the parallel lines of imitation must converge toward a single point. The mimetic model is both model and (potential) obstacle; it is at the moment when this contradiction prevents action that the human linguistic sign appears.

The cessation of action in the situation of mimetic crisis is more radical than in that of hierarchical submission, where the non-alpha animal acts out its submission by its very stasis—and where it would normally expect to take its turn after its superiors. We need a more general word than "action" or even "behavior" to describe what is prevented in a truly paradoxical situation—*habitus*, perhaps—a term that designates simply a coherent mode of being. The psychological correlate of the paradoxical state of mimesis is anxiety, as was the case with Pavlov's dogs. The situation is obviously similar, but here the feedback loop is minimized; it is not determined by the interference of two conditioning factors that drive the subject to two incompatible actions at the same time, but by an internal contradiction in the (mimetic) mode of behavior itself. When mimetic attraction has reached a sufficient intensity, behavior as such becomes impossible.

What is done in this circumstance is no longer to "behave," but to produce a sign. The triangular model of the hypothesis permits a more rigorous analysis of how the function and character of this designating sign differ from those of the original appropriative gesture. In the naturalistic model, the clearest function of the sign is apotropaic; it averts potential violence from the group by demonstrating to it that the emitter no longer intends to appropriate the object. To designate is to renounce, to defer possession through representation. This still leaves unclear the nature of the link between renunciation of appropriation on the one hand and imaginary possession through representation on the other. The very fact that we talk about a "link" between what appear to be two wholly distinguishable operations is proof enough that this is not yet a minimal exposition of the hypothesis. This is the appropriate point at which to recall the Aristotelian notion of mimesis as (theatrical) representation. This notion leaves the potentially conflictive horizontal imitation of others to the subject matter on stage and retains as its formal definition only the conflict-free vertical representation of reality. In the originary scene, the Aristotelian concept of mimesis applies, not to the original appropriative gesture, which depends on the other as its mimetic model, but to the new designative-representative gesture of the sign.

The sign emerges as a turning away from the other as model to the object of desire as model. In the transformation of the mimetic relationship wrought by language, the subject displaces the intention of his gesture from (unconsciously) imitating the other to (thematically) imitating the object. Signing remains a mimetic operation in the older sense; the sign in its otherworldliness, its "arbitrariness," can be learned only from others. But unlike even the most stylized of animal behaviors, the sign is intended to make present a referent other than itself.

How does this doubling of mimetic models resolve the "paradoxical state" of mimesis, the originary mimetic crisis? Prehuman imitation, whether one-on-one or in a herd, has a two-place structure of actor and model; the only difference in the latter case is that the model has many bodies. Animal imitation, lacking in triangularity, can only be the basis of a dualistic order, a "pecking" order of one-on-one relationships. Unlike the triangle of human mimesis, it cannot be expanded into a communal circle in equilibrium around its center. If a central object is the actors' common goal, they go to it in accordance with the pecking order; the appropriative gestures of the non-alphas are not converted into signs but merely postponed. Hence the circular structure of the scene of representation, fundamental to human cultural phenomena, is unknown among animals, except as it may have evolved in hard-wired form for a single purpose—as in the famous waggle-dance of the honeybee.

The formation of the triangle of human mimesis, the minimal structure in equilibrium, resolves the crisis by permitting the resumption of mimetic activity. The sign begins as the same physical action as the aborted gesture of appropriation, but the intended deferral of horizontal interaction with its object allows it vertically to "intend" this object in the phenomenological sense, to take it as its theme. What unblocks the mimetic process has its source within mimesis itself. As the appropriative intention of the original gesture makes its imitation impossible within the framework of animal relations, it increasingly focuses attention on the object to be appropriated. When I imitate the other in his appropriation of an object, my attention focuses on him if I have my own counterpart to his object, but on the object if it is the same for us both. The intensification of mimesis, by putting into question the equivalence between my object and the one that partakes of the aura of the mediator, makes it increasingly less satisfactory for me to choose an object different from his. The normal child chooses a mate in imitation of his father's choice; Oedipus, the mimetic archetype, can take no wife other than his father's.

The movement toward the object—and concomitantly away from the model—is inherent in mimesis as such. The appropriative gesture is so to speak already "predisposed" to re-present the object even as it performs its practical function.[4] What remains for the originary scene to accomplish—but it is the accomplishment that makes all the difference—is the thematization of the intention to represent and defer appropriation. Once attention to the object and its interdiction by the other have increased to the point of rendering appropriative action impossible, the mimetic shift to the object formalizes—in effect, brings to (human) consciousness—this already-existing tendency.

This analysis moves in the opposite direction from Girard's original exposition of mimetic desire in *Mensonge romantique*, which consists in bringing to light the mediating third element behind the "romantic lie" that conceives of desire as a dual object-relation. Here it is the object of desire rather than the mediator that is exposed as central to what had appeared to be a one-on-one relationship of behavioral imitation. This counterintuitive result requires explanation.

Appetitive behavior normally directs itself to objects, and it is not stretching the analogy too far to say that it "intends" these objects. A cat hunting a mouse knows what object it is looking for as much as a human hunter stalking a deer. But the cat's behavior, unlike the hunter's, is an unlearned routine that includes its object categorically within it— not hunting behavior that happens to alight upon a mouse, but mouse-hunting behavior. When imitative learning does take place with respect to such behavior, the object, as part of the behavior itself, does not fall under the spell of the imitation; if one cat learns from another a new mouse-hunting technique, no particular mouse receives thereby a supplementary value. The supplement that comes from re-presentation of the object can only arise when it is not already present as an element of the learned activity.

Desire is always mediated desire. The movement of appetite toward desire is that of an intensified mimesis that discovers not only behavior but the goal of behavior in the other. What causes the late emergence of the object into the mimetic equation is not indifference to it but, on the contrary, the practical object-orientation of animal behavior. Because the object as source of food, shelter, sexual release, and so forth is less freely chosen (more "scarce") than the behaviors of the subject by which it may be appropriated, the techniques of appropriation are subject to mimetic learning before there is any need to "learn" the object of appropriation. It is only at an advanced stage of mimesis that not merely the action itself but its goal falls under the influence of the mediating other.

Why should the intensification of mimesis lead the subject away from the other's behavior toward the object to which it is directed? This movement reflects an internalization of the model's motivation, the self's closer assimilation to the other's own reality. The more closely I imitate my model's goal-directed action, the more I share the goal of this action, which is not located in the action itself but precisely in its external object. (This analysis applies as well to self-directed actions; a higher level of mimesis will lead me, for example, to imitate the other animal's "narcissism" and groom it rather than myself.) Whence the apparent paradox that as imitation becomes more intense, it prefigures the triangular structure of human representation, focusing less on the model's behavior and more on the object to which it is directed.

The Paradox of the Sign

The sign, as we have noted, is the conversion of a gesture begun in imitation of the model's appropriative gesture into the "imitation" of the object that was the aim of this gesture. In performing the sign, I abandon my imitation of the other's original intention of appropriating the object; I turn back from the object we desire in common. In consequence, my situation in performing this gesture is once again compatible with that of the other, whose action can take place simultaneously with mine without any danger of convergence on the object. The two gestures are not parallel as before; they are both directed toward the object, but they no longer seek to remove it from its central position. The object has now become the center of a *scene*.

The emission of the sign creates verticality out of what was previously a horizontal relationship of appetite and appropriation by combining the roles of model and object in a single behavior. I imitate the other in my *énonciation* and the object in my *énoncé*. Instead of my action being a simple means of self-expansion into the world through the incorporation and obliteration of external objects, it becomes a means to preserve these objects by reproducing them within myself. I can now continue to imitate the gesture of my model despite the presence of an obstacle to appropriative action. Because the model does not disturb my signing behavior, it is the object that is perceived as the obstacle to its own appropriation; this is what we call its sacrality.

This model of the first emission of the sign is that of its "early" or "thoughtful" emission. In the sense that I emit the sign as the result of my own abortion of the gesture of appropriation rather than in imitation of my model, the decision to emit the sign is the originary example of thinking, as discussed in Chapter 7. This may be contrasted with the emission of the sign under the mimetic influence of the model by the "late" participant still seeking to appropriate the object. This exercise of influence is discussed in Chapter 12 under the rubric of "originary rhetoric."

Once again, the specific difference between these two moments of the emission of the sign is clarified by the use of a minimal rather than a naturalistic context. The originary sign is the first instance of the free, conscious, intentional thematization of an object. Our analysis cannot be content with showing that the sign is freely performed, but must show how freedom is born with the sign. Like the birth of verticality from horizontality, the birth of freedom from necessity is another statement of the paradox of originary signification. Its explanation can never be complete; as the birth of a new level of complexity, it is irreducible to any earlier configuration. But rather than lament the futility of intellectual bootstrapping, we should take such paradoxes—and all paradox reduces to this one, the paradox of the human-as-such—as guarantees of the inexhaustibility of originary thinking.

In a brief discussion of the question of freedom in the Introduction to *Originary Thinking*, I used Kant's formulation of the esthetic judgment ("without a concept") as my model for the freedom of the signifying intention: the subject was influenced by the "beauty" of his gesture, that is, by its ability to re-present the all-desirable central object. This is a suggestive formulation; but it complicates the matter by introducing the category of the esthetic, in which the subject's attention oscillates between sign and referent. The esthetic is dependent on the sign; it perpetuates our paradoxical experience of the sign's thematization of its referent as already significant. To grasp the originary freedom of the sign prior to the reinforcement provided by the esthetic, we must attempt instead to define "freedom within the limits of mimesis": to understand how a mimetic act can free itself from "instinctive" or nonreflective dependency on its model.

The transformation of the aborted gesture into a sign is a movement from the imitation of a human model to the "imitation" of an appetitive object. In the mimesis of the object, the subject is not copying another's gesture, but representing the object itself.

Let us consider for a moment the subject-object relation. I appropriate an object in order to fulfill an appetitive need. Whether or not I am imitating a human mediator is not critical so long as I indeed have this need. Up to this point, mimesis is merely a beneficial way of learning the technique of such necessary appropriative gestures.

We might then be tempted to call even the appropriative gesture "free" when it arises in a nonmimetic context. I may have learned it from another, but my performance of it is dictated by my own needs, and in higher animals these needs themselves need not obey a strict physiochemical calculus of stimulus-response. For example, animals engage in various kinds of play. Here we come up against the traditional question of "free will," which is, along with the existence of God, one of Kant's antinomies of pure reason.

Generative anthropology offers a new understanding of the concept of freedom as well as of that of God. Ours is a strictly anthropological explanation; it makes no cosmological claims. The question of freedom versus determinism, like that of the existence of God, is really a purely anthropological question. One can no longer take seriously the nineteenth-century "science of religion" that wanted to derive the concept of God from our awe of the cosmos. The reality is just the opposite: having sufficiently deferred human violence by means of the concept of God, we become interested in the relatively dangerous cosmos on the model of extremely dangerous humanity. Religion tends to apply to the cosmos a model of divine power that is indeed of value in anthropological situations but has little functionality in cosmological situations. In times of crisis, cosmic or otherwise, we appeal to God because in our fundamental, originary model of crisis, the sign as name-of-God provides the solution.[5]

The problem of freedom versus determinism is equally anthropological rather than cosmic, "cultural" rather than "natural." To say that the future movement of a particle is "determined" is to conceive a mind potentially aware of this determination. The simple anthropological test of determinism is the following: if after calculating the future state of a system, I can inform the system of my calculations without leading it to deviate from them, that system may be called determined. If, on the contrary, I must hide my calculations to avoid such deviation, then the system is free; for someone within the system could eventually perform the same calculations as I have.

The obvious objection to this definition is that it is biased in favor of language users; how could I convey the results of my calculations without language? But the burden of proof should lie not with the definition but with its critics. It is for them to show why, if human language is just one among many means of communication that makes no real difference to the matter of free will, it has such an effect on the system that contains it, why the animals whose languages they study so intensively are incapable of such feats. Nor should the question be deflected by bringing in artificial intelligence. *Jusqu'à nouvel ordre*, computers have been constructed by human beings for their own benefit.

The freedom of signing as an act of representation distinguishes it from imitation as a new, human variety of mimesis. To imitate is not to represent. I imitate you because we are analogous beings; I need make no conscious effort to follow your gestures, to thematize them as objects of representation.[6] The mimetic crisis leads to stasis precisely because prehuman imitation is nonreflexive; the subject has no knowledge of itself as a self imitating another. In contrast, my representation of the object is a conscious thematization. I am not like the object; I cannot follow it by analogy. When I imitate you, I imitate your action, make movements analogous to yours; but when I represent an object, I designate *it*, not a particular action of it. My intention of the object is an intention to recall it into being, to double it using only my own resources. I cannot perform the sign, as opposed to the gesture of appropriation, without thematizing the purpose of the sign to represent its object.

The key to the freedom of the sign lies in the detemporalizing/retemporalizing movement discussed in chapter 6 of *Originary Thinking* ("Narrativity and Textuality"). Imitation has no inherent form. The practical gesture is "horizontally" contiguous with its object; its lack of end-in-itself is visible in its outward formlessness. Because appropriation ends with the object, not with the act itself, if I imitate you successfully, I have no awareness of the limits of my gesture, which are imposed upon it from without. The nonformal quality of the practical gesture is reflected in the continuity between its temporality and that of the life-world to which it is subordinate; the hunter's movements must obey the rhythms of the animal he hunts rather than his own. In contrast, the sign is detemporalized, cut off from its natural aim and therefore from the time in which such aims are realized.

In the discussion in *Originary Thinking*, the sign's detemporalization of the original appropriative gesture was considered tantamount to its constitution as form, even esthetic form (for example, "In the originary scene itself, in the presence of the sacred, the esthetic contemplation of the sign is the complement of the sign's desiring prolongation toward the center" [103]). But in the present discussion, we stand at the origin of form, which we must explain without recourse to the notion of the esthetic. This explanation will return us to the question of freedom.

Abortion of the gesture is not in itself detemporalization; it is such only when the aborted gesture becomes an action in its own right—an action of a new kind, devoid of direct worldly aim. We may say that it defers this aim, that its very existence as form is a worldly realization of deferral, by which I refer to the fundamental equivalence, pointed at by Derrida's seminal term *différance*, between differentiation as marked by the sign and deferral of the mimetic conflict that the loss of difference risks bringing about. The sign re-presents the object as what may truly be called an object of desire, now that its potential appetitive attractiveness is cut off from practical action. Desire is not first experienced and then "repressed," as in the psychoanalytic model; its thematization of its object is itself a product of the repression of the possibility of discharge in appetitive satisfaction.

The detemporalized gesture possesses a new, formal temporality.

The beginning and end of a form are within the form itself. At the origin of formality is the new aim of the aborted gesture, which is transformed from a practical into a representational act. Within the practical realm, the goal is no longer to appropriate the object in imitation of the human mediator but to imitate the object to the latter's satisfaction, that is, well enough to make him understand the new sense—which can already be called the "meaning"—of the gesture. This is an aim external to the gesture itself, but one that depends on its formal closure as a representation. This closure is not perceived within the practical world but on the other's imaginary scene of representation. In practical terms, this imaginary aim mediates the deferral of conflict, averting the potential wrath of the other-mediator toward his disciple-rival.

It is justifiable to follow past practice in calling this originary form of representation "designation" and the utterance that performs it an "ostensive," with its connotation of pointing. (But it is useless in this context to speculate on the oral versus manual character of the "aborted gesture"; we may just as well assume it to have both.) In principle, any appropriative gesture will "point" toward its object in the sense of serving as a natural sign that draws attention to it, but this within the continuum of worldly action that leads ultimately to its appropriation. Now that the latter course has been foreclosed, the sign does nothing but "point," not in anticipation of further action, but as re-presentation, calling to attention. The aim of the action now having shifted to communicating a representation of the object to the other, the beginning and end of this action, whatever feedback is available from the other, are ultimately determined by the internal or formal coherence of the gesture itself, since it is this coherence that makes *it* an object of perception and thereby communicates to the other the intention to represent the object. The formality of the signifying gesture, however different its form may be from that of the object it designates, is of the same kind, in contrast to the nonformality of the practical gesture—the normal aim of which is rather the de-formation of the object, the destruction of its form for the benefit of one's own, as is the rule in appetitive operations.

The formality of the gesture is an objective quality analogous to that of the forms of objects in the real world; the gesture as part of a sequence having its principle of coherence outside itself becomes an au-

tonomous object of perception or *Gestalt* in itself. This alone is sufficient to allow us to speak of the sign as an imitation of its object. At
the same time, the creation of a formal object in the sign requires that
the criteria for formal closure be imposed by the subject. A feedback
loop connects the progress of the sign with the perception of its completion, something not required either in prehuman mimesis or in the
performance of life-world routines. This loop anticipates the oscillatory structure of the esthetic, but it determines the specificity of the
signing action as the creation of form-in-general rather than beautiful form. The sign is well-formed rather than beautiful; it does not call
for "a second look" as does esthetic form. This first loop of formal judgment, in which the relation between sign and object is thematized so
that we examine our sign and "see that it is good," is the minimal structure of human free will.

Gesture and Object, Speech and Writing

Originary freedom is the mimesis of form. The vertical doubling of
object-form by significant form is won from the horizontality of appetitive object-relations by the impossibility of pursuing these relations in the context of prehuman imitation. This sheds new light on
the problem raised by Derrida concerning the relative primacy of speech
and writing.

Despite its author's extraordinary philosophical sophistication, there
is a *glissement* between the empirical and the a priori in *De la grammatologie* that at times almost suggests a return to Engels's "dialectics
of nature."[7] In particular, the exact status of the categories of "speech"
and "writing," whether historical-empirical or in some undefined sense
"ontological," is never made clear. This is not due to arch coquettish-
ness, as Derrida's more superficial critics suggest, but very simply to
the limitations of his anthropology, limitations of which he perversely
makes virtues.

The placing in doubt of the priority of speech over writing is exemplary of a powerful but frustrated anthropological intuition. Derrida's preference for writing over speech as a model of human language
is based on his critique of the illusion of the speaker's self-presence. In
writing, the subject is absent; in speech, he appears to be present. But
because language operates only through *différance*, the differentiation

of signs through the deferral of their individual meaning within the paradigm with respect to which it is determined (so that, for example, we cannot understand "green" until we know "blue" and "yellow"), language is more faithfully exemplified by the overtly "deferred" form of writing than by spoken language's illusory immediacy.

What is primarily deferred/differentiated in language is the conflict potentially aroused by the fact that the subject and his model both occupy the same position with regard to the object. The deferring function of the originary sign is not dependent on a plurality of signifiers; this is a Saussurean, "structuralist" notion accepted uncritically within Derrida's critique of Saussure. Nor need we dismiss the notion of (self-)presence as pure illusion, despite its inclusion of a central moment of self-absence, in order to appreciate the paradoxes of deconstruction. All these elements acquire a clear anthropological meaning in the light of the originary hypothesis. In particular, the opposition between writing and speech may be situated within the originary scene at a more fundamental level than Derrida's discussion suggests.

The difference between the sign and the worldly gesture from which it is derived is most simply explained as the difference between an act and an object. The gesture of appropriation is an act that directly intends a worldly result; its temporality is that of the practical world. In contrast, the sign does not intend its referent directly, but through mimesis of its formal closure. The sign is an object, a product, a whole imitating another whole. The sign points to its referent, but in order to do so, it must be cut off from the possibility of attaining it, must mimic the object's closure in its own. What is new about the human sign as opposed to the most complex animal signals is that it is the product of a formal consciousness. The sign is a form in that it turns back on itself in order not to appear to be pursued as a gesture of appropriation. The maker of the sign is not performing a genetically inherited stylized action, nor even a learned stylized action; he is creating an action-object from his blocked action, in imitation of the object that has become the obstacle to this action.

This distinction between action and object is the real anthropological point of Derrida's distinction between speech and writing. Unlike speech, writing is clearly the production of an object; the *act* of writing is of no independent interest. Even when we see someone writing, we only want to know the result, not observe his performance. In speech, on the contrary, performance and production of the language-object are one and the same. Once the *énonciation* is over, there is no more *énoncé*. Whence what Derrida refers to as the speaker's illusion of self-presence. To the extent that what is essential is the language-object and not the process of its creation, our analyses are in agreement. The self-presence of speech is blind to its own constitution; if language were indeed mere self-presence, it could not function within the intersubjective triangle of mimesis. As we have observed, mimetic performance requires no self-consciousness whatever; I can follow your movements without being conscious of any self, yours or mine. The self can only emerge in the context of the forming of the sign-object. But this "object" is, in Derrida's scheme, the equivalent not of speech but of writing.

This is the justification for the claim that writing qua trace is prior to speech. Yet the dismissal of self-presence as illusion throws out the baby with the bathwater. The originary sign qua writing can only emerge from within the worldly temporality in which it is performed; its existence presupposes the reality and suspension of this temporality before its metaphysical abolition or "forgetting." The sign is writing only because it is first speech; it has form because it first became form by emerging from the nonformal in the aborted gesture. Only once the event of this emergence has taken place does the completed sign transcend the worldly temporality in which it was enacted to become "vertical" form, "written" form, if we like.

This critique has its psychological corollary: the illusion of self-presence *is* the self. The self is never self-present in the metaphysical sense of Aristotle's unmoved mover, but it subsists as that which experiences itself as self-present (whatever the philosopher may think of it). It is Derrida's metaphysical view of paradox that leads him to reject the self as an illusory category because it is founded on an "illusory" experience. Deconstruction constitutes the very anthropological reality that it thinks it has abolished. The speaker-as-writer uses the specifically human language that the deconstructor has in his own way defined, all the while thinking he has subverted this very specificity.

The real truth of originary self-presence is the presence of the participants to each other as mutual communicators of the sign. The mediator cannot retain his hierarchical distance from the subject in the presence of the sign. In the naturalistic or "circular" version of the originary hypothesis, this goes without saying. But this is explained by assuming that the intensity of mimesis is such as to break down or "dedifferentiate" the old animal hierarchy. The triangular version avoids this supplementary postulate. Because it posits only the minimal hierarchy of mediator and disciple from the outset, it provides a model of the establishment of their reciprocal, dehierarchized presence under the sole weight of the sign.

The scene of mutual communication of the sign, whether between two beings or ten thousand, is determined by the active stasis of sign production. What is centrally present to me is not myself nor even the other participants but the central, sacred object of desire. The signing self defers its self-presence through identification with the object as its giver of form; this deferral of self-identity breaks the paralysis caused by mimetic paradox. "Presence" comes into being filled with absence, difference, and differentiation; but it is presence nonetheless, the only kind possible, whatever more perfect models the imagination can conceive by extrapolating from the positive moment of this paradoxical process.

From Thought to Rhetoric

The subject's emission of the sign is the origin of conscious reflection, or thinking. In contrast, the subject's persuasion of the other-model to transform his own gesture of appropriation into an imitation of his former disciple's sign exemplifies what will be discussed in Chapter 12 as rhetoric. In a collective context, it is easy enough to understand that the single dominant figure would be persuaded by the example of his inferiors to renounce his prior claim to the central object. But like all arguments that rely on the contrast between a group and an individual, this one uses *force majeure* to foreclose a more nuanced explanation.

No doubt a single creature, however powerful, is incapable of physically dominating a united collectivity. But the picture of a collectivity of inferiors bound by the sign opposing a single individual of superior status is suspiciously like Freud's scene of the murder of the primal father. Freud keeps the mediator as the mimetic center throughout, begging the question of how the one-on-one relations characteristic of animal hierarchies were transformed into a many-one opposition. Nor do we learn how the sons are able to thematize their common resentment against the father. Unless we accept Freud's thesis, the "alpha" figure must be included along with the others in our model of the originary human collectivity. The triangular model of mimesis makes clear why the relatively independent mediator's sign must be "late" in comparison to the relatively dependent subject's; what remains to be explained is how the latter's rhetoric, independently of superior numbers, can persuade the former to imitate his disciple's gesture. The single parameter of the originary hypothesis is intensity of mimesis. We have been gauging this intensity by the mimetic passion of the subject for the mediator; but mimesis is contagious. The convergent trajectories of the two gestures are not attributable to the disciple alone; the evolving increase in mimetic intensity affects both parties alike. At the moment at which the subject's gesture of appropriation is aborted, the other's gesture, and the intention behind it, can no longer be distinguished from it.[8]

The "slave" thinks for himself, the "master" lets himself be persuaded; this is the originary version of Hegel's master-slave dialectic, stood on its feet not in the universe of matter but in the scene of mimetic interaction. The subject thinks to represent the central object by imitating its form; the mimetic model is persuaded by the subject's example. One might ask why, on the contrary, he would not be encouraged by this example to appropriate the object unencumbered by his disciple's competition. But at the level of mimetic intensity that blocks the subject's gesture, the only trace of the master-disciple relationship is the latter's precedence in renouncing the object. The former cannot help but follow his lead; to break the symmetry would require a differential movement of qualitatively greater magnitude than to imitate the subject's renunciation.

To think is to abandon the closer, human model for the more distant object, to pass from what Girard calls "internal" to "external" mediation.[9] The historical progression from formal to implicit hierarchy, from external to internal mediation, generates ever more intense resentment. But modernity has in the mass media its own institutional means for externalizing mediation. The solution to the problems of internal mediation is the establishment of an external mediator; this is the lesson of *La violence et le sacré* and of generative anthropology as a whole. This lesson is even clearer in the triangular model. The direction of the movement that defines thinking is opposite to that of the historical movement of internalization and self-delusion depicted in *Mensonge.*

To think is to liberate oneself from an idolatrous form of mimesis, never absolutely, but by replacing it with another, less pathological form. In animal mimesis, thinking is unnecessary precisely because imitation is unproblematically internal, concerned with the model rather than the goal. The mediator is qualitatively easier to imitate than the object, so much so that the question of imitating the object never arises. But at the moment of the aborted gesture, imitation of the model-subject has become dangerous enough to threaten the equilibrium of the mimetic triangle. Hence the liberating shift to the object.

Thinking is the distancing, the deferring of mediation. It takes its great leap forward in Socrates' turn from the polemic dialogue of forensic rhetoric to the *elenchos* that substitutes the Idea for the practical object of a lawsuit. Rhetoric, in contrast, is the foregrounding of mediation. The subject persuades the other to imitate his use of the sign by emphasizing not the sacrality of the object but the appropriateness of his own gesture. The addressee of rhetoric is the "late" participant in the scene who observes that the other(s) is/are already using the sign. He converts his gesture of appropriation into a gesture of signification in the intention not of representing the object but of imitating his fellows.

This analysis is sharpened in the triangular model, which dispenses with the subject's fear of being outnumbered. The sign is "contagious" because it is easier to imitate its producer than to pursue an independent path to the object. Rhetoric reverses the mimetic switch made by thought from other to object. The reversal is not absolute; every reproducer of the sign mimics not a practical gesture but a form closed in imitation of the object. The captive of even the most powerful rhetoric, in other words, has done a minimum of thinking. Rhetoric comes after thought, which it can never wholly expel. In this it is analogous to the violence of the sparagmos, which it paradigmatically serves to incite.

Mimetic Paradox

Paradox is a structure of language; it cannot be conceived without the sign. But neither can the sign be conceived without paradox. The horizontal and the vertical cannot be cleansed of one another. The doubling of reality by the sign-world cannot follow either the Saussurean or the Peircean model. The sign that is in the world represents the world it is in; the sign that stands above the world remains within the world of the sign.

There is more than an analogy between this situation and that of the mimetic subject who finds the doubling of his model's gesture blocked by the collision of converging trajectories. There are neither two places in the same universe nor two separate universes for the one to find room to mimic the other. The constitution of the sign is the creation-and-deferral—the *différance*—of paradox. Paradox itself is paradoxical; that is what makes it paradox. It cannot be reduced to "lowest terms," only deferred. But neither is it ever present before our eyes; it is *always* in a state of deferral.

The subject sets the process in motion by imitating the object, doubling within his own action the inaccessible goal of his mimetic gesture. This action liberates the gesture from its stasis by separating the components of the mimetic blockage. On the one hand, the signing gesture, unlike the gesture of appropriation, can be imitated without further difficulty, since it has its end in itself and not in the material world. On the other, the object is designated, represented as an obstacle to the very appropriative action its designation incites. Instead of two hands converging on the object, we have two coterminous gestures cut off before they can interfere with one another, but which thematically reject the practical aim that incited them in the first place.

What this transformation generates is a radical redefinition of the "practical," a program for the stabilization of the human community through signification the validity of which has been demonstrated by our continued use of it for at least 30,000 years. This program creates paradox by deferring it. The referent is no longer a simple object of appropriation but an object of signification; there is no way to maintain a barrier between its "natural" and its "cultural" being. Formally to designate the object through language is inevitably to designate it as an object-of-designation; the object I mean is always already an object-meant. This is not an artifact of mimesis that can be overcome with the benefit of a lucid theory of desire; it is already the case for the first sign, the originary aborted gesture, at the first moment of human thought.

*

The exploitation of our experience of this paradox, the recuperation of the difference between the object and the object-as-designated-by-the-sign, is the role of the *esthetic*, which I have described as the state of contemplation that oscillates between these two "versions" of the object.[10] The use of language in situation forecloses the esthetic, which flourishes only when time is allowed for this oscillation—time that serves the further deferral of action. Esthetic institutions specifically valorize this time, which ritual inserts into its own practical context of sacrifice.

Other loci of revelation of the originary paradox of the sign—irony, signification, being, the Platonic Idea, thought, the erotic and the unconscious—will be discussed in the chapters that follow. It remains an open question whether a more schematic exposition of the ensemble of these categories is possible.

The Necessity of Paradox

Why is there such a thing as paradox? To ask the question in this manner is to collude with metaphysics in making it impossible to answer. The parasitic Other of truth is in fact the generative principle of truth, the truth of logic as well as that of the originary ostensive sign. There is a prelogical and even a prehuman form of paradox, although the latter can only be so called from the perspective of the sign that resolves the crisis it engenders. Pavlov's experimentally induced "paradoxical" state, although confined to the stimulus-response mechanism—and something of an experimental artifact—is not without analogy to the nascent paradox of mimesis. But the stasis of the mimetic subject as described in the previous chapter, unlike that of Pavlov's dogs, is structured vertically as well as horizontally. The subject is not torn between two independent mimetic programs, but between imitation of the other and rivalry with the other grounded on this very imitation. Mimetic paradox lies on the frontier between the prehuman and the human. The sign resolves prehuman paradox, but only to create true, human paradox.

Paradox is an elusive category in which metaphysical skeptics find support for their assertion of the inadequacy of human thought. Not even Russell's theory of types can insure against it.[1] But the real import of paradox is anthropological. The scandal of paradox is that the transtemporal proposition-based language of metaphysics should be subject to it. Paradox is the emergent structure of human language, and its reemergence reminds us of our language's intrinsic historicity.

One may well assume that if language-using beings were discovered in some other galaxy, we would find their logic identical to our own. But this would be because their system of representation would have evolved in a similar way to our own. What metaphysical thought cannot conceptualize is that human language, from which logic is abstracted, is not an eternal reality like mathematics but a historical one. No doubt there must be enough freedom in any practical sign-system to permit the formulation of statements like "'This statement is false" or "The barber shaves every man who doesn't shave himself," but this is because human needs determine what systems are practical and what statements interest us in them. Our fascination with paradox has historical roots far deeper than the sort of difficulties that concerned Russell. The place of paradox in human representation is older than the possibility of logical thought; it is older than language itself.

The structure of the originary crisis deferred by the emergence of humanity is the "pragmatic paradox" or "double bind" of mimesis, which gives rise in the human context to the triangle of mimetic desire.[2] In this configuration, the subject-disciple takes the mediator as his model in an attempt to duplicate a behavior that has led to a favorable result. There is no need to supply an ad hoc explanation for the role of the human mediator, let alone to indulge in Freudian mythology. Animals that are capable of modifying their behavior do so by imitation, and inevitably some members of a group—older, stronger, sexually dominant—are more valuable objects of imitation than others. But A's peaceful imitation of B's food-gathering routine ends when A challenges B for the last piece of food. The disciple becomes a rival; peaceful imitation, "the highest form of flattery," turns into conflict. The mediator who at first welcomed the disciple now rejects him. However vertical/metaphoric the latter's conduct with respect to the former, there can be no guarantee that it will not impinge horizontally/metonymically upon his being; true verticality is the product of the doubling of the real world by the world of human language.

The prehuman protoparadox of mimetic stasis discussed in the previous chapter arises when mimesis becomes so intense that, on the one hand, the only possible action is the imitation of the model, but on the other, this imitation, once it extends to the specific object of the model's appropriative praxis, comes into potential conflict with the latter's aim. This stasis is broken by the sign, which defers all appropriative action. But with signing comes true paradox: the sign cannot represent the object-as-such, only the object-represented-by-the-sign. "Culture" cannot thematize "nature" except as nature-thematized-by-culture; the thing represented by the word is not just a thing, but a thing-represented, a *representamen*. The logical paradoxes we will take up later are merely thematizations of the paradoxical structure of representation as such. One might wish for a better term than "paradox" to describe this unavoidably self-referential feature of representation, but no other term better captures the essential instability of the relation that representation establishes between subject, language, and world.

There is no true paradox, not even pragmatic paradox, prior to the existence of the sign. Only the signification-relation establishes within the world the vertical separation of levels of being that makes paradoxical self-referentiality both possible and necessary. The category of paradox designates what signification is created to avoid or, more precisely, to defer: the reimplication of model and obstacle. The sign is to be imitated; the referent is to be avoided. It is already clear from this dichotomy why the danger of paradox arises when a sign is taken as a referent. But the problem is not confined to such specific cases. The real-world referent is always already the designatum of the sign, a relationship whose dynamism the metaphysical vocabulary, from Idea to *signifié*, can never fully capture.

Originary paradox—as opposed to logical paradox, which is born with the declarative sentence—takes the pragmatic form of the double bind of model and obstacle. The originary sign is no sooner cut off from its referent by the most sacred of separations than the dissolution of this separation in a fall from transcendence into immanence becomes conceivable. This occurs in the first place in the nonappropriative domain of the esthetic.[3] Esthetic experience is not an experience of conflict, but of contradictory modes of perception. In the originary scene, the referent is ontologically primary; the sign is merely a transparent means of indicating what is already there. But once we put aside the "transparent" sign, we discover that there is no object for us to be with, that our real desire was not for the referent at all but for the

center of the scene of representation that the sign brought into existence. The referent vanishes, to be restored through the renewed mediation of the sign.

The esthetic is the primary self-contained experience of the paradox of mimesis. Its oscillatory pattern temporalizes the contradictions
that led to the originary stasis discussed in the preceding chapter. Esthetic paradox is peaceful because the conflation of model and obstacle remains confined to the imagination. What forces us to turn our
desire from the content of the artwork to its form is not its sacred power
and even less the violence of a model-rival, but its existential nullity as
a mere representation. The sacred object can produce an esthetic effect, in anticipation of artworks specially designed for this purpose,
only because its inaccessibility prefigures existential absence. The sacred object's repulsion of the movement of desire provides the framework for esthetic experience by forcing us to turn back to the sign; this
is the movement of return that will later be generated by the imaginary referent of the artwork.

In the structure of paradoxical experience in general, it is the subject's turning back rather than the object's repulsion that is primary.
Hence we should not speak of a "paradox of the sacred" distinct from
that of the esthetic. Sacredness is experienced as really inherent in its
incarnation; the return from the latter to the sign is experienced as the
effect, not of the paradoxical sign-referent relation of signification—
in which the referent is always already inhabited by the signing relation—but of the obstacle of sacred presence. No doubt this presence
is itself a "paradoxical" inherence of the transcendent in the immanent, but when we try to describe sacred revelation as paradox, we must
fall back on the structure of signification—on the sacred as a form of
representation—thereby in effect eliminating the specificity of the experience of the sacred. Girard's neglect of language as a primary constituent of the human is no doubt traceable to his decision to grant
primacy to the sacred over the linguistic—in the vocabulary of *The
Origin of Language*, to institutional over formal representation.

But the esthetic turning back is also a turning forward; the esthetic
returns to the sign, but it also anticipates the de-figuration of the referent in the sparagmos (see Chapter 10). The resentment generated by
the return from the object is an anticipatory movement, however long

deferred, of appropriation. The resentful imagination would linger indefinitely on the margin of the scene of its exclusion; but exclusion from the center is also the deprivation of what are ultimately appetitive needs. Hence, within the operation of esthetic deferral, oscillatory movements in the direction of the center have the marginally greater effect; an inevitable gradient leads to the sparagmatic consumption of the central object.

Paradox is the form taken within the world of representation by the conflict that representation was created to avoid. Pragmatic paradox realizes within human behavior what irony reveals to its detached observer: the impossibility of maintaining a strict separation between words and things, language and metalanguage. Just as the mediator cannot designate an arbitrary object to his disciple without its becoming significant as the object-designated-by-the-mediator, so the sign cannot designate a referent that is not the referent-designated-by-the-sign. In the difference between these two homologous structures lies the specificity of human representation as a means for deferring the originary crisis of mimesis.

Logical Paradox

The protoparadoxical stasis in which the subject oscillates between mimetic attraction and repulsion, between model and obstacle, is the originary state of crisis that language emerged in order to defer. Likewise, new linguistic forms emerge as means of resolving paradoxes that arise in the usage of earlier forms.[4] In contrast, logical paradox is the explicit failure to formalize this oscillation in the detemporalized language of metaphysics. The oscillation that time permits in the world of experience is incompatible with the consistency required of a logical system.[5] Conversely, no attempt to eliminate paradox from language can retain the freedom of reference that is an indispensable characteristic of natural language.

Logical paradox is late in relation to pragmatic paradox, but not simply derivative of it. Logic, metaphysics' most objective achievement, is not a "cultural form" like the religious and esthetic forms that find their model in the ostensivity of the originary scene. Logic can be construed as a pure system invulnerable to anthropological reflection, on the model of mathematics with which it has so much in common.[6] But the historical function of logic is to serve as a model of signification relations; because logical propositions presuppose a world that they are true of, logical systems cannot exclude paradox.

It is in the very nature of logic to be obsessed by and wish to expel paradox; the protection of form against its dissolution in the chaos of content is the essence of all cultural operations. But the analogy between logical paradox and Girard's emissary victim, however illuminating it may be in a broader anthropological context, is not helpful in the domain of logic itself. The originary hypothesis can tell us why we are interested in paradox; it cannot supply its own technique of logical analysis.

Logical systems can be used to construct paradoxical statements because the Achilles' heel of metaphysics is its inability to prevent the mutual contamination of form and content, language and reality. The confusion of levels or "logical types" is unavoidable once language becomes able to take itself as object. Logical paradox articulates the inevitable interference between language and metalanguage into a contradictory self-reference, as epitomized by the archetype of logical paradox, the common denominator of all the others: the Liar paradox— "This sentence is false."

Negative self-reference is not merely an occasional possibility of language in its "linguistic universality," its capacity to take anything whatever as its theme. In the hypothesis of linguistic evolution formulated in *The Origin of Language*, it is precisely negative self-reference that is constitutive of the declarative sentence, which is to say, of the logical proposition. The declarative emerges as a linguistic rather than pragmatic reply to a previous imperative. The declarative "topic" is the object demanded by the imperative, and its simplest "comment" or predicate is the negative: "No, the imperative object is not available." Because its reference to the world is mediated by the words of a previous utterance, the original declarative sentence is metalinguistic. Mature language is from the start metalanguage; the clearest evidence of this is the interrogative, which is an imperative adapted to the expectation of a verbal reply. It is also from the start negative; originary predication is negation, the denial of imaginary presence. "This sentence is false" conflates linguistic self-reference and predication-as-negation, the constitutive elements of the declarative, its means for expressing and averting the consequences of desire. The declarative sentence thus contains from the beginning the elements of self-reference and negation that join to create logical paradox.

Originary negation is a potentially dangerous operation—it is the contradiction of a preceding imperative. For a logician, to assert the falsity of a proposition is merely to append a negative sign to it, the exact equivalent of asserting the truth of the contrary proposition. In contrast, in the emergent declarative, what is negated is the (imperative) expression of the interlocutor's desire. The declarative speaker risks setting off just the kind of crisis that language supposedly permits us to avoid. The imitable sign has become not merely the designation of the obstacle to desire but the thematic articulation of its unfulfillment.

This articulation gives rise to the possibility of logical paradox within the sphere of the declarative. With predication, truth and falsity are thematized; self-reference is found at the very heart of language. As an utterance-form that arose in response to another, the declarative is language in dialogue with language, and, as the inevitable result, language affirming or contesting language. It should not surprise us that language in its mature form contains within itself the trace of the paradoxical state of mimesis from within which it first emerged. Logical paradoxes are not typically replies to any conceivable imperative or interrogative. The theme of the sentence that constitutes the Liar paradox is the sentence itself, not a preexisting reality that a previous sentence might have asked about.

Sentence paradoxes such as the Liar are simpler than set-inclusion paradoxes such as the Barber paradox, the self-referentiality of which is not explicit but must be discovered through reflection on its semantic content. In the statement of the Barber paradox, we understand the predicate as a typical detemporalization, the description of a state rather than an action; it is this understanding that becomes the locus of paradox. Although this paradox occurs at a lower level of our decoding of the sentence from the Liar, this is a sign rather of derivative than of primitive status. The predicate involved in the barber "who shaves everyone who doesn't shave himself," or more rigorously, "all those and only those who do not shave themselves" includes within itself lower-level propositions ("clauses"). The paradoxes of set theory, which, because of the need to define set membership, are always constructed from complex predicates of this kind, are not primary paradoxes of language; their existence is dependent on the prior possibility of semantic paradoxes.[7]

Once falsification is permitted, one cannot avoid paradox: one sentence's denial of the truth of another sentence cannot insure against the vulnerability of its own. It is no accident that this denial is the basic form of the verbal duel or agon. "You're a liar!" "You're another!" The symmetry of such dialogues, which tend to lose their content and degenerate into exchanges of empty accusations, should not make us forget the essentially "vertical" nature of each assertion with respect to the preceding one. The series avoids paradox only so long as each speaker maintains an identity separate from his rival's; paradox arises when A says "You're a liar!" but B, countering the form rather than the content of his rival's statement, replies "No you aren't!" Such turnabouts are a frequent source of comedy routines. Russell's theory of types would make impossible the agon of verbal conflict by establishing a strict form-content hierarchy. We could not call each other liars in typed sentences; *I* might, but then the *you* who accuses me in return does not bear the same index as the *you* I accused, who has no right to talk about my language at all. In Russell as in Plato, metaphysics defers conflict through the establishment of a hierarchy of signs.

In the normal dialogic use of "this sentence is false," "this sentence" would refer to another sentence than the one being asserted—it might, for example, be accompanied by a deictic reference to a sentence on the blackboard. No doubt the ambiguity can be reduced by more explicit specification, as in "the sentence you are currently reading/hearing is false." But natural language is not equipped for the unambiguous designation of the sentence one is in the process of speaking or reading. The ambiguity can never be wholly eliminated without the use of artificial terminology, and any such specifications would weaken still further the connection with any conceivable contextual imperative/interrogative. It is precisely the imposition of decontextualization that produces the self-reference indispensable to paradox. Just as Oedipus's pragmatic paradoxes stem from the lack of reference of the notions "rival" or "bride" outside his immediate family, which is so to speak their original context of enunciation (*tout Freud est là*), so logical paradox arises when the declarative sentence is enclosed within such a context, cut off from the worldly topic of a preceding imperative/interrogative, real or implied. The enunciation of a declarative presumes a prior interest in its topic. It is not a serious problem if this presupposition is in error, the interlocutor's interest being an empirical matter; but what is implied ontologically is that the topic, "interesting" or not, already exists within semantic space, that is, is constructed from previously existing linguistic material that the two speakers share. A declarative without an external context in this sense is a deliberate anomaly.

Our first reaction to "this sentence is false" is to accept the truth of the proposition: the sentence is false. Then we observe that this is what the sentence says, so it is true—and so on ad infinitum. But this kind of "esthetic" analysis of our temporal experience of the sentence has no place in the world of logic, where an oscillation between undefinable moments of truth and falsity on the model of esthetic experience cannot be tolerated. The question is how to eliminate such sentences a priori, how to recognize them in advance of this oscillation. But this discovery may be indefinitely deferred. Instead of "this sentence is false," we may extend the paradox to two sentences: A: B is false; B: A is true, or to as many as we like.[8] In a well-known variant, the two sentences are printed on opposite sides of a card: "the sentence on the other side is true," "the sentence on the other side is false." Here, in the absence of self-reference, nothing in the individual sentences reveals their paradoxicality. Because each proposition depends for its truth on another, each must be read as meaningful. But if the discovery of the final circularity that leads to paradox may be indefinitely deferred, there can be no hope of eliminating paradox *ab ovo* as a defect of the propositions themselves.

*

Paradox is crucial for generative anthropology because it is the distinctive feature of human mimesis. Because mimetic paradox presides at the creation of the "vertical" human sign from the "horizontal" continuum of worldly experience, it stands at the center of a constellation of categories—irony, comedy, tragedy, evil, and so on—that are conceivable only in a universe of speakers of (human) language. As is demonstrated by our analysis of the protoparadoxicality of prehuman mimesis, paradox is the most critical because the most liminal of these categories.

The term *paradox*, or even *logical paradox*, can have no precise definition, since paradox is only such because it exceeds formal systems. Our intuition of the paradoxical alerts us to the insertion of the "cultural" element of human desire into systems of representation that appear "natural." What must be added to this intuition is the understanding that this apparent intrusion is precisely what makes these systems so historically resilient. It is their very deconstructability under the pressure of desire that permits them to reconstruct themselves as the containers of desire. We have nothing with which to compare the forms inaugurated by the first sign of human language, surely not the computer languages that have shown themselves to be fundamentally incapable of modeling them. An appreciation of the structuring function of paradox should cure us of the fashionable pessimism that has attended the passing of the modernist utopias—the exemplary model of which is not Marxian socialism but Hilbert's dream of the completeness of mathematics—that were intended to realize the metaphysical dream of a paradox-free human universe. The paradoxical foundation of our systems of representation is a sign not of failure but of openness.

Two Illustrative Paradoxes

Because paradox cannot be contained by logic, it is not truly a logical category. Paradoxes of less logical rigor but more pragmatic content provide clearer illustrations than the Liar paradox of the "cognitive dissonance" by which desire transgresses formal systems designed to contain it. Let us consider two familiar examples: the "Petersburg" paradox and the paradox of the "unexpected examination."

1. *The Petersburg paradox* is a result of probability theory that for the modern mathematician is not paradoxical at all. Yet its paradoxical effect exemplifies in a pragmatic context the same structure as the fundamental human paradoxes of desire and signification.

It is usually formulated as follows. A player flips a coin until it comes up tails and is paid according to the number of heads thrown: $1 for no heads, $2 for one, $4 for two—in the general case, 2^n for n heads. This looks at first sight to be a playable game, comparable to one in which, for instance, the payoff would be $n for n heads, where the player's expectation would be ½+ ¾ + ⅜ . . . = 2. Yet simple arithmetic shows that the expectation of 1 + ½ + ¼ . . . is infinite. Thus in order to make the Petersburg game fair, the player must put up an infinite sum of money to play even once, a result that is clearly "paradoxical."[9]

Because of the properties of infinite series, this result could be presented in much more striking fashion: the payoff could begin only after the trillionth consecutive head, at only one trillionth of a cent, and yet the player's expectation would remain infinite so long as it doubles with each successive head.

In most probability questions, the gambling model can be applied without reflection on the specifics of human behavior. If I claim that to break even at roulette one should receive 38 times one's stake for a single-number bet, and that by paying off at only 36 times the house makes a profit, I can then go to the roulette wheel and illustrate my model. Or when you flip a coin once, you know immediately that in a fair game the player must put up half of what he stands to win if he guesses right. Such examples naturalize a gambling model based on equating expectation and entry price, and make it appear applicable to any apparently comparable game, such as the Petersburg game.

Without being exhaustive, among the unspoken presuppositions of these games are: (1) the bank always has enough money to pay off, and (2) the game lasts a short amount of time in human terms. Since the player's expectation from the Petersburg game comes from the infinite tail of the series, an infinite amount of time and money must be available to provide the winnings that will provide the return on his investment.[10]

The Petersburg paradox, first proposed in the eighteenth century, is no longer of mathematical interest; it does not throw into question the foundations of the theory of probability. Its usefulness to us is in foregrounding the ostensibly neutral behavioral context of the paradox, a domain in which it functions exactly like the paradoxes of self-reference that deconstruct the ontological separation between word and thing. In the general case, we conceive of the "fairness" of gambling games as a simple function of mathematical expectation; as a result of exposure to the Petersburg game, we are forced to consider this model's tacit presuppositions. Similarly, when we hear "this sentence is false," we are forced to consider the tacit presupposition behind "truth-falsity games" as they are usually played, which is that an assertion of falsity (or of truth, for that matter) refers to a sentence other than the one that makes the assertion.

The difference between the two cases is that the contradiction of the gambling example is empirical, whereas that of the sentence is inherent in autoreferential representation.[11] One paradox is pragmatic and the other is logical. But we should not be too quick to assimilate this difference to that between the necessary and the contingent. The "empirical" Petersburg paradox, which depends for its existence on the current state of mathematical theory, differs from the Liar paradox only in that, in the latter case, no conceivable evolution of the metalanguage can do more than defer by further explanation—as opposed to eliminating—its fundamental instability. The autoreferentiality of language is not an ontological requirement of sign-systems. It reflects the mimetic-paradoxical origin of human language and, in particular, the metalinguistic origin of the declarative proposition as a response to a previous imperative.

Ultimately the ontological-ontic or form-content distinction that separates these paradoxes breaks down because the forms of representation are indeed derived from their content; words were originally, and can always be shown still to be, a species of things, which in turn can never be spoken of independently of their role as the designata of words. The existence of the unstable oscillation between the horizontal and the vertical, even in the rule-bound domain of philosophical language, guarantees that logical paradoxes are ultimately pragmatic ones. The idea that sentences should not negate themselves is no more anomalous than the idea that gambling should not require infinite sums of time and money: it is simply an implicit assumption of a certain representational operation. At what is still the everyday level of mathematical sophistication, the expectation of winning money is supposed to be an unproblematically formalizable reality, independent, like the use of language, of the details of its material context. It is a secondary matter that the contextual rules have been made more explicit in one case than in the other.

2. The "unexpected examination" paradox is as follows. A professor announces to his students that they will be given a surprise examination during the following week, that is, that they will not be able to tell

on which day it will fall. This means that Friday is ruled out, since if the examination has not yet been given before Friday, the students would know for certain it must fall on Friday. But once Friday has been eliminated, the same argument holds for Thursday, and subsequently for every preceding day. Yet on whatever day the professor gives the examination, now declared impossible (on any day other than Friday, a point I shall return to), the students will be "surprised."

This paradox may be simplified by reducing the number of days to two, because the significant difference in reasoning falls between Thursday and Friday. If the day chosen for the exam is Friday, then once Thursday is over, either the students know it will be on Friday or the professor has lied. To say "I will give you an examination today but you won't know on what day it will be given" is a self-contradiction rather than a paradox. To "know" that the exam is on Thursday in the two-day case requires a chain of reasoning from the premise of (non-)knowledge; to know it is on Friday in the one-day case is a direct consequence of the professor's assertion. But the latter situation is exactly the same as that which occurs on Friday in the two-day case when the exam has not yet been given. Then too we know on Friday that it will be today, because the professor has promised an exam this week and this is the last possible day for it. The Friday argument depends only on our knowledge of the facts of the case, whereas the Thursday argument requires reasoning from the premise of non-knowledge of the professor's intentions.

But suppose the examination is set for Thursday. The students can reason as above that it must take place on Thursday, and it is true that, since it cannot take place on Friday without the students knowing it, the professor is obliged to give it on Thursday. Yet they cannot *know* it will be on Thursday because the chain of reasoning that leads them to conclude that it cannot fall on Friday is not included within the set of criteria established by the professor. This is yet more obvious when more days are allowed; as the chain grows longer it becomes increasingly impossible to distinguish between, say, the impossibility of Wednesday and that of Tuesday. The result of the two-day case is alone significant, because the argument of the student who predicts on, say, Wednesday morning that the day must be today depends on the validity of the prediction in the two-day case that the day "must" be Thursday rather than Friday. And the unconvincingness of the Wednesday—

or Tuesday, or Monday—argument reflects the formal invalidity of the Thursday argument that is its basis. The two-day result bears more than a superficial resemblance to Gödel's famous proof of the incompleteness of mathematics: the necessity that the exam fall on Thursday is a true statement unprovable within the system.

This paradox illustrates, in a completely different way from the Petersburg game, the foregrounding of contextual elements on which one suddenly discovers that a formal relationship depends. Instead of a set of fully formalized propositions, we are faced with the problem of demonstrating our knowledge in an opaque interaction. If I tell the professor on Thursday morning, "I know the exam is today," he can listen to my reasoning and simply answer, "Perhaps, but you don't really know I won't give it tomorrow." And on Thursday, I don't. I can deduce that the exam will be given today, and yet I will not *know* it. As the multiday version shows, pretending to possess this knowledge leads to the absurdity of claiming that the exam will not be given at all.

What we discover is that there is a difference between formal and informal knowing that cannot itself be formalized within a given system. My declaration about your knowledge is a piece of information that contributes to a knowledge beyond the reach of that declaration.

It is no accident that the villain of the tale is a professor. This paradox, because it reveals the ineluctably interactive nature of all knowledge of human behavior, may be read as an allegory of the inadequacy of positive social science. Like the emission of the sign in the originary scene, the professor's setting the exam on Thursday is an act both free and necessary, coerced on the level of content but voluntary and contingent on the level of form. Our intuition of paradox is our reaction to the undecidable self-reflectivity of human representation that is both the mark of its origin and its guarantee of survival.

The Two Varieties of Truth

There are two fundamental conceptions of truth: the ostensive and the declarative, the truth of faith and the truth of reason. Today's reader is likely to deny this symmetry; the believer even more than the secular intellectual will reject the idea that these two "truths" might be discussed in the same context. Yet both derive, and in that order, from the originary use of language.

Human language does not begin with the declarative sentence, but with the ostensive. To go beyond the declarative of propositional thought to the ostensive reference that ultimately founds it is the gesture of originary thinking. This operation of liberation from the metaphysical "prison-house of language" is not a romantic return to the nature that stands behind our fallen culture. The ostensive lies within the realm of human language. Originary thinking liberates thought from metaphysics by returning it to its minimal presuppositions. Because the originary moment of thought precedes the declarative, we are not prisoners of the formal propositions of metaphysics; we may deconstruct them through the procedure of originary analysis. In revealing the incompleteness of metaphysics, deconstruction turns us toward anthropological concreteness.

In a language lacking the declarative conception of propositional truth, to conceive the ostensive that lies behind the declarative is already to "believe" it, to accept on faith its presence-as-truth. There would be no declarative truth without ostensive truth; no truth of reason without the truth of faith. This has always been known by religion, but not in a way that has permitted it to be understood by philosophy. Originary thinking explores the locus common to the cognitive operations of these two domains.

*

What is ostensive truth? On the model of the familiar declarative conception we might suppose that it is the correspondence between the ostensive sign and its referent. The child who points to a cat and says "dog" is using the word incorrectly. But this easy parallel with the declarative is misleading. The originary truth of the ostensive cannot be understood as simply equivalent to the use of the correct sign. The world in which everything has a name and one need only get the names right is that of the secure metaphysical separation between words and things given its final consecration by Saussurean linguistics. In the world of the ostensive—and there is no life-world that is "beyond" the ostensive—significance is prior to signification; the question of whether it is appropriate to use a sign at all outweighs that of the appropriate sign to use.

The truth of the originary sign is not understandable as its correspondence with a meaning, for before the act of signing the sign had no meaning, no signified to get wrong. No doubt the association of the sign with its designatum in the act of signing subsequently provides the basis for correspondence-truth. But what we seek is a notion of truth that need not await the second use of the sign, one that already applies to its originary emission. Here the truth of the sign is its designation of something worthy of being re-presented, of what may be taken by the nascent community as the source of its unity precisely because it is an agent of potential disunity. Because the very fact of the production of the sign is a demonstration of the significance of its designatum, this definition of ostensive truth is self-demonstrating or "autoprobatory."[1] But this is not to say that it is tautological; it is not the utterance (*énoncé*) that demonstrates its own truth, but the fact of its being uttered (*énonciation*) in the specific circumstance of the originary scene.

The truth of the originary sign is the birth of the human. The sign is what protects the human community against its potential self-annihilation in mimetic conflict. In the face of this danger, its truth as a gesture of representation rather than a gesture of appropriation is not a foregone conclusion. It is only because the members of the originary community accepted this truth as the revelation of central Being that we are here to speculate about it. They drew back from conflict because they were able to interpret their own acts not as spontaneous movements toward the center but as ostensive signs designating the agent that prevented this movement.

Thus the sign does not represent a certain kind of object, but recognizes an object that *can only be* represented. Significance is not a quality independently possessed by the center that the sign acknowledges, but one attributed by the sign to its referent in the mode of already belonging to that referent. This is not a paradoxically circular definition of significance, but a description of the paradoxically circular procession that constitutes significance. The truth of the originary sign is neither the correspondence between a preestablished meaning and an object that fulfills it, nor that between a preestablished significance and a sign that recognizes it. The usefulness of the notion of "truth" is to thematize the stability of the relation established by the sign, so that its utterer can stand back from it and "see that it is good." The truth of the originary sign is the rightness of the sign-signifying-the-significant or designating-the-designatable, the designatum as a *designandum*.

The originary relation between the sign and its object is not transparent to intuition. It is one that requires thought, that is indeed a defining condition for real thinking, as opposed to models of ratiocination that can be performed by computers. Since it is religion rather than metaphysics that has been concerned with the commemoration of humanity's historical origin, it is not surprising that the best analogy in traditional cultural practice to the operational identity of the originary sign is the name-of-God. The originary sign *names*, in all the ambiguity of the term—at the same time giving a name to and repeating the name of. The idea of God is the originary source of this ambiguity; the sign names what is already worthy to bear the name, what therefore already possesses it, for were it not already God's name it could not be used to name him. The name-of-God is on the one hand infinitely "proper," confined to the unique object that occupies the center, but on the other, it is infinitely generic, designating a central locus that may ultimately be occupied by anything whatever.[2] But as this is understood and other signs for other referents become available, the generative relationship between the unique central being and the anything-whatever of significance—God as the source of language— becomes itself a theme for cultural preservation in ritual and subsequently in mythical narrative.

Ostensive truth is the result of standing back from signification to view the "goodness" of its results. This goodness is that of the human community united by the sign; but it is mediated through the signifying relation to the central object. The identity of the Word with God and of both with Truth is thematized in the partial synthesis of metaphysical and religious thought carried out within early Christianity.

Truth from Paradox

Paradox, as has already been made clear, is anterior to truth; it is the problem that truth resolves, or more precisely, defers. In the crisis that stands at the threshold of the originary scene, all previous dominance relations are annulled; all become imitators and rivals of each other in the same moment. As we have seen in the preceding chapters, the pragmatic paradox of mimesis that had led to stasis is resolved by the transformation of the gesture of appropriation into a sign, and of the blocked appropriative action into a new, uniquely human praxis of signification.

In this revised understanding and performance of the gesture as a sign representing the central object, renunciation of its appropriative aim becomes not a turning away from the object but a new form of turning toward it. The object that had been the occasion of pragmatic paradox has been removed from the terrain of the participants to an— as yet provisionally—transcendental realm accessible only through the act of signification. "Truth" is our name for the guarantee of this accessibility as mediated by the sign. The sign is adequate to designate its referent because, as we have observed, the referent is uniquely adequate to call forth its designation. This is not "correspondence-truth" but its originary source: the truth of faith in the significance of the designatum.

The ostensive sign becomes in turn open to paradox when its truth is conceived independently of the communal scene. The mutual adequacy of sign and referent that constitutes the truth of the ostensive makes scandalous the possibility of performing the sign without its referent. What corresponds to falsity in the domain of ostensive truth is inappropriateness. Because the sign signifies the referent in a mode of inaccessibility—so that it would be better to say that the sign signifies-as-inaccessible—not merely the presence of the referent, but its perceived absence provokes the sign as an expression of desire. Conversely, when one perceives the sign, one imagines the referent. But this imagination corresponds to no perceptual reality; the sign is "false." Only its connection with its referent remains true in the imagination. This is the context of emergence of the imperative, which seeks to abolish the paradoxical oscillation between the falsity and the truth of the "inappropriate" ostensive. The paradox forces the thematization of the distinction between absence and presence, with the result that instead of mere imitation of the ostensive sign, the acceptable response to the imperative is the making-present (the transformation of absence into presence) of its referent.[3]

The truth of the imperative, like the truth of the ostensive, is the adequacy or rightness of the sign for its referent, but now this adequacy is no longer given in advance but must be produced by human agency. The tension of the ostensive without a referent is transformed into the awaiting characteristic of the imperative. The imperative's truth is beyond it; in the terms of ostensive truth, the imperative is a lie. As a consequence, it can fail in a way unavailable to the ostensive. The inappropriateness of an ostensive without the proper referent is in principle verifiable, since the interlocutor is presumed to be able to see for himself whatever the ostensive designates. The imperative as a sign without a referent, an expression of desire, cannot be inappropriate in this sense, even if its object is unrealizable or logically impossible ("get me the round square"). On the contrary, because the awaiting of the referent is inherent in the imperative form itself, violation of its commandment is, at the very least, a crime against language. And the penalty for this crime is eternal, for, in the case of nonperformance, even the interlocutor's intent to obey the imperative could not efface the scandal of what would be in effect an ostensive without a referent.

Ostensive truth, the rightness of fit between sign and referent, is experienced in a mutually reinforcing movement between the two. The imperative profits from the stabilization of this sign-referent relationship to extend it in time; but this extension is in effect its destruction as a functional truth conception. The circulation that defines truth in the ostensive sense is completed only with the satisfaction of the imperative, that is, with the presentation of the referent. The temporal coincidence of the two halves of the original experience, the utterance of the sign and the presence of the referent, is broken; the experience of rightness that was an element of language is now extended into the world as a guarantee of the temporal continuity of the linguistic community. Truth becomes a function not of the speaker but of the hearer: for me to speak the (imperative) truth, you must carry out my request.

This development presupposes the internalization of the old ostensive truth function as no longer the truth of an utterance *en situation* but as a "definition" that atemporally associates the signifier of the sign, not yet with a signified, but with a worldly referent. The imperative tests the validity of the definition. No doubt the sign, in order to *be* a sign, must have from the beginning an imaginary signified, the object of the utterer's formal imitation or intention to represent, but this is not thematized in the act of utterance itself. The originary nondistinction between *énonciation* and *énoncé* is recalled by the crime of "taking the name of God in vain," which among Orthodox Jews reaches the point of refusing to write the word "God" or the equivalent even as an element of a declarative sentence. What remains deliberately unthematized because of what is ultimately fear of mimetic contagion is the concept or Idea of God as opposed to the name. "God" still exists within the internal lexicon of the believer, but he will not *use* the name as though it were a mere dictionary entry because in his eyes it permanently retains its ostensive force.

The emancipation of meaning from the originary presence of the central locus passes through the temporal detachment of the imperative before reaching fulfillment in the transcendental model of the declarative. The open-ended truth of the imperative corresponds to an overestimation of the power of language over the world. This truth cannot be counteracted by the world outside language; instead a new, metalinguistic operation emerges, that of *falsification.* Instead of the oscillation, infinite in principle, between the understanding of the meaning of the imperative and the (inexpressible) renunciation of the attempt to fulfill it, the subject replies with an "objective" predication of nonfulfillment. With the declarative comes the notion of propositional truth familiar to philosophy. Because the declarative provides a model of reality, a predicated "other scene" on which the desired referent can be found, it can be verified against this reality. That is, its *truth* has become independent of its *meaning*.

The Two Schools of Metaphysics

In the elementary linguistic forms, meaning and truth are not formally distinguished. When the child points to a cat and says "dog," lack of rightness in the designation coincides with unclearness of intention. If the listener, uninterested in details, finds the utterance sufficiently right—ostensively true—for his purposes, he will take the meaning of this utterance as the animal the child is in fact designating. The inappropriate ostensive becomes an imperative precisely because it is felt that meaning and truth are identical; that if the speaker intends an object, that object *should* be present. With the emergence of predication, truth and meaning become two different qualities of utterances, determined by entirely different means. It is this separation that permits the "strong" propositional definition of truth as correspondence.

For analytic philosophy as a systematic variety of metaphysics, this definition, formulated with appropriate rigor, is sufficient. If paradoxes creep into the language-games admitted by this philosophy, they can be either foiled by draconian measures like Russell's types, treated on an ad hoc basis, or simply dismissed as parasitic. For the "Continental" variety of metaphysics, haunted by a more profound intuition of the primordial, ostensive form of truth, meditation on the limits of the metaphysical permits one to work one's way through to the originary. But the quest is hampered by the impossibility of referring to the latter except in terms of a metaphorical "negative theology" (e.g., *sous rature*; Heidegger's entire philosophical vocabulary could be cited here, from *Verworfenheit* to *Lichtung des Seins*). This working-through, however rich in anthropological insight, fails to construct a model of the emergence of the declarative from the ostensive because it cannot grasp the independent anthropological significance of the latter, which it understands solely as an instrument for the deconstruction of the former.

The return from the declarative to the ostensive, more specifically, from declarative truth to ostensive truth, is the master problem of post-Hegelian philosophy, a problem first given prominence by Nietzsche and one that preoccupied Heidegger throughout his career. Truth as *aletheia*, as unveiling, is ostensive, not declarative. This does not mean that ostensive truth is a guarantee of presence. On the contrary, presence is itself deferral; to be present on the scene of representation is to be no longer an object of appetite and appropriation, to be cut off from the immediacy of such objects. Presence (on the scene of representation) as the deferral of (worldly) presence is the reality of language; on this point, as we might expect, the naive experience of the ostensive is rendered self-aware by the declarative. Language is always already nonpresence; we have no quarrel on this point with Derrida. But unlike the presence of metaphysics, which subsists within the context of the declarative, ostensive presence is not conceivable as the presence of the sign alone.

The pseudoreligious ontology of Continental metaphysics is no substitute for anthropological minimality. Metaphysics ultimately cannot tolerate the existence of another minimal discourse than its own. Derrida's often brutal attacks on anything that resembles a positive science of discourse, whether in linguistics or analytic philosophy, is perhaps metaphysics' final attempt to enforce the ontological-ontic dichotomy inherited from Plato via Kant's distinction between the empirical domain of the understanding and the a priori one of reason.[4]

Metaphysics' ultimate ground for claiming mastery of the *logos* is its control over the concept of propositional truth. The religious conception of revealed or ostensive truth is unable to contest propositional truth on its own terrain. This is no doubt why Girard's attempt to reclaim primacy for the Judeo-Christian component of the Western tradition over the Hellenic, although grounded in a qualitatively superior conception of mimesis, has fallen short of its goal and retreated into quasi-prophetic rhetoric.[5] Girard's key limitation is a mirror image of that of Derrida: where the latter can only comprehend declarative truth, the former sees only the ostensive. Because the Girardian scene of origin is not a scene of the origin of language, the ostensive language of revelation is never linked to the declarative language of reason, let alone shown to constitute its source.

The late metaphysical working-through begun most visibly by

Nietzsche is the deconstruction of the Platonic separation of ideas and things that is at the foundation of the metaphysical concept of correspondence-truth. Generative anthropology traces the emergence of truth through paradox; Continental metaphysics is uninterested in paradox because it is uninterested in logic, which can give it no assistance in its task of assimilating the revelatory. Or to put it less sympathetically, in its effort to assimilate its mimetic intuitions to the laws of metaphysics, Continental thought has made paradox so much a part of its connotative pathos that it is unable to stand back from it in order to grasp its structure.

The effects that dazzled the generation of 1968—largely faded today in the harsher light of cultural politics—are expressions of the quasi-aporetic situation of the metaphysical thinker trying to think himself out of metaphysics. That such a thought process requires a guarantee outside the realm of metaphysics itself is an idea too dangerous to be entertained, for pushed one step farther it would destroy the resentful attachment of the deconstructive enterprise to its ancestral thought-form. The obsession of deconstructive thinking with attacking the father masks a filial relationship with metaphysics that resembles Hamlet's relationship with Gertrude more than Oedipus's with Laius.

By recurring to paradox, we abandon the stormy Continent for the dry terrain of Anglo-Saxon analytic philosophy. The usefulness of this displacement is strategic; the failure of declarative language to exclude paradoxical statements is a chink in the armor of metaphysics, one through which, after a little prying, there appears a glimmer of anthropological light.

Predication

The defining operation of the declarative is predication, the most elementary form of which is the negative reply to the imperative. Predication, the attribution of a predicate to a subject or "topic," affirms the validity of a model of reality in which the subject-topic is declared to inhabit the universe of the predicate. But the worldly referent does not participate directly in this model, in which the simplicity of the ostensive truth relation is deferred to a linguistic "other scene." The declarative is in principle subject to verification through the examination of the real-world association of subject and predicate. But this verification is not, as for the ostensive and imperative, implicit in the intentional structure of the form itself, which creates an imaginary or "fictive" reality independent of the real world. Verification belongs to the reference-world, the conformity of which to the model given by the sentence—which determines the latter's truth—is wholly independent of the meaning by means of which the hearer understands the sentence prior to verifying it.[6]

The predicate's relocation of the topic of a preceding imperative from the world to the imaginary scene of a linguistic model leads to the thematization of truth as the "value" of the declarative proposition. Predication inserts a *différance*, a deferral-differentiation, between the understanding of its meaning and the verification of its validity. The anthropological understanding of predicative truth turns on the specific nature of this deferral.

Ostension is pointing; the ostensive begins as a movement-toward, albeit one that has renounced its appropriative aim to turn back on itself in formal closure, detached from the temporality of worldly praxis. The ostensive is intended to be immediately confirmed, not verified, by the experience of its hearer. The function of the ostensive is to mobilize communal attention toward an object of particular appetitive interest, whether positive or negative. Its failure to justify such interest would not be an incorrect affirmation but an inappropriate demand for action, a public scandal likely to arouse a violent reaction. In the imperative, which cannot be confirmed before the performance of the task it sets its hearer, a temporal deferral is opened up between sign and referent that liberates the language user from the immediacy—the "presence"—of the ostensive. But this deferral retains its direct connection with worldly reality; it is not an element of the intentional structure of the imperative qua representational form.

What is distinctive about the verification of the declarative, which is to say, about its criterion of truth, is that whether it be carried out immediately, indefinitely postponed, or never even conceived, its structure contains deferral within itself. To understand the declarative is to abandon the scene of real-world performance for the imaginary scene of representation. Predication, unlike ostension, requires the construction of a synthesis in the hearer's imagination. This synthesis is most evident in sentences like "the grass is green," where a noun and an adjective are connected by a copula. First we think of the grass, then we move toward greenness. But predication incites the deferral of understanding even in subjectless sentences like "it's raining." When I hear, "it's raining," I move from my previous intuition of a weather-neutral world to one in which rain is falling. There is no immediate imaginary experience of rain, as would be the case with "Rain!" but the creation of a model of reality.

Depending on circumstances, I might look out the window to see for myself. But this empirical act is essentially late with respect to my synthetic understanding of the meaning of the sentence. The linguistic expression is self-sufficient; its understanding includes within itself the synthesis that the elementary forms found and/or created between the word and the world. The confirmation that was inherent in the linguistic experience of the ostensive and a reality of praxis for the imperative becomes a secondary truth-verifying operation on the already-constituted declarative.

We have noted that the gap between the understanding and the verification of the declarative has the temporality of deferral. The originary utterance of the ostensive sign deferred conflict over the central object by substituting a sign that all could possess for a thing that had become inaccessible. The declarative doubles this linguistic process by proposing a second sign—the predicate—that locates the object within a linguistic model. This model is in principle verifiable; all language eventually leads back to the world. But verification is no longer contained within the intentional structure of the linguistic form itself. On the contrary, the deferral of verification is central to its intention; to test the linguistic model against reality is to reopen the potential for conflict inherent in the unfulfillment of the original imperative. Verification provokes interpersonal tension because it demonstrates worldly desire's dissatisfaction with the merely linguistic response that the declarative provides.

We may distinguish between two kinds of verification of the predicate, only the second of which really merits the name. In the originary case, the hearer of the declarative performs the verification as a prolongation of his former imperative, that is, in order to fulfill his intention of acquiring the object. As a result of the information conveyed by the declarative, the original speaker is better equipped to find the object he seeks. This form of verification does not question the veracity of the predicate, but merely seeks to transcend the predicative situation toward the topic about which the predicate supplies new information. The second kind is carried out independently of praxis because the speaker's predication is suspected of being false. The first case contains the second nonthematically; my need to act on the information tests its truth as a matter of course. Conversely, the expulsion of the practical concern of originary verification by the second form coincides with the establishment of metaphysical philosophy, the love of wisdom for its own sake.

The thematic notion of truth emerges when the two types of verification are recognized as distinct, so that disbelief in the predication is distinguished from mere dissatisfaction with predication as a response to the imperative. At this point, the declarative has become an acceptable answer to the imperative, which has become a de facto interrogative. Only if the predicate is false does it now bear a potential for conflict; if true, its speaker would presumably have nothing to fear from his interlocutor's disappointment.

Verification in the first case, that performed out of impatience to possess the referent, dismisses the specific pertinence of the declarative at the same time as it makes use of the information it imparts. It avoids conflict by substituting the first interlocutor for the second in the performance of his own imperative. The association of the (ostensive) sign with its referent in the immediate mode of presence has been stretched to the limit, but it has not been broken. The second case, however, introduces the possibility of untruth where in the first we could still speak of "inappropriateness." The untrue predicate does not designate an absent presence, a locus in which the referent may be found; it hides a definitive absence. What is significant is not untruth itself but the predicate's suspicious potential for untruth, its fundamental fictionality.[7] Not only is language capable of misleading, but even when true, it constructs a fictional world separate from reality. But this gives no comfort to the superficial postmodern tendency to use the fictionality of the declarative as an excuse to ignore its correspondence with the real. On the contrary, it is precisely its fictionality that makes the declarative the locus of a new form of truth.

Truth is the result of the secondary deferral accomplished by predication, of the gap between understanding the predicate and verifying it. The predicate depresentifies; to make present the depresentified takes real time. In the meantime, the status of the predicate remains unclear. We justifiably call it fictional—and the in principle indefinite deferral of correspondence-truth implied by this term is precisely what permits the existence of esthetic fictions—so long as we remember that fiction is from the beginning the deferral of truth; one has no conceptual existence without the other.[8]

*

Since declarative truth is in essence deferred, not present in the utterance itself, it cannot foreclose the possibility of the radical form of fictionality we call paradox. The deferral of empirical verification risks being usurped by a form that transforms the fictional hesitation between truth and falsity into an oscillation in which understanding itself, made to depend on this verification, is indefinitely deferred. Yet to consider paradox a danger to language is perversely to ignore that the source of all logical paradox is the formal verticality of representation that defers the originary protoparadox of mimesis, the antinomy of imitation and rivalry.

Metaphysical thought founded on declarative language opened up the whole domain of nature to the power of the truth function, gradually delimiting, if only by default, the fundamental anthropological domain in which paradox reigns as a constitutive principle rather than an anomaly. If today's metaphysicians have become suspicious of the declarative truth concept that underlay their predecessors' achievements, this reflects their intuition of the paradoxical truth that the stability of truth in the human community depends, both originarily and historically, on the dynamic interactivity of paradox.

On Irony

The standard treatises on rhetoric tell us that the figure of irony consists in saying the opposite of what one means. For example, Pierre Fontanier's *Figures du discours* (1827): "L'ironie consiste à dire . . . le contraire de ce qu'on pense, ou de ce qu'on veut faire penser" [Irony consists in saying . . . the contrary of what one thinks, or of what one would have one's interlocutor think];[1] or as my (American Heritage) dictionary puts it, "The intended meaning of the words used is the direct opposite of their usual sense." One might wonder what could be the possible use of such a figure, why anyone should bother to express an idea by affirming its direct opposite. Yet the expression "the irony of fate" suggests a direct connection between the catastrophic occurrence of "the direct opposite" of one's expectations and the opposition between the words of the ironic tenor and vehicle. And we designate by the expression "romantic irony" an attitude toward life that consists not so much in anticipating the opposite of one's expectations as in a knowing superiority to the ironies of fate that await us in the real world.

Irony attends us everywhere, always gifted with prestige, although its association with meaning makes the term sound just a bit quaint in comparison with such postmodern terms as *différance* or *scriptible*. No mere figure of speech, irony is central to all thought, for the use of language as such is essentially ironic. The Greek *eíron* is the (apparent) fool, the dissembler, but the root of the word is the same as that (*eíro*, from IE *wer→*word*) of speech itself.

*

The idea that one can mean the contrary of what one (ostensibly) says, that a sign can be made to bear the opposite of its normal sense, is clearly dependent on the prior existence of a sign-system. But it would be metaphysical naïveté to affirm that irony is inherent in sign-systems-in-general, as though irony existed independently of human forms of representation. Irony is a characteristic of the historical human sign-system of language, and any ironies to be found in "fate" or elsewhere are derivative of this system.

The primary characteristic of the sign is that it occupies a different level of being from the reality it designates. This vertical difference, the basis of the opposition within the sign-system between signifier and signified, can only be thought concretely from an originary perspective. The sign as an abortive gesture of appropriation is on a different level from its referent because although it remains a physical gesture, it renounces the physical assimilation of this referent in becoming a representation of it. The separation between the sphere of the sign and that of the referent is no longer merely physical; the gesture that was to abolish this separation has been transformed into one that consecrates it. In phenomenological usage, the sign "intends" its referent precisely in the sense that the referent remains outside the immediate sphere of action of the intender.

What role could be played in this originary context by irony, by intending the opposite of the sign? How indeed is the "opposite" to be defined? The strange prestige of irony in the domain of communication is only revealed through originary analysis.

Irony is the expression, necessarily indirect, of the fragility of the absolute or "vertical" formal difference inaugurated by the sign with respect to its source, the relative or "horizontal" difference in the real world between the subject and the object of desire—ultimately, between the eater and the potentially eaten. We should beware of characterizing this difference metaphysically, as in the Hegelian phenomenology of consciousness where subject and object interact directly without the mediation of the collectively determined sign. From the standpoint of the peripheral community of subjects, the sign indeed creates a universe of signification that is absolutely other than the real world, but the absolute nature of this otherness is only an instrument of deferral; it is ultimately subject to deconstruction.[2] Irony is the necessarily indirect and allusive expression of the deconstructability of the formal structure of language that is the model for all formal structures, all of which are in the last analysis structures of representation.

To think a formal structure is to conceive both its levels on the same plane, to deconstruct it—to ironize it. True thinking, originary anthropological thinking as opposed to the positive thought that unconditionally respects formal difference, is thus always ironic. But because humanity depends on the maintenance of formal structures in order to defer conflict, ironic thinking is potentially tragic. Once the absolute formal barrier between sign and referent has been shown to be vulnerable, an end is made to deferral and the central figure becomes subject to sparagmatic violence. The fate of the tragic hero is irony incarnate.

How does this anthropological concept of irony square with the standard rhetorical definition? To say the opposite of what one means is not so simple a phenomenon as the words make it appear. Not all statements have "opposites"; nor is the ground of opposition simply logical. Were irony a mere matter of reversing truth value, it would be impossible to detect and would in fact make language wholly indeterminate; the assertion of any proposition p would also be the ironic assertion of not-p. Clearly this is not the way irony works.

If I look out the window and see that it is raining, it would not be ironic to say "It's not raining"—unless this statement repeats a previously made claim that my observation would falsify. ("No, it's not raining! Those raindrops are just figments of my imagination!") The normal ironic remark would be something like "What a lovely day!"[3] This remark requires no preestablished context because fair or "good" weather is normatively felt to be desirable. My irony expresses disappointment; I would like to be able to say "What a lovely day!" sincerely, but under the circumstances I can only say it ironically. My words reflect my desire, but at the same time, through a change in tone, they are "quoted" rather than asserted, so that I am merely pronouncing the (ostensive) phrase in the absence of its referent. My language points to the rain but declares it to be sunshine.

We recall from the preceding chapter or from *The Origin of Language* that this is precisely the intentional structure of the derivation of the imperative from the ostensive: the ostensive, which normally designates a referent actually present to the speaker, is uttered in the absence of such a referent in order to make it appear. This intention depends on a magical conception of ostensive language: since the word is pronounced only in the presence of the object, pronouncing the word alone is expected to produce the object. In the ironic situation, we know better. Saying "What a lovely day!" is not going to put an end to the rain. It expresses my disappointment; but the focus of this disappointment is less that the weather is contrary to my wishes than that my language is unable to alter it. The hierarchy of form over content, words over things, by means of which the imperative is derived from the ostensive, has no effect on the things themselves. This is a reproach directed against the originary project of language, which in the case of the weather may easily enough be attributed to the will of God. The ironic sign expresses originary resentment, the human reaction to the withdrawal of the center that language both commemorates and supplements. Irony makes explicit the resentment that is at the heart of all language, the disappointment of the originary aborted gesture that reveals itself in the sparagmos once the danger that blocked the gesture's original aim is past.

We do not ironize when faced with the real power of the sacred center to defer human conflict. But whatever the flourishes of the cosmological imagination, this power is not transferable to the natural world; God lets it rain on the just as on the unjust, which is really to say that he can do nothing for or against either. By our irony we reject *ad maiorem Dei gloriam* this attribution of impotence to God, implicitly reproaching him with deliberately choosing not to grant our wish for sunny skies. In demonstrating the impotence of language to grant our wishes, we at the same time imply that the Being who gave us language does not lack the power to do so, with the result that we are justifiably dissatisfied when this Being does not use this power for our benefit.

The pleasure of irony is truly an esthetic pleasure, functioning through the same oscillatory movement as esthetic experience between ascetic form and seductive content. The fact that I can express my wish and imagine its fulfillment depends on the unreality of this fulfillment. My subsequent ironic statement is an ex post facto "artwork" that is given form by the preexistent denial of my desire—a desire that need not even have been previously formulated. By exclaiming "What a lovely day!" I transform the simple frustration of my implicit desire for clear skies, scarcely more than an appetite, into an esthetic experience that "drowns" my resentment of the central power from which I am excluded. Who has not experienced the disappointment of having one's ironic outburst voided by the sudden realization of one's purported wish? If the rain immediately ceased, could the sunlight be bright enough to compensate me for the vanished pleasure of irony? The ironist is a masochist; his proof of being is furnished by suffering. Rather than an expression of divine favor, the reappearance of the sun would be for him a demonstration that God does not exist.

On the one hand, irony demonstrates our independence from the constraints of the sign-referent hierarchy: form cannot dictate to content, language has no ontological privilege with respect to reality. On the other, by its very expression, irony resentfully affirms the authority of the form it has denied. The ironic deconstruction of the hierarchy between words and things pays homage to this hierarchy by implying that it presides over its own deconstruction. By pretending that my words are not powerless to realize my desires, I confront the scene of representation with my own powerlessness as a reproach, as though the power were available but arbitrarily withheld. This withholding is what provides the peaceful resolution of the originary event; but now it no longer appears to be necessary, since all I desire is a nice day. (Think how strange—and unironic—it would be if the object of my desire were openly conflictive or resentful. Only in a world of black comedy can someone say ironically, "Nice torturing, Bob!" to an insufficiently cruel—as opposed to a barbaric but inefficient—torturer. Or is our meta-ironic postmodern culture loosening our grasp of this distinction?)

Irony is like a black Mass, a mode of disbelief that only a believer can engage in. But its pervasiveness as a cultural mode in a world that proclaims the "death of God" suggests the unlikelihood that there exists a still more sophisticated, more atheistic mode from which irony itself is excluded. The persistence of irony is proof that resentment of the divinity outlasts faith in it; the ironist is an atheist who condemns God for his failure to exist. Raised to the status of a life principle, this atheism becomes "romantic irony."

Romantic Irony

The world's failure to meet the ironist's expectations becomes proof of his victimary centrality. The historical origin of this phenomenon is in Rousseau's *Rêveries*, which begin with the immortal words, "Me voici donc seul sur la terre, n'ayant plus de frère, de prochain, d'ami, de société que moi-même. Le plus sociable et le plus aimant des humains en a été proscrit par un accord unanime" [Here I am, then, alone on earth, deprived of brother, neighbor, friend, any social contact other than myself. The most sociable and loving of men has been banished from society by a unanimous agreement]. The romantic subject's worldly role of hapless victim hides a divine self-consciousness for which the worldly separation between form and content, sign and thing is an illusion. This is not yet an ironic position. Because the romantic recognizes that qua human subject he contains within himself the totality of the scene, the center as well as the periphery, he is content to smile down from above on the follies of human praxis, without considering that these follies include his own since he too is forced to live in the world.

Romantic irony is a "late," second-generation phenomenon that in France corresponds to the disillusionment of the failed romantic revolution of 1848. Even when the first-generation romantic—speaking not just for himself but for the whole of humanity—utters ironically, "What a lovely day!" he is not yet a romantic ironist. Chateaubriand or Hugo say such things, not Baudelaire or Kierkegaard. The early romantics fail to see the contradiction between the formal superiority over the world conferred on them by the sign and their use of the sign in futile contestation of the forms of worldly superiority. The romantic ironist knows that his extraworldly stance makes him complicit in the worldly iniquities he denounces. He more than anyone is aware of the fragility of ontological hierarchies, which all begin from the hierarchy of signs and things. Thus the Olympian posture of the romantic ironist is itself ironized—which does not mean that it is abolished. The writer of the lines

Tu le connais, lecteur, ce monstre délicat
Hypocrite lecteur, mon semblable, mon frère![4]

has in no way renounced the privilege of the writer's position. What he derides is the reader's complicity with this position, and his own complicity with that complicity. Baudelaire mocks us all for pretending that language can transcend reality, and that he as the writer can use language to transcend even that transcendence.

As opposed to the naive romantic, the victim of the *mensonge romantique*, the romantic ironist is aware of the nonoriginality of worldly desire. Nor is it fair to condemn his transcendental stance as mere illusion when it displays the understanding that he is condemned within the world to imitate the very conduct he has unmasked. The romantic ironist grasps from above the unity of the scene that he cannot experience in the world. His is an authentic mode of anthropological thought.

Romantic irony is not immediately dependent on language because the subject no longer identifies himself as a mere peripheral language speaker; his participation in the scene of representation is central and originary. Romantic irony plays on the contrast between material triviality and spiritual importance; the individual is powerless, ignored, yet a possessor of the whole through the intermediary of the sign. This is Pascal's *roseau pensant* in a secular world; irony is as close as the late romantic will come to a belief in divine providence.

The Irony of the Esthetic

It is because the esthetic effect is the direct experience of irony that the greatest artworks are the most ironic. The oscillatory structure of esthetic experience, ever circulating between form and content, realizes the same paradox that the ironist enacts in speech. Esthetic form dissolves as the mere revelation of content, but content can possess significance only by recalling the form in which it is revealed.

But although the esthetic incarnates irony in experience, popular art, the most general model of esthetic experience, ignores the formal necessity of this incarnation; it takes the order of the sign for granted. In contrast, high art is explicitly ironical; that is perhaps its sharpest definition. It is informed with the understanding that the peace procured by the vertical separation of signs from things is merely a deferral, a *différance*, that form offers only a distraction, not a barrier, against the chaos of indifferentiation.

In the terminology of *The End of Culture*, popular art takes the attitude of consumption rather than production. This point may be sharpened by reference to the sparagmos as satisfying not only alimentary appetite but originary resentment. The individual both participates in the collective disfigurement of the central object and acquires his own portion of it. In the former respect, the sparagmos is a success; the central figure is indeed destroyed. Insofar as I feel myself a mere member of the collectivity, my resentment against the center has been fully satisfied. But as an individual defined in a one-on-one relationship with the center, my satisfaction is concentrated in my individual portion, which bears to the central figure as a whole the same paradoxical dependence/independence relationship as the sign to its referent: the part expresses the power of the center only because of the totality that was destroyed in order for the part to come into existence. As a representation, the part is ironically superior to the whole, but only because the reality of the whole is prior to that of the part. Popular art expresses the collective satisfaction of the sparagmos as though there were nothing to mourn for in the destruction of the originary totality, as though there were no more to the individual than his existence among the "people," whereas the irony of high art reflects the individual's paradoxical relationship with the totality that must be destroyed in order for him to possess it.

The Irony of Fate

Suppose a man runs to catch a train and boards it just as it is pulling out of the station. Shortly after, the train is derailed and he is killed. The fulfillment of his desire to catch the train has led to his death. An ironic element is introduced by the fact that his desire was fulfilled only in extremis, as if by miracle. Destiny appears to favor him, but ultimately does the opposite. This sequence is analogous to saying "What a lovely day!" in the rain, with the significant difference that it follows a narrative temporality. In both cases there is an appeal to an implicit divine promise of the satisfaction of desire, in one case through the sign, in the other through the grace experienced in the in extremis realization of a project—a sentiment conceivable only because human projects are not merely programmed but thematized, reflected on. In the case of the rain, the linguistic capacity that allows me to formulate my desire is a reminder of this promise; in that of the train, the promise appears first to be realized, then to turn into its opposite.

The irony of fate does not require language in order to manifest itself, but it is only understandable through a representational lens; the pursuit of the train is an allegory of desire-in-general. To obtain one's desire is fatal—this is the deepest irony of tragedy, that of Oedipus.

We may define tragic irony more precisely. The tragic situation is the reductio ad absurdum of mimesis, the failure of representation. Oedipus is so mimetic that he no longer understands that mimesis is representational. He can only imitate by literally usurping the other's place. Hence at every turn, when Oedipus seeks otherness, he arrives at sameness. He leaves home—but he returns home. He abandons his mother—but he finds his mother. The irony of the *Oedipus* recurs again and again to the failure of initiation, the impossibility of finding an object outside the family circle, of transforming the specificity of family reality into a representation of behavior in general. Language cannot provide its usual assistance in avoiding conflict because for Oedipus the universe of representation is ironically indistinguishable from the life-world. The sign cannot realize its ontological privilege of detachment from the referent.

Hence when Oedipus condemns the murderer, it is himself whom he condemns. This is sometimes presented as a failure of "intelligence"; as with the man who catches the doomed train, Oedipus's fabled reasoning powers only help realize the oracle's prediction. Thought is always ironic, that is, it deconstructs vertical difference into horizontal sameness; but this very fact makes thought useless to one whose desire is confined within the scene about which he thinks. All I learn from thinking my categorical desire for women cannot help me understand my specific desire for my mother.

Irony performs the same function in tragedy as in the simple scene of "What a lovely day!" but tragedy shows us that the impotence of representational difference can have more dangerous consequences than the frustration of desire. In revealing the ultimate common source of form and content, sign and referent, sacred and profane, ontic and on-tological, tragedy represents, and thus again defers, the failure of de-ferral, the inevitability of conflict. The extraordinary stability of lan-guage and representational systems that permits us to appreciate three-thousand-year-old texts and thirty-thousand-year-old paintings is due to the resiliency of the paradoxical structure of signification, of which irony is the experiential component.

Irony is more fundamental than the esthetic effect, which should be considered a particular form of irony. It is the fundamental cultural mode or "trope" because all culture is grounded in nature, the *hylé*, where the sign and the referent are cut from the same cloth. Decon-struction inhabits structure from the beginning; irony continually knits up what it has undone, as is the case for the whole family of paradox-ical structures that make up the human. Irony both points out and re-pairs the inadequacy of the deferral of violence through representa-tion that is the essence of human culture. Ultimately all formal differ-ence breaks down, but we can only learn this from within a new formal difference that has not yet broken down. The ironies of tragedy can only be contemplated in a state of ironic—but untragic—repose.

Irony removes the security of the sign and returns us to originary chaos, but this chaos is accessible only through a system of represen-tation that remains intact. Our sympathy with the victims of tragic irony does not prevent us from knowing that it isn't really a lovely day, or from knowing the true identity of Laius's murderer. This is the vul-nerable point of tragedy and of the esthetic/ironic in general as a model for anthropological understanding. Tragedy's insight into the inevitable dangers of human indifferentiation leads it ultimately to reaffirm—however ironically—the arbitrary victimizations it inherits from its mythical sources. Its demystifications are always finite and ultimately self-liquidating.

The esthetic depends on finitude, spatio-temporal decisiveness, how-ever arbitrary. To remain undecided within the symmetry of the agon is to renounce art's formal promise to defer our resentment. We iden-tify with the hero on the level of content while we await his demise on the level of form; it is this ironic, paradoxical structure that has made human culture capable of lasting as long as it has. All the postsacrifi-cial wisdom of the Gospels cannot prevent the Passion narrative from taking on the very tragic structure it denounces. The secret of the historical success of Christianity lies in this paradox, not in the eternal truth of the moral Kingdom that shares the fragility of all utopias. Irony is built into the formal representation-relation that is the basis of human culture. In this sense, it is truly a transhistorical phenomenon, one that annuls its own historicity in the very act of producing it. Not that irony does not have its own history as a cultural mode. From classical tragedy to romantic melodrama, the cultural subject anticipates through representation the demise of the scenic center, but his efforts to escape its fate only encounter the same ironic structure on a higher plane. Postmodern culture takes ironic anticipation to a still higher level, where the very reality of the sign-referent relation is denied in advance. But this denial, in its formal abstraction, changes nothing essential; regardless of wisdom or cynicism, in order for the esthetic to function, we must experience irony through our own lived illusion and disillusion.

*

Does generative anthropology, in laying out explicitly the paradox of cultural form, escape deconstruction through irony, or does it fall subject to the facile but suggestive schema of Paul de Man's *Blindness and Insight*, where each insightful demystification has its own blind spot? The best answer is that like all cultural operations, generative anthropology works not by dichotomy but by deferral. Unless we believe in the chimera of the "end of history," we are forced to anticipate a future understanding of irony and paradox (which may not necessarily use the terms "irony" and "paradox") from the standpoint of which our own analysis is *structurée* without being *structurante*. In contrast with de Man's schema, which is, like everything else in his work, a radically nihilistic denial of history, our model respects the human labor, material and intellectual, that the resiliency of our cultural structures permits us to carry out. The continual deferral of our ever-present propensity for self-destruction is the highest or, in any case, the most necessary of human achievements. May God, or the ironic contemplation of his absence, save us from the utopian search for final solutions.

Plato and the Birth of Conceptual Thought

For over a century, thought has attempted to free itself from metaphysics.[1] A certain philosophical postmodernity has declared this a vain endeavor, having decided that metaphysics is the indispensable form of any coherent reflection. Yet since humanity existed before metaphysics, we should be able to survive its demise. It suffices that we oppose to it a form of thought sufficiently powerful to be able to think both its beginning and its end.

Primitive, egalitarian societies function by means of ritual distribution systems guaranteed by the symmetrical differentiations of mythical speech. With the appearance of social hierarchy, the mastery of ritual distribution becomes fixed in one place and refuses to circulate; the new task of cultural language is to justify this disequilibrium. But in the society of the "Greek miracle" that arises in the margins of the archaic empires, the accelerated circulation of goods and ideas loosens hierarchical rigidity and gives language a competitive value. The Sophists learn to manipulate speech for the purpose of persuasion. Yet, whether out of indifference or self-interest, they do not seek the a priori conditions of this manipulation; language is for them simply a tool in the hands of man who claims to be "the measure of all things."

The Concept as Ethical Content

Following Socrates, Plato understands that "free" speech, far from being gratuitous, is the sign of a new, implicit ethical order. In order to understand this order, it is necessary to reflect not on what language refers to but on what it signifies to the community. We may roughly express this distinction by contrasting the ensemble of worldly referents of a word (its "denotation" in analytic philosophy) with its "signified" or meaning (its "connotation"). But for Plato, the latter is not an abstract meaning but a substantial *content* that the users of the word possess in common. The intuition that the usage of certain words reveals an ethical content that is more than an abstract signification is the very foundation of philosophical reflection. This intuition is already implicitly that of the Socrates of the early dialogues, and was no doubt that of the historical figure who irritated his contemporaries by forcing them to define courage, beauty, friendship, and the like. It is by deepening his understanding of the content of words that Plato will transform Socrates' open interrogations into conceptual thought, which is only another name for metaphysics.

In order to grasp the ethical point of departure for this way of thinking, let us listen to the debate between Socrates and Callicles in the *Gorgias*:

1. [Callicles:] For by nature the ugliest thing is also the worst: to suffer injustice; whereas it is only because of the law that it is worse to commit it. . . . Unfortunately it is the weak and the masses who have created the laws. . . . They say that it is unjust to wish to have more than the others. . . . For, as they are inferior, it suffices for them to have equality! (482abc)

What is by nature beautiful and just, is that . . . he who wants to live his life rightly must . . . give to each desire that may come upon him its fullness of satisfactions. . . . Should they who are able to enjoy without restraint all that is good pose as a master over themselves what is decreed . . . by the multitude?. . . . Sensuality, license, unreserved freedom . . . that is virtue and happiness! (491e, 492c)

2. [Socrates:] But [the pleasures] that are good, are they also those that are useful . . . ? Now, pleasures as well as pains, it is those that are useful that one must choose and practice? [Thus] it is for the sake of good things . . . that we should do everything. . . . Do you not agree . . . that the good is, without exception, the end of all our acts and that it is for the purpose of the good that

all the rest must be done, but not the good for the purpose of the rest . . . ? Is it not therefore for the purpose of good things that one should carry out all acts, including those that are pleasant, but not the good for the purpose of the pleasant? (499de, 500a)

For Callicles, to satisfy one's desires, assuming one can get away with it, is a clearer path to happiness than obedience to the law, which this proto-Nietzschean sees as the instrument of domination by the weak over the strong. All other things being equal, the "unjust" person who disobeys the law to promote his own satisfaction has the advantage over his obedient opposite number. But the unjust does evil, and evil is harmful, whence Socrates demonstrates that no one can knowingly be unjust. No one can intend the harmful, therefore knowingly do evil, even if the harmful is "pleasant." Any conflict on this point is not real but illusory, an error of ignorance.

Of the two arguments, it is rather Socrates' that strikes us as contrived. The question Socrates avoids is how he knows that "the good" is always the same for all. In the practical (ontic) world, the concepts of good and evil are "indexed"; what is good for me is not necessarily good for you. Indeed, if my good and your good involve the possession of an identical object—a person we both love, an honor we both covet—the two goods cannot be identical. This is the very structure of mimetic rivalry. We will not be able to avert conflict merely by pronouncing some magic word ("good," "just," or "beautiful") as we might the name of a god in a rite.

There is nothing sacred in the words themselves. Plato's new sacred is the *concept*. At the time of the *Gorgias*, the Eidos/Idea/Form has not yet been conceived. But what Plato has already discovered is that the concept of the Good, to which the Just and the Beautiful are related (and which ancient philosophy never really distinguishes from it), contains something more than the meaning of the word. The eirenic sharing of the concept that founds the identity of your good with mine is not a product of the meaning of the word "good," but of its ethical content, a notion explainable only within the framework of an originary anthropology.

Plato's doctrine of the good-as-concept, the decisive moment of the forgetting of the sacred-ontological denounced by Heidegger, is not yet fully developed at the time of this not altogether persuasive refutation of the anti-idea of Callicles. When the latter's argument is taken

up again by Thrasymachus in Book I of the *Republic*, the insufficiency
of the old answer of the *Gorgias* motivates the displacement of the subject, in the sense of the Subject of the Good, from the individual human soul to the political collectivity. The capstone of Socrates' argument is that "no ruling authority works for his own benefit, but . . . for
the benefit of him who is under his authority" (346e). This is the beginning of a necessary but incomplete return to the communal origin
of the Idea, where alone the notion of a commonly possessed, conflict-
deferring content makes sense.

What separates us from Plato is supposedly his "realism." But the reality of the Ideas is nothing but what we have been calling their "content." Let us forget for a moment the heaven where the Ideas with a
capital "I" are supposed to dwell. Their reality has a more concrete
meaning, which the lesson of the *Gorgias* can help us to uncover. A
"real" idea is an idea that intervenes in reality between desiring beings.
It is an apotropaic object that serves to defer potential conflict. The reality of the Idea is the substantiality that makes it capable of replacing
the thing that provokes the conflict. It is because Callicles and Socrates
possess in common the Idea of justice that they cannot rationally come
to blows. Those who do are only the ignorant who do not possess the
Idea, or rather, who are unaware that they do so.

The concept is a representation; ultimately, nothing more than a
word. But the word is not a simple duplicate of the thing. The thing is
unique, or, to speak more prudently, reproducible with difficulty. The
word is multiple, or, let us say, reproducible with ease. Where we would
have to divide the thing, we can share the totality of the word. Where,
between you and me, the good-as-thing would pose a problem, the
good-as-word would not; it is neither your word nor mine, but everyone's. As though a word could replace reality, the cynic will object. But
it can, on the condition that the good-as-word acquire the reality that
will transform it into a concept, that is, an entity of another order,
which is, like the word, infinitely shareable but which, being substituted for the good-as-thing, stands in the path of conflictual desire.

The Originary and the Metaphysical Logos

Plato does not seek, does not want to recognize the configuration
of the originary scene of language in which alone such a substitution

is conceivable. The linguistic sign comes into being to substitute for the thing that the multiplicity of appetites makes inaccessible—not forever, but for a certain time. The sign defers—this lesson we have learned well—but we forget that what it defers is in the first place the violence of the desires converging on a common object. The collective possession, division, and distribution of the thing are all deferred; the thing-totality remains only as the remembered referent of the sign. We need no psychoanalytic scenario to understand this idealization of the object as totality, to which we preferentially give the name of God.

The sign defers conflict, offers instead of the thing an imaginary substitute. One might object that this hypothetical sign is hardly the equivalent of Plato's Idea. Plato did not formulate an originary anthropology; on the contrary, his doctrine promoted the suppression of the originary anthropologies he knew in their ritual form. No doubt Plato retains, by attributing it to the concept, the essential function of the originary scene he denies: the deferral of conflict through representation. But in affirming the reality of the concept, he inverts the ontological priority of word and thing. The entire doctrine of Ideas that derives from this affirmation and that will be elaborated beginning with the *Cratylus*—to which I shall return—maintains this inversion, which prolongs and preserves in the form of an ontology the sacred difference attached to the scenic center. This prolongation, this fetishizing of the word in its difference from the thing, is an alternative, equivalent characterization of metaphysics.

In our hypothetical originary scene, the role of language is reduced to its strict minimum: the momentary hesitation between the (chaotic) beginning and the (minimally ordered) end of an act of collective appropriation. The minimal linguistic act is the re-presentation of an already-present object by means of an ostensive sign that will preserve the memory of the object after its disappearance. The ostensive word is not yet a concept; it is the name of an object-in-situation, a phenomenon that we can no doubt better understand as the "name of God."[2] It is by means of the ostensive that we teach words to children; they subsequently learn to use these words as imperatives to make appear objects designated in their absence, and finally to construct "complete sentences," that is, declaratives. In the declarative sentence, language achieves its mature capacity to create imaginary models on the "other scene" of representation. We may then give a preliminary definition of the concept as the word/noun understood as necessarily an element of a declarative sentence, cut off from the original act of naming. ("Noun," like "name," comes from the Latin *nomen*.) Metaphysics, by denying the existence of an utterance-form more primitive than the declarative, incarnates the refusal to think the origin of language as an event.

This metaphysical sacrifice of the elementary linguistic structures institutes "logocentrism" in the precise sense of domination by the declarative sentence or proposition, the strong meaning of the word *logos*. It is this, rather than the strategic marginalization of writing, that is the founding expulsion of Western philosophy. The ostensive exists only in situation; spoken or written, it cannot detach itself from the place in which it is uttered. The arrow on the signpost, the sign on a door of the toilet constitute an ostensive form of writing that presupposes on the part of its reader the same (virtual) copresence with the referent as the living word. The inaugural gesture of metaphysics, which makes possible analytic thought, suppresses the ostensive that attaches us to the trace of the historical presence we continue to commemorate under the name of God. The concept, the Platonic Idea, is something we all possess without having to point to it, that is, without needing to perform the ostensive sign that defers potential conflict among those who covet the same object. It is not in its role as a grammatical form that the ostensive is dangerous. What is protected against by its exclusion (and not merely from grammar books) is the renewal of its originary function of designating the sacred center of the communal circle.

The fundamental circular structure of ritual reveals the connection, not obvious in the abstract, between ostensive language and religion. The oft-repeated notion that philosophical logocentrism is in complicity with religion misunderstands the communal operation of the sacred. Traditional metaphysics redefines the sacred in its own terms as a "first principle," as though the universe itself were deduced from a master proposition. The *logos* of the conceptual sacred of metaphysics, whose gods, beginning with the demiurge in the *Timaeus*, have never been worshiped by anyone, is not the *logos* of the historical religions. The deferred, discursive presence that presides over metaphysics is not the real presence that the rite claims to realize. The ostensive is banished by the linguistics of the philosophers, who replace faith in the divine presence it designates by confidence in the self-presence of philosophical language.[3]

The two *logoi*, that of religion and that of metaphysics, the one that refers to originary revelation and the other that denies it, can only be reconciled in the discourse of originary anthropology. There is, however, a fundamental parallelism between the conceptual "forgetting of Being" inaugurated by metaphysics and the new, similarly "declarative" conception of the name of the divinity that a few centuries earlier in Judea had become the point of departure for a religious revolution. Their common replacement of predeclarative linguistic structures by the declarative sentence establishes between Hebrew religion and Greek metaphysics the founding homology of Western culture.

I have proposed elsewhere an exegesis of the *ehyeh asher ehyeh* by which God names himself to Moses in Exodus 3.[4] By refusing the ostensive-imperative name by which the divinity can be called, Moses liberates his people from the sacrificial system that commands divine presence. God is the central being of the scene of representation that survives the disappearance of the central object of the originary scene; in the terms of *Originary Thinking*, he is the subsistence of the central locus of the scene remembered as a being. In Exodus, the divine being, whose concrete origin is recalled by the ritual fire of the burning bush, becomes "transcendental," detaching itself from any specific historical locus. But this detachment itself is an event that takes place in a specific historical locus. The liberation provided by revelation has the strength and the weakness of never being able to deny its historicity. The two "universal" religions born from Judaism, Christianity and Islam, remain as attached as their ancestor to a historical place of foundation.

To eliminate the ostensive is to expunge the local historicity of the deferral of collective violence by means of the sign. The originary opposition between center and periphery that founds and is founded by language is the source and model of all the great philosophical dichotomies: word and thing, form and content, Idea and copy, ontological and ontic, and so forth. But if all these oppositions are already latent in the sign as such, it is only from the time of the declarative sentence that they can be thematically expressed. To understand a declarative sentence, one situates it on an "other scene" that is not a simple prolongation of the present scene but a mental scene inhabited by imaginary objects.

The Mosaic revelation distances the corporeal presence of the divinity that was formerly accessible to invocation by means of the imperative. But in contrast to metaphysics, religion cannot demand the exclusiveness of the declarative. The God who names himself "esoterically" as a sentence (*ehyeh asher ehyeh*) in Exodus 3 consents, in a second "exoteric" moment in Exodus 6, to condense this sentence into a single word/name (YHVH).[5] This inversion of the historical order of linguistic evolution is analogous to that of the grammar books, which define the imperative as a "transformation" of the declarative.

But whereas the inversion of the grammars is a simple forgetting of linguistic origin, that brought about in Exodus puts linguistic form in a dialectical relationship with the divine will, for which it proposes a paradigmatic model. To the request for a (magical) name, the answer is a sentence, which is only then recondensed into a (religious) name. The God who maintains himself in the "other world" chooses to manifest himself to a man, to let himself be called by him. Our knowledge of God's choice determines the nature of our address; we are no longer commanding God but appealing to him.

The Euthyphro and Philosophy's Eventless Ethic

Although metaphysics is a fundamentally antireligious mode of thought, as we have observed, it has its own conception of God. It is not certain whether the metaphysical divinity was the God of Socrates but it was certainly that of Plato. Attempts have been made to associate the latter with the religious movements of his era: orphism, the Eleusinian mysteries, and the like. But from its earliest formulations, Platonic religion is essentially delocalized.

In the *Euthyphro*, Plato-Socrates attacks the traditional conception of the sacred that leads his interlocutor to bring an accusation of murder against his own father. Euthyphro affirms that his action is pious; Socrates asks him to inform him then as to the "form" (*eîdos, idéa*) that makes pious things (*ta hosía*) pious. Some have gone so far as to see in this manner of formulating the question a primitive version of the doctrine of Ideas. Euthyphro attempts to define the pious as what pleases the Gods, but lets himself be tricked by Socrates into agreeing that, on the contrary, an act only pleases the gods because it is pious. In the last analysis, the pious, like all the other virtues in the Socratic dialogues, is indistinguishable from the just (*díkaion*); the consequence is to eliminate from religion the very revealed element through which it preserves humanity's originary historicity.

For anyone who takes religion seriously, it is the divine will that determines what is pious and not the reverse. The god who would be satisfied with the Platonic definition of piety is one no longer capable of being worshiped. The fact that the metaphysical God has no proper name—not even the sentence-name revealed by Moses—is an indication of this. The philosophical divinity covers over a profound contradiction: he is a person-subject possessed of a will, yet this will, like the content of the Platonic concept, never reveals itself in any specific time or place. It is by means of this construction that metaphysics conjures away the paradoxicality of its "declarative" sacred.

Plato's God is a weapon against the narrow humanism of the Sophists, which he interprets as a radical individualism, indeed, an anarchism incompatible with maintenance of the social order. For the Plato of the *Theaetetus*, he who affirms that "man is the measure of all things" would deny all values that transcend the individual. In the face of this danger, Plato relocates the foundation of the human community outside of it, but this "outside" is no longer revealed in the localized history of religious revelation. In this manner, he creates the no-man's-land that metaphysics will inhabit for over twenty centuries— that it has not yet abandoned.

The *Euthyphro* is the only Platonic dialogue in which the argument is directed not at the opinions or attitudes of the interlocutor but at a specific act, an event of ethical significance. Euthyphro accuses his father of having brought about the death of a *thête* or dependent (of Euthyphro), who suffocated when the father had had him bound and imprisoned because this dependent had himself been guilty of the murder of a slave (of the father). Socrates is surprised that the death for which Euthyphro is requesting punishment was not that of a member of his family: only this would justify so great a lack of filial respect. Thus Plato gives us to understand that the father's murder of a murderer through negligence should be left without punishment. No doubt the piety that demands this punishment is mechanical, formalistic, blind respect for tradition rather than true justice deserving of divine approval. Nonetheless, a man has perished. The traditional piety of Euthyphro recognizes in its own way, by speaking of "pollution" (*míasma*), a disequilibrium that Plato prefers not to acknowledge. In the place of the old logic of pollution, which obliged Orestes to appear before the Areopagus even though he too had only requited a murder, philosophy substitutes a logic of neutralization. In either case, we fall short of a moral judgment that views any murder as a crime against human reciprocity.

The *Euthyphro* presents a paradigm of the opposition between philosophy/metaphysics and sacrificial religion. Where the latter prolongs the chain of revenge by making use of the very judicial institutions that were designed to break it, the former puts an equilibrium of injustice in the place of genuine moral reciprocity. Sacrifice consecrates the event of the murder; philosophy evacuates it. If one side finds it too easy to point the finger of accusation, the other finds it even easier to accuse no one. But the second case is not really any more eirenic than the first; the accuser finds himself accused in the place of the one whom he accuses. Not only is Euthyphro, like so many others, intellectually humiliated by Socrates; he is implicitly charged by him with a murderous design against his father.

Socrates himself, as Plato's readers will know, must answer an accusation of impiety before the archon, in whose palace his interlocutor is surprised to encounter him. To bring a lawsuit is to designate a victim, whereas, in its historical origin, metaphysics is the refusal to designate (the victim)—the refusal, at its Platonic point of departure, to participate in the sacrifice of Socrates. However, as the example of Euthyphro's father shows, to decline to bring an accusation does not prevent violence. In contrast with Judeo-Christian morality, whose refusal to designate a sacrificial victim goes together with an insistence on communal reconciliation, philosophy tacitly approves of an equilibrating violence.

Is it a simple matter of chance that in the example chosen by Plato as a counterexample to true piety, the father did not kill deliberately, or that his victim was both of inferior status and himself guilty of murder? In this manner, the original murder is punished without its perpetrator being designated as a criminal. Just as in ritual executions, where care is taken so that no individual be made "unclean" by the blood of the victim, justice has been done without any individual carrying out an overt act, or even a thought, of violence. He who would destroy this providential equilibrium is the patricidal son who accuses his father within the traditional ritual context.

Thus the judicial system of metaphysics eliminates the designation of the guilty party on analogy with the declarative proposition's elimination of the ostensive of religious revelation. The suppression of the ostensive is magically compensated by a justice, and by extension a social order, that is both effective in punishing crime and yet nonviolent. The evacuation of the event—which is in principle always a murder— permits the intellectual negation of Socrates' execution in the *Phaedo*. It is the suppression of *this* event that is the anti-evenemential origin of philosophy.

The Cratylus and the Discovery of the Signified

The *Euthyphro* speaks of the *eidos* of piety, but only as a substrate for pious things, not as an Idea existing in itself. The order of composition of the dialogues will probably never be sufficiently well established to permit us to determine from historical evidence at exactly what point the doctrine of Ideas came into being; our hypothesis must consequently be based on the internal logic of Platonic thought. By this criterion, I shall follow those who locate the first appearance of the Ideas proper in the *Cratylus*.[6] Even if it is impossible to prove that this dialogue precedes the *Symposium* or the *Phaedo*, the progression from Cratylic reflection on language to the Ideas is attractively parsimonious. It is logical that, at the moment when Plato is meditating on the arbitrariness of the linguistic sign, he should be led to separate explicitly the concept-signified from the word-signifier that designates it.

The *Cratylus* devotes a very long digression to the fabrication of "motivated" etymologies, the real significance of which is that most of them construct, like the God of Moses, names out of declarative sentences. To name is to designate, and as in Genesis, the distribution of names is carried out by a "legislator." But Socrates finds "primitive words" too distant and obscure to reveal their object clearly. In answer to this objection, Cratylus attempts to guarantee the revelatory power of names by appealing to the sacred, proposing a Heraclitean derivation of primitive names on the basis of universal movement. The raison d'être of this derivation has never been satisfactorily explained. It is in fact a nascent semiotic that marks a crucial step in the dialectic leading from pre-Socratic thought to Platonic metaphysics. If names are given to things "insofar as they are borne and flowing and becoming" (411c), it is in order to permit us, since we are unable to immobilize this becoming, to observe it from a stable "Archimedean point." It is only when we possess the unchanging word "river" that we can affirm that we never put our foot in the same one twice. The Heraclitean flux generates in the sign its own antithesis. In this view of signification, the name preserves its ostensive function; it points to an ongoing worldly movement, as the just-quoted passage from 411c indicates—a remark made by Socrates himself, who informs us that he was in his youth a student of Cratylus.

But Socrates no longer accepts as univocal the Heraclitean derivation; basing himself on a few etymologies as apparently arbitrary as those which preceded them, he insists on the equal plausibility of the derivation of words on the basis of "immobility." By forgetting the implicit raison d'être of the Cratylean-Heraclitean doctrine—the opposition between atemporal words and their temporal referents—Socrates slips from the idea that the name is made necessary by the impermanence of things to the idea that the name must "signify a movement and a translation," that is, that rather than imposing its stability on the flux of things, the name must itself be a model of the thing-in-movement that it designates.

But if *this* is the point, then it is easy enough to find examples of word/things that are "immobile." The still-ostensive name of Heraclitus thus becomes the conceptual name of Plato, which expresses or "contains" the quintessence of an action—movement or the stopping of movement—attributed to the thing by Socrates' fantastic etymology. His first example of an "immobile" word says it all: it is the word *epistémè* (knowledge), which he would derive from *hístesin epí* ("[it] stops on"), "the sign that knowledge 'stops' our soul 'on' things" (437a). In order to refute the Heraclitean who claims that knowledge has a stable existence only in relation to the instability of the things to which it refers, Plato derives the very name of "knowledge" from the already-theorized action of knowledge-that-arrests-movement; like the God of Exodus, he arrives at the name only by the detour of the sentence. The endpoint of Plato's reasoning is the demonstration that, since nothing in the words themselves could universally impose a revelation of their referents as being either in movement or in repose, our sole source of knowledge concerning the accuracy of words is the things (*ta prâgmata*) themselves. But it is precisely at the moment in which Plato abandons words for things that he discovers the fundamental relationship between the word and the thing it designates. For the deconstruction of the originary opposition between the stable word and the unstable thing does not for all that render the things of this world capable of offering to the word the solid basis that would permit it to function within a semantic system. Once the semiotics of Cratylus-Heraclitus has been refuted by a declarative conception of language, Plato finds himself obliged to present a stable correlative for language that would not only be other than things-in-movement, but *of another nature* from them. As he puts it, in order that there be knowledge, there must exist not only beautiful and good things, but something that would be "beautiful and good in itself" (*ti . . . autó kalón kai agathón,* 439c).

It is thus upon the stability of the *signified* that Plato constructs his theory of knowledge. Heraclitus, in remarking that things constantly "translate" themselves, would not have been able to think that this state of flux makes them incapable of functioning as correlatives of the linguistic sign. Heraclitean ostensive nomination depends in fact on a subjacent sacred model. The originary ostensive is not the name of an impermanent thing, but the name of permanence itself—the name of God. To rid himself of the sacred Being that lurks within the Heraclitean flux, Plato must ground the sign not upon its worldly referent but upon the signified, which is by nature in a state of extraworldly repose.[7] The impermanence of each beauty is unimportant, provided that the Beautiful remain in place.

Plato is the first real theoretician of signification. Without the signified, there can be no linguistic sign; Plato was the first to understand this capital fact, the foundation of all semiotics.[8] But metaphysics is not content to be a theory of the sign, nor a fortiori a linguistics; it wants to found an ontology. The signified "beautiful" will consequently be transported beyond the region of perishable things to become the Form-Idea "the Beautiful."

Plato realizes that language cannot be explained on the basis of ontological monism. The word is something other than the thing, and not merely another variety of thing (an "imitation" like that of the artisan, for example). But lacking the possibility—ethical as well as intellectual—to return this dualism to its anthropological source, he fetishizes it and consequently degrades it. To affirm that the Ideas alone are real is not to distinguish them absolutely from worldly things, but on the contrary, to assimilate the two. As soon as one imagines a "heaven" inhabited by the Ideas, one makes them play the same role in the other world as things play in this one, just as they do in the myth of the Cave. The other world is in fact the "other scene," the scene of representation, on which only signs appear.

What then is the relationship between the world of Ideas and the other world of souls, that imaginary locus consecrated by religion, described at length in the *Phaedo*? Let us not be too hasty to naturalize the religious heaven as an instrument of priestly manipulation of the credulous or as the fantastic wish fulfillment of some inborn desire for immortality. Its model is clearly, as Plato reveals, the (signified of the) sign. But Plato fixes this model in a dualistic ontology by suppressing the originary link between signifier and referent, a connection the syntactic trace of which is precisely the ostensive.

So long as the sign serves as a means for the revelation of the central object of desire, the other world of permanent Being will appear to be inhabited by that object rather than by the sign itself. The originary model of immortality is that of the sacred center of the scene of representation. To use language is to institute a relationship that is from the beginning formal and consequently liberated from the force of time. Those who would put a transcendent Language in the place of the Christian or Hegelian *logos* forget that language *is* not, but that it is constructed, and that the point of departure for this construction cannot well be the declarative sentence that crowns it. No doubt some of the responsibility for this lapse is attributable to Saussure's emphasis on signification at the expense of syntactic structure. But it is more profoundly the responsibility of metaphysics itself, whose disillusioned adepts believe even today that it must magically furnish them with the entire set of tools needed for its own deconstruction. It is the formality of the linguistic signification-relation that engenders the world of the Forms. Immortality in this realm is not a beatific prolongation of lived time into eternity, but an extratemporal form of being. Although he did not understand the other world to be originarily that of linguistic signification, Plato is the first to have realized that it is inhabited by beings accessible solely through meditation on the sign—beings that we call in a formalist vocabulary "signifieds," but that merit their Hegelian name of *Begriff*, concept, for they "grasp" and preserve an originary content.

The concept is born when the formal immortality of signification becomes separated from its origin in ostensive designation. We proceed from immortal gods to immortal Ideas, in such a manner that when the gods themselves are invoked in the mythical passages of Plato, they are creatures rather than creators of language. The judges of the myth of Er at the end of the *Gorgias* are fictions that illustrate the idea of Justice, not gods who incarnate it. Their distributions of compensatory pleasures and pains reveal by the "logic of the supplement" the inefficacy of Socratic morality; the tyrant Archelaos suffers in the underworld in order to embody a moral truth that cannot be exemplified on earth.

Liberation from Metaphysics?

Now that we have seen by what dubious stratagems Plato imposes order on the seething Heraclitean universe, we can well understand the impatience of those who would liberate us from the grasp of metaphysics. The late Jean-Marie Benoist, in his *Tyrannie du logos* (1975), sets out the postmodern indictment. Socrates has only freed our language from Sophist "technocracy" in order to enslave us to a repressive *logos*. What a wonderful opportunity was lost for a linguistics of the signifier, for a community founded on the pleasure principle. The doctrine of the always-already remains haunted by a myth of origin, always the same: the myth of difference and desire "polymorphous and perverse"—the dream, inherited from modernism, of a Being anterior to language. It bears the influence of the Lacanian schema in which language imposes a paternal order on the fragmentary turbulence of "imaginary" desire.[9] However, in the model of historical evolution that Benoist follows, it is not the unmentioned origin of language but that of metaphysics which institutes repression. This permits him to regret the repressive domination of metaphysics without admitting that its *logos* is human language itself.

The originary-without-an-origin language of deconstructive thought is a free play of the signifier that, by returning us to the material reality of the sign, puts signification and therefore metaphysics into question. Heidegger could conceive of a "thinking of Being" that would stand opposed to metaphysics as the ostensive is to the declarative, that would designate Being itself rather than creating fictive models of it taken from the realm of the ontic. The disappearance of this pre-Socratic paradise in the postmodern era has relegated ostensivity to the religious domain in which it originated, and where no philosopher is likely to seek it out. As a consequence, Benoist has recourse to psychoanalysis as postmodernity's official originary anthropology—an anthropology in which the substitution of ontogenesis for phylogenesis permits the evacuation of the ethical. But *chassez le religieux, il revient au galop*: what psychoanalytic authority supplies is nothing other than a myth of origin. Within the horizon established by the author's concluding reference to Heraclitus, the reign of the mythical is all the less contested for being entirely unavowed.[10]

It is time to return *la dépense* to the ritual context where Georges Bataille found it.[11] Benoist's summary reference to the potlatch reflects a typical postmodern failure to understand—as Bataille did in his lucid moments—that this marvelous flux, this outpouring of energy beyond all reason, is born not in the delicious polymorphism of individual desire but in the ritual "cruelty" (to use Artaud's term) of societies far removed from our intellectual utopias. The pre-Socratic chaos expelled by metaphysics is the decadence of a ritual order subject to a control far more rigid than latter-day metaphysics imagines. When Plato attempts to constrain the tyrannical excesses of individual desire, it is to avert crisis in a barely postritual society, not to put a phallocratic brake on the pristine appetites of originary humanity. Originary humanity already knows language and order in their most rigid sense; our dream of anarchy is conceivable only on this basis.

*

The metaphysical conception of language is defined by the expulsion of the elementary linguistic forms. But Plato does not expel the ostensive as such because he does not theorize it as such. Had he been able to theorize it, he would not have had to expel it. Plato fears the immediacy of language that itself acts on the world. The Sophists are dangerous because their rhetoric restores to language its originary power of creating meaning, but in a context where the speaker is no longer subject to the transcendent communal order incarnated in ritual. The stability of the Ideas that maintain the social order is founded on a deeper, albeit still mystified vision of the originary event and of the scene of representation that preserves it.

The formal logic of signification justifies the founding gesture of metaphysics. The concept is indeed immortal because it does not belong to the real world, whatever its point of entry into human language. But if the nominalized virtues of the early dialogues and the Ideas themselves of the later ones possessed only the formal immortality of the sign-in-general, they would fail to meet the ethical requirements that Platonic thought imposes on them. In attempting to find in language the basis of a conflict-free community, Plato creates a form of thought that effaces the historical origin of language as the human community's means to defer conflict. In order for the concept to be immortal, it must be without origin and therefore without history. On the contrary, the real immortality of the concept is in its evocation of the scenic sharing of the sign in the originary event as a transtemporal guarantee of communal peace.

Originary Being, Originary Thinking

"To be" is to be in the center, at the locus of significance; "to do" is to act on the periphery. The substantiality and subsistence inherent in the verb "to be" are those of the originary center. To be present in the center of the scene is to be uniquely significant precisely because it is to be absent from any project of action. Being is present-to-consciousness because it cannot be made present-to-hand. It is the foundation of the specifically human form of knowledge because it introduces the stasis of representation between the imitator and his mimetic model. To imitate the central being, I cannot simply mimic its behavior; I must re-present its self-substantial form.

Because being is the chief preoccupation of metaphysics, it is the key locus of its deconstruction, which undermines the metaphysical duality of idea and reality through the revelation of being's ostensive nature. For Heidegger, being can "reveal" or "hide" itself because it resides in a locus that can be pointed to rather than in the transcendent Platonic realm of Ideas. The return to Being from the preoccupation with beings is a return to originary scenicity from the ideal scene of metaphysics; in a still-mystified form, thought returns from the world of concepts to its ground in originary language.

Being is not identical to sacrality, nor to significance. The central object is sacred insofar as its inaccessibility defers mimetic conflict, but this deferral is effective only because the quality of the sacred is attributed to the object rather than to the peripheral humans whose mutually repelling desires render it inaccessible. In contrast, being inheres in the role of the center-as-mimetic-obstacle. There is no adjective analogous to "sacred" to describe the object that "has" being, because being is precisely not a quality but a form of action. Unlike the sacred, it cannot be conceived as subsisting in a transcendent realm, but is only realized in the mimetic context. The third term, significance, is the status of the object qua referent of the sign; the referent's significance "expresses" its prior being. Significance is for the user of language; being is in and for itself.

The relationship between the ostensive being of the central object and the use of "to be" as the copula parallels that between elementary and mature language. Ostensive language contains no predicative description of being; being is what is being "done" by the objects to which the ostensive refers. In contrast, the declarative sentence, by subordinating the presupposed significance of its topic to the new information provided by the predicate, permits us to thematize the notion of being as such by extrapolation from the copula "to be." The thematic understanding of the ontological (Being) must be won through the ontic (beings).

It is useful to trace the various words for being back to the more concrete terms like "bear" (*bhṛ* →? *bhū* → to be) or "stand" (*stare* → Sp. estar) that have been pressed into service as copulas. Many such words other than "be" exist in our vocabulary: "he looks good," "it appears correct" express a restricted sense of being. But this passage from the concrete to the abstract is only possible because the notion of being as we have defined it is implicit in language from the original ostensive designation. To re-present the object is to imply that it *is*, in the sense that the term has in the *cogito*: being as the mark of potential thematization. It is because being is already implicit in the ostensive that we experience the substantiality of the topic (the "substantive" or noun) as existing prior to predication.

What *is* is what stands before us as the forbidden goal of our (originally appropriative) mimetic behavior. In this standing-before or standing-against our desire, the central being appears to be in-itself; in our concentration on the object, our former (human) mimetic model is forgotten. This is no mere illusion that the originary hypothesis dispels. The resistance of being to imitation in action (and not simply its resistance to physical appropriation) makes it imitable only through representation. Whereas mimesis of others is unproblematic, representation of central being is the originary act of self-consciousness. The ritual reproducer of this act, for example, the shaman in a trance state of "possession" by the divine figure whose costume he wears, is at the other end of the mimetic spectrum from the unaware subject of everyday mimesis; where the latter merely prolongs the prehuman imitative pattern, the ritual performer's concentration on his task takes him beyond consciousness.

Being is the foundation of the internal-external scene of representation on which all formal activity—language, desire, thought—takes place. Our interest in the object is ultimately always the same, but the scenic manifestation of the object-as-being opens up between it and the subject—whose subjectivity is thereby established—a space-time of deferral, what Sartre called a *néant*, within which a new set of mimetic behaviors toward the object may be elaborated. There is no simple mimetic fit between the behavior of the subject and the being of the object; in contrast with the imitation of a human mediator, the formal "imitation" of the central object has no a priori content. The sign provides a minimal representation of the referent's formal closure; ritual and secular art will incarnate it and temporalize it in various guises. The appropriation of central being through mimesis is the human project par excellence.

The Ontological and the Ontic

What is the historical significance of the Heideggerian return from the ontic to the ontological, from beings to Being? This movement began with Brentano and Husserl in reaction to a naive empiricism that sought to derive the laws of logic inductively from experience.[1] There are times when we cannot rely on our experience because it is not the source of the being of what we experience. This is obvious in domains like geometry, which are concerned with ideal objects constructed according to parsimonious rules, the role of which as models of reality has no place in their ontology. It is not obvious at all in anthropology, where no boundary can be drawn between the human reality we invent and the human reality we discover. We have no empirical experience of the human that is not mediated by our human originary intuition.

We need not linger over the gaps in Heidegger's conception of the ontological-ontic opposition. Lacking a theory of human origin, he generates an ontology of the human from *Dasein* or being-present-(to) without providing a theory of the scene on which this scenic presence-to might have emerged. Dasein's presence to time in the form of Death remains a figure of Hegelian phenomenology; for a person to know his own death, it must be revealed to him in specific circumstances of the kind that the originary hypothesis proposes. But we can accept the fundamental ontological intuition of Heidegger's "existentialism": that real thinking—which is to say, anthropological thinking—is about Being rather than beings. Empirical anthropology rests on a generative foundation. We cannot understand humanity in its diversity if we have no understanding of its originary unity. But the "fall" from Being into beings is originary as well; we need not await Socratic or Platonic metaphysics in order to witness this fall's cognitive and ethical consequences.

The Being/beings opposition is one case in which English is a more philosophical language than either German or French. In English as in Greek (*to ôn/ta ónta*), this dichotomy hangs entirely on the difference between singular and plural, unlike the German *Sein/Seiendes* or the French *être/étant*. We need seek the origin of this opposition between singular Being and plural beings no farther than the originary scene itself. Being becomes beings in the sparagmos; we may formulate in this manner the central insight of the second part of the present volume. It is the return to the inextricably appetitive-cum-resentful division of the central object among the participants that sends originary humanity back to its worldly concerns from the otherworldly unity that obtained during their deferral.

Heidegger's question as to why there should be being(s) rather than nothing should not be understood in the cosmological mode in which it is stated. The existence of the cosmos is not a problem for human ontology, nor (whatever profundities may be offered on the subject of the "anthropic principle")[2] does the human phenomenon add anything that can help us explain it. But within the anthropological domain, the beings versus nothing question is indeed dramatically relevant: Why are there *things-for-us* rather than nothing? Why is there, rather than not, a species that can represent things to itself, that can use language? Positive thought does not know to ask such questions;

philosophers ask them, but they cannot be answered in merely philosophical terms. At the origin, protohumanity indeed had a choice between being and nothing; this choice hinged on its ability to intend a Being that would through *différance*—deferral of conflict, differentiation of meanings—make available to humanity a plurality of beings.

Our reading of Heidegger's question in anthropological rather than cosmological terms should not induce us to interpret "Being" as "*human* being." The Being that the philosopher seeks is external to the human and can be exemplified by humanity only at the horizon of its historical trajectory. Being, *to ôn*, the most abstract concept of metaphysics, bears the same anthropological burden as more obviously human concepts like truth, thought, God, or morality. The apparently unshakable stability of the concept of Being, invariant under any conceivable transformation, is misleading; this invariance is the object of a resentment always ready to incite the sparagmos in which self-contained Being is violently fragmented into a plurality of beings. Being is inhabited by the tension of this threatening resentment, a force far more potent than the much-touted anticipation of our individual death that is merely a derivative of it. The ultimate ground of the priority of anthropology over philosophy is the impossibility, sensed for over a century by the critics of metaphysical thought, of protecting the concept of being, and a fortiori all concepts, from the deconstructive force of resentment.

Originary Thinking

As the species whose propensity to mimesis makes it its own most serious problem, humans must think because they are too mimetic to act peacefully otherwise. The aim of thinking is not to reproduce the originary unity that obtained during the emission of the sign, but rather to reconstruct it in such a way as to reduce the tension between periphery and center, subject and object. Thinking deconstructs the figures by means of which the sacred center defers the establishment of reciprocal relations with the profane periphery. Thinking reduces "outward" to "inward" form, visible to invisible; it struggles to maintain the fundamental arbitrariness of the sign in opposition to the cultural institutions, ritual and esthetic, that would take advantage of the sign's materiality in order to motivate its relationship with its referent. Where the sign minimally re-presents the formal closure of the object, thinking prolongs representation into analysis. Originary signification defers the sparagmos, but thinking is the antisparagmos that reunites the object's scattered remains, recomposing Being from beings. On this point, two directions are possible. Metaphysical thought conceives of the scene of representation on which it manifests itself as an atemporally stable locus, denying the mimetic tension that is its historical raison d'être. Such thought remains within the limits of the declarative proposition, in which "to be" is merely a copula linking a noun with its predicate. Because this model of language cannot figure the (ostensive) interest in the noun-topic that precedes and provides the basis for predication, it cannot conceive originary being. The being in a proposition cannot merely be; it must always *do* what is predicated of it, the archetype of which predicative doing is, as we have seen, to be absent. The limits of metaphysics are not those of the declarative sentence itself; they are those of the model of language—and the thinking that it generates—that takes this sentence-form as its originary basis.

In contrast, originary thinking—practiced throughout most of history exclusively in the religious sphere—privileges the ostensivity of central Being, its presence. Generative anthropology is a new way of thinking, but only in the sense that it thematizes an activity that has gone on since the origin.

The most obvious originary model for thinking would be that the first thought is expressed in the first sign, and that the content of this thought is the central object, the object of Girard's "first noninstinctual attention." Once the gesture of appropriation has been transformed into a sign, the central object becomes an object of desire situated on an internal scene of representation where we may contemplate or "think about" it.

But this is not really what we mean by thinking. Thought is not reducible to the desiring contemplation of the imaginary referent of language. It is an activity of reflection on the contents of one's mental processes, an effort rather than a pleasure. Indeed, this effort requires us to renounce our pleasure in the immediate contemplation of the mental image from which our desire constructs the image-as-we-would-like-it-to-be; thinking is a deconstructive search for the original and ultimately for the originary components that underlie the idea/image. To think about a concept is not to contemplate it in the imagination

but to analyze our immediate idea of it into the more primitive notions that the idea's figurality has occulted. The Socratic *elenchos* is an
exercise in thinking that requests, as against easily imagined figures of
courage or beauty, an analysis of its prefigural essence. All thinking is
originary analysis.

Thinking as a renunciation of pleasure, as a form of deferral, is the
mental correlate of the physical abortion of the originary appropriative gesture. The thought that gives rise to language is the thought-not-
to-appropriate the object. The pleasurable image of the object-as-ap-
propriated must be thought through to the separate components hidden by the image, notably the copresence of the mediating others and
the danger they represent. This first act of thinking that motivates the
production of the originary sign acknowledges the presence of others
within the sphere of the apparently binary relationship of appetite; it
is the originary deconstruction of desire *avant la lettre.* The result of
this first thought is the turning-back of the appropriative gesture as an
imitation/representation of the object. This movement is not "instinctive" but reflective; thought produces not a mere turning-away
but a modified turning-toward. The gesture is aborted as appropriation but pursued as representation.

The originary position of thought is complementary to that of
rhetoric. In the "rhetorical" moment of the originary scene, the already
constituted community of emitters of the sign successfully attempts
to influence by their example the isolated individual who has not yet
joined the group. The "late" phenomenon of rhetoric mimetically persuades the "last" emitter of the sign to join what he takes to be an al-
ready-formed community that threatens to exclude him.[3] In contrast,
thought is "early"; it is through thought that the "first" individual aborts
his gesture and creates the sign, before there could be any question of
a constituted human community. Although it takes place in a collective context, this "early" act of renunciation is grounded in individual
thinking. Both thought and rhetoric characterize in principle all the
participants of the scene; they are moments of the whole rather than
the activities of specific individuals.

To think the appropriation of the object is to think the dangerous
presence of the others and therefore to defer it. But deferral through
thought is not simple abandonment. To think the others' presence in
the context of the gesture is to redefine the gesture as a means of communication with them. Because thought has placed the others' ap-

petites in the same context as my own, my movement toward/back from the object is also a signal to them. Arresting the movement begun for my own benefit converts it into a deferred movement for the benefit of my fellows. But I do not abandon my gesture in order to withdraw attention from myself; on the contrary, its prolongation as representation attracts the attention of the others to the referent. The self-conscious operation of human representation contrasts with semiautomatic animal signal systems, where the connection of the signal not merely with its object but with the animal's own relation to that object cannot become an object of reflection. What is now realized beyond mere signaling is that the self can intend a gesture as a sign.

Although I can imagine the danger of the others' aggression without a sign, I cannot otherwise imagine turning their attention away from myself and toward the object. For the gesture to be a sign for them, it must first be a sign for me. I must notice that my gesture turns *my* attention in a nonappropriative mode to the object as a formal totality before I can assign to it the formal operation of representation. The final result of thinking through the originary appetitive context is the establishment of the sign as a means for deferring, and for mutually communicating that one is deferring, the act of appropriation that would fulfill the original expectations of this context.

The gesture-sign thematizes the central object, reveals it to me and to my fellows as the sole object worthy of our attention. In the formal closure of the sign, thought incarnates itself and thereby abolishes, or rather defers, itself. Thought is detachment from appetite that is not yet sign. It takes place in the space between the prehuman, unthematic interest of appetite and the sign's externally directed thematization. In the moment of thought, there is no gesture toward the object, either as an appropriative act—in which case there would be no thought, only the actualization of appetite—or as a sign—in which case the thinking would be over, and the resolution of the crisis communicated to the others.

The designation by the sign of the object of mimetic attraction articulates the triangular structure of mimesis: the sign communicates itself to the interlocutor as it represents the object of their common desire. To designate the object, to represent it in its formal inaccessibility, is also to oblige the others to copy one's gesture, which at the same time copies theirs. Thought, once aroused by the emergence of the mimetic obstacle, exteriorizes its unconscious, unthematizable "objectivity" in the attribution of significance to the object that incarnates this obstacle. This attribution by "projection" indirectly acknowledges the primacy of the mimetic model provided by the collectivity in creating my original interest in the object.

Thought in the universe of language begins not with appetite but with human desire, which already contains its own obstacle. Instead of finding pleasure, as does the esthetic, in the formal perfection of the inaccessible figure, thought deconstructs the figural relation that maintains the obstacle in order to seek a way around it.

In worldly or practical thinking, we deploy for the reduction of an external obstacle resources first developed in the more problematic sphere of human interaction. The difficulty that prevents access may not be mimetic or human at all; it may be conquerable through a purely positive, instrumental analysis. But the fact that the practical thinking institutionalized in the scientific method need not retain contact with its anthropological roots should not allow us to forget the originary use to which the "technique" of thinking was put.

Originary thinking, religious or secular, always reverts to the mimetic nature of the central obstacle. In the "early" thinking that produced the first sign, each individual, under the pressure of the danger of mimetic conflict, seeks to create, and thereby anticipates, a human configuration that cannot be subverted by the parallel anticipations of the others. The result of successful thought is the originary scene of representation, the first configuration that succeeds in maintaining itself under the feedback that human mimesis necessarily provides. But thinking does not guarantee a priori the deferral of mimesis. Just as one cannot write a computer program to decide in the general case whether another program will conclude or "return," there can be no law to determine if and when thought will "return" to the world of action, or, if it does, in what relationship to desire its object will reemerge.

*

What we think about, and why we think it, is an open matter; but this very openness is understandable only in the context of its origin. We began to think, as we began to speak, not to fulfill the destiny of an *élan vital*, but to defer the intraspecific problems that would otherwise have prevented us from existing.

The scene of representation is the locus of desire, religion, and art; it is also the locus of thought. Where religion operates through submission to the power of a preestablished center, in thinking we put aside our desire for central being to construct a hypothetical model of its interaction with its human periphery. But it is not surprising that the most fundamental and consequently the most dangerous kind of thought, reflection on human origin, has historically been confined to the context of established religion, where speculation on fundamental anthropology is constrained by theological dogma.

In contrast, thought independent of institutional authority has been throughout Western history virtually synonymous with metaphysics, the forgetting of the ostensive movement toward the center. Socrates' conceptual analysis, rejecting the cosmic globalism of his predecessors, constitutes a new stage in the separating out of thought from the religious elements of the scene. As we saw in the preceding chapter, in posing the "reality" of the Idea-concept exemplified by the Good, Socrates-Plato attempts to define the basis of the human community independently of religious revelation. As the founding model for over two millennia of metaphysical reflection, the Socratic *elenchos* creates a propositional agon with respect to which the transcendental status of the Idea plays the role of deus ex machina.

Generative anthropology, which is originary thinking founded on hypothesis rather than revelation, explicitly locates the deconstruction of the object of thought within the minimal configuration of the originary scene. It thereby comes qualitatively closer than its predecessors to the unreachable ideal of intellectual self-generation: to be a way of thinking that includes paradoxically within itself the content of any conceivable metathinking about it.

But the only valid demonstration of this claim is to be found in the work that realizes it. One recalls from the opening of the preface—over sixty pages long!—to Hegel's *Phenomenology* that a truly "philosophical" work cannot expound its truth in a preface. Hegel lacked only the distinction between ostensive and declarative, anthropology and metaphysics, to be able to articulate this paradox. We may express it thus: Generative anthropology must be its own originary analysis.

The Origin of Signification

The great discovery/invention of the originary scene is significance: the concentration of the attention of the nascent community on a unique center. But the crux of a theory of originary signification is posed by what the scene cannot illustrate directly: the *plurality* of language. Although significance must precede signification, no theory of language, even of its origin, can be complete without a theory of the plurality of signs.

The problem may be posed in Heideggerian terms: if the originary sign designates Being, how do we arrive at the signs for beings? However strongly we emphasize the priority of the ethical, of the human community's internal relations rather than its interaction with the natural world, humanity's ethical success can only be demonstrated in the Darwinian terms of survival within this world. Humanity may be its own greatest danger, but if it remained wholly preoccupied with this danger, it would soon be engulfed by the others. Whatever else it produces, the solution of the originary ethical problem must be the source of an opening toward nonhuman reality.

Thus the single sign of originary language must be not only the name-of-God but the origin of the name-of in general. The accrual of new signs is not a dilution of originary theology but, on the contrary, a demonstration of its success. The Mosaic revelation, in which the religious moment of the scene becomes self-consciously independent of all imaginary objects, is also the moment at which the name-of-God can no longer function as the model of the sign. The name of God is too sacred to pronounce; this ultimate proof of the power of the Verb can only be conserved unused, outside of spoken language. What is revealed is that the word-in-general is not indeed the name of God but of a worldly object, not of Being but of a being among others.

Our task in this chapter is to understand how the unique originary sign provides the opening to this plurality. If representation were nothing but designation-as-significant, it would require no more than a single sign of ostension-in-general—a pointing finger. We have assumed that the sign originates in the mimesis of the formal closure of the object that has been cut off from direct appropriation. The object is placed on a scene where it can for the first time be contemplated and its formal articulations explored; the potential scenic contemplation of other objects follows as a consequence. This "disinterested" contemplation of the object as form, in tension with its appetitive interest qua content, prefigures its later transfiguration via the sparagmos into the Being of the center-in-itself in the "religious" moment of the scene.

The deepest mystery of metaphysics is its repression or forgetting of the relation between the Being of the scene, to which religion attributes personhood as God, and the metaphysical scene-as-such on which objects present themselves to our "objective" contemplation. It is the mark of the Continental-existential school of philosophy to have remained aware of this mystery, which Anglo-American analytic philosophy dismisses as meaningless because its criterion of meaningfulness takes the institution of the metaphysical scene as its unexamined precondition.

Personhood is the quality of the being that defers its own appropriation, that opposes its will to the appetites of the members of the community, whose own sense of self is given to them as derived from this deferring force. In the face of the resistance of the center, the human self discovers its own relation to it as desire. Religious understanding detaches the personhood of the center from the object that inhabits it and attributes it to a being existing prior to the scene and ontologically independent of it; the central object becomes the locus in which this being chooses to reveal itself. It is this detachment of being from scene that provides the context in which the scene of representation is opened up to beings in general. Any object that appears on it is capable of arousing mimetic desire and thereupon of being endowed with significance and represented by a sign.

The originary sign is singular and, in its origin as a gesture of appropriation, motivated rather than arbitrary. Its change of motivation from practical-appropriative to theoretical-signifying is the source of the so-called arbitrariness of the signifier. Insofar as the sign is a material act, it has a worldly reality that is subject to variation. Our question is how some such variation could come to be understood as constituting a *significant* difference, the distinguishing criterion between two different signs. This is only conceivable because from the beginning signification is not a pure unity but a bringing together under tension of disparate elements: the absolute of significance and the specificity of the worldly referent imitated by the sign.

Originary designation is not a mere pointing at whatever happens to appear in the center but a recognition that centrality itself is dependent on the particularity of the central object. A residual appetitive element always remains in the center of the circle of desire. The uniqueness of the first sign gives proof, not that it is a designation of absolute Being, but that it is incapable of distinguishing the absolute Being of centrality as such from the specific being of the central object. By thus conflating Being and beings, the originary sign is already supplementary to itself; its particularity supplements its universality. (The paradoxical experience of this supplementation is what we call the esthetic.) In this autosupplementarity or doubleness of the sign lies its potential for future self-differentiation.

The question might well be asked whether there is any way of signifying centrality without thus evoking a specific being. Mystical thought remains in meditation before this question. The philosophical gesture of putting a capital B on Being cannot encompass the religious intuition expressed in the Mosaic revelation, which not so naively retains the personal nature of God. The real language of being is anthropological; we can come no closer to absolute being than to formulate anthropological models of its origin.

At the origin, signification operates through the incarnation of significance-as-such, which religion will make its domain, in a particular sacred object. Central Being is experienced as incarnate in *a* central being. The deferral of the Being-beings dichotomy by the originary sign is analogous to the dialectic of the Christian trinity, in which the subject oscillates between the unknowable otherness of God-the-Father and the contemplation of the incarnate Son. But in its originary form, this deferral is unstable. The sacralization of the central object does not convert it irreversibly into a sacred being; it remains an object of appetite, with the consequence that in the sparagmos, deferral gives way to appropriative violence.[1]

The sparagmos demonstrates the necessary inadequacy of the central object to bear the full weight of significance. On the one hand, the specific object represented by the sign (the referent) gives way to the empty locus that preserves its form (the signified); but on the other, the object's specificity provides the originary opening to a plurality of significations. The difference between potential occupants of the center is accessible to prehuman cognitive faculties; what concerns us is the recuperation of this prehuman "knowledge" by the human process of signification.[2] But originary designation is not simple pointing; the sign already embodies the return of the appropriative gesture upon itself in the re-presentation of the closed form of the object.

The preservation of the originary scene in memory is the basis not merely for the renewal of the scene itself in ritual and the cultural forms derived from it, but for re-forming the sign to the form of a new object of potentially similar concern. Because the originary sign is not only form-as-such but is motivated by the specific form of its referent, the renewal of the scene is the occasion for the pluralization of signs.

Plurality in this context is a form of "supplement," but without the negative connotation of the term in its metaphysical context. In relation to the desire for absolute being, Derrida's supplement is a figure of disappointment; it is the inadequacy of the first relation that obliges it to be supplemented by a second. In contrast, from the standpoint of originary anthropology, the inadequacy of the single sign reveals not the failure of signification but its success.

The opening of conscious attention to other objects and of signification to other signs is the product of what I called in *The Origin of Language* the "lowering of the threshold of significance" that follows on the success of the originary sign in maintaining the cohesion of the human community. The expansion and diversification of language, like that of the community, is not a simple triumph over obstacles; human progress is better understood as a *fuite en avant*. Significance spreads not by rational analogy but by mimetic contagion, which serves as the discovery principle for any such analogies as are later established. The historical cost of the success of the originary sign is reflected in the intensification of mimetic danger in an object-world that contains increasingly diverse objects of desire; this intensification, rather than a mysterious drive to conquer new provinces for knowledge, is the cause of linguistic universalization.

If the first sacred object was a buffalo and at a future moment a bull was permitted to play a similar role, this "lowering of the threshold of significance" would reflect an acceptance of the historically inferior bull to play the role that had belonged to the buffalo. The analogous qualities of the bull as an object of desire would be felt to outweigh its nonidentity with the buffalo in the ritual renewal of the originary scene. Previous to the appearance of the bull, the sign remained materially motivated by the form of the buffalo, but the specificity of this form as re-presented by the sign is merely supplementary to its role in representing its referent. Now the sign's supplement of signification, beyond the mere indication of significance itself, becomes part of a paradigm capable of conveying differential information.

The larger the paradigm, the more bits of information can be conveyed. But the supplementary function of the sign in representing the specificity of the object, however conceived, must already exist at the origin. The originary sign is not simply the sign of Being but of the specific being that is its worldly incarnation; were it not, it could not acquire this specificity at a later time.

Being and Significance

The philosophical critique of anthropology is conceived in the spirit of the phenomenological critique of psychology. As noted in the preceding chapter, where positivists like John Stuart Mill thought that all mental objects were of the same nature, so that the truths of logic and mathematics were ultimately only statements about mental operations, Brentano and Husserl defended the specific ideal status of logical and mathematical constructs as being independent of the mind in which they are constituted. Similarly, Heidegger defends the priority of Being with respect to the humans whose role on Earth is to concern themselves with it, open themselves to it, act as its guardians and "shepherds."

But Being is not an ideal object like a triangle. The intuition expressed by the term derives from the communal need to preserve the peace-bringing effect of the sign after the sparagmos has destroyed its originary referent. The laws that apply to triangles derive from the nature of the objects thus defined, and it is meaningful to say that we discover rather than invent them. But there are no such laws of Being for us to discover. Unless we would fall into the classic religious confusion between anthropology and cosmology, the only Being that should interest us is that revealed to and by the human community.

In the originary event, the single sign bears the entire weight of signification; its "meaning" includes on the one hand the significant as such, Being or the name-of-God, and on the other, the specificity of the central object. The significance of the central object and its sacrality refer to different relationships: the object is sacred for resisting the gesture of appropriation, it is significant for demanding the gesture of representation.[3] It must be represented not because it cannot be appropriated but because the only praxis afforded me in the situation of mimetic crisis is this representation, which communicates to the (mediating) other(s) that I am renouncing my potentially rivalrous act of appropriation. But whereas the sacred resistance of the object is a property of the central locus in which it is found, its significance, its demand for representation, requires that it be represented in its specificity, its "thisness."[4]

The separation of significance from signification has already begun in the originary act of language, yet it is never complete. The word is always both unique and plural. The Cratylist dream is to explain this plurality by the antecedent plurality of the world of experience; the characteristic pluralities of sounds and of things, signifiers and signifieds, are explained as being simply of the same nature. Cratylism observes correctly that the sign, like its referent, is in the first place a material reality. But, basing itself on a few onomatopoeias, it leaps to the antithesis of the right conclusion. Motivation is useful only for explaining the origin of the sign, not its function. As Saussure explained, even the most clearly motivated sign is "arbitrary" in the sense that the system of language is not a part of the natural world and is not subject directly to its motivations. (Thus the sign will tend to evolve in conjunction with the language in which it is found rather than with the worldly object that supplied its original motivation.) The paradoxical relationship between the sign's "horizontal" materiality and its "vertical" ideality is irreducible to its projection on either plane. But of the two projections, the vertical real-ideal duality reveals the major articulation of the signification-relation, whereas the horizontal assimilation of the sign to the materiality of the thing obscures it.

The materiality of the sign accounts for the originary possibility of culture as a supplement to language.[5] It is the cultural-esthetic domain that fully exploits the motivation of the sign, its capacity to multiply itself to the limits of the universe of material experience. In the formal realm of language, the materiality of the sign is of operational value only in the minimal sense that it provides a substrate for the formal distinctions, for example, those among phonemes, that enable the plurality of the signifier. Yet this minimum of materiality can never be altogether detached from the cultural supplement it enables; all language is, to some extent, poetry.

The Constitution of the Signified

The mental representation that Saussure baptized the "signified" can be an element of communal language only if, at the origin, the community as a whole shares the same defining experience. But because the signified is an internal trace that maintains itself in the absence of its worldly referent, the crucial moment of its constitution is the moment in which the referent ceases to be present. In the originary event, this moment is that of the sparagmos. Following the annihilation of its referent, the signified qua mental image becomes the sole subsisting correlative of the sign.

The sparagmos is the radical making-absent of the object. The object is destroyed as unified figure, as formal and personal whole, not merely as edible flesh. Thus what we call the persistence of the figure of the object in the signifying imagination should be understood as its *return*, on the model of the "return of the repressed," or of Jesus's return from the world of the dead. Despite the defiguring intent of its original sacrificers, the figure retains its existence through the sign. By the same token, the ritual commemoration of the originary event gives proof that the sign has defeated the praxis of originary resentment that the sparagmos was meant to realize. Like Saul on the road to Damascus, the member of the originary community discovers that annihilation consecrates rather than obliterates the central figure.

The signified is the trace of a referent made absent by the violence of the sparagmos. But this violence, in which Girard finds the source of the object's significance, is a secondary product of originary representation, a reaction to the resentment aroused by the object's resistance to appropriation. The sparagmos does not create significance, but when it destroys the already-significant referent, it leaves the signified in its place. The destruction of the central figure, to be replaced only by the imaginary figurality of the signified, is the originary withdrawal of the divinity. God's withdrawal in Exodus from the figure itself signifies the revelation that the basis of human scenicity is not figural, that it inheres in the circular—minimally, triangular—structure of mimesis.

The unique central being is destroyed in the sparagmos; the sign remains because, indefinitely repeatable, it defers the resentment inspired by the unique center. The passage from the unique sacred referent to the signified via the sparagmos is the originary passage from "proper" to "common" noun. Now that the ostensive sign has survived the destruction of its single privileged referent, the sparagmos's ultimate aim of obliteration has become both impossible and unnecessary.

The retention of the sign as signified depends on the sacrifice of its exemplary object, which religion reinterprets as the withdrawal of the sacred Being that inhabited this object. We accept this sacrifice because we have in fact anticipated it, indeed, participated in it. To give significance to an object, to show interest in it, to desire it, is to retain its figure at the same time as we engage in its imaginary de-figuration. The signified, as the residue of the violence of the sparagmos, remains the locus of the tension between the figure as a specific incarnation of desire and the negation of this specificity in the generality of the sign. If I say "tree," the tree-figure that my imagination conjures up is neither specific nor general but oscillates between the two. As soon as I form an image, it possesses a thisness that must immediately be denied by the universal nature of signification.[6]

The paradoxical, oscillatory nature of our relation to the signified determines the historical openness of the semantic system of language. Although the signifieds of language do not possess the concreteness of communicable images, each depends on the potential availability of this concreteness within the reference world. When it is lacking, the sign falls into disuse and loses its place in the system. By placing a premium on the vividness of the figure that a given signifier evokes in the interlocutor, language provokes a renewal of its signifiers. The selection of the more colorful or vivid expression is never definitive, however, since the latter requires of the subject a supplementary effort that becomes impossible to justify once the effect of novelty has been lost.[7]

*

The signs of language coexist in a state of rivalry for the privilege of attracting the unique and exclusive attention that is accorded to the significant. Saussure's image of the sign system as a piece of paper divided into territories hides the fact that significance is indivisible, incarnated whole in each uttered sign. This is the consequence of the centralized configuration of the originary scene.

What makes this configuration human is not its scenic structure as such—all living creatures congregate around "significant" objects—but the internalization of this structure within the individual signifying imagination, an internalization reflected back upon the public scene, and one that only the sign makes possible. But because the originary scene of significance can be internalized, or from the worldly standpoint, deferred, it can also be "forgotten," first by the construction of the extraworldly model of the declarative sentence, then by the declarative's canonization in the propositional ontology of metaphysics, and finally by the structural theory of signification that finds even the scene of metaphysics too eventful. It is the dangerous ostensivity of this structure, a hair's breadth from the violence of the sparagmos, that long made its forgetting a prerequisite of intellectual progress. Only the postmodern era's disillusionment with the power of the center, the esthetic as well as the sacred, has made it possible to recall it.

Two Psychoanalytic Categories:
Eros and the Unconscious

To what can we attribute the extraordinary success of the Freudian paradigm in our era? By formulating its generative hypothesis in terms of individual development, Freudian thought avoids the problem of defining the anthropological status of its constitutive categories. The Freudian theory of desire is ambivalently a critique of Western capitalism and a description of the unchanging reality of human relations. By defining the human in a narrow enough fashion so that its model can be attacked for its phallocentrism, psychoanalysis permits the postmodern intelligentsia to espouse an individual-centered theory that flatters the bourgeois ego, while denouncing the theory and its "white male" outlook at the same time.

Yet beneath the surface, the Freudians, most explicitly those of the Lacanian school, are seeking what all postmodern thought is seeking: an originary anthropology centered on language. Our common faith is that the institution of human language and all it implies is able to shed sufficient light on the human to permit us to formulate anthropological hypotheses independently of historically revealed truth. The politics of resentment aside, our projects are not incompatible. The following originary analyses of two psychoanalytic categories have been undertaken in this spirit.

The Erotic

In the originary scene, it is reasonable to assume that the birth of human desire induces a state of sexual excitement in the participants.[1] The central desire-object would then be the first object of human sexual desire as well. In this context, sexuality does not lose its specificity; yet the sexual is not, as in psychoanalytic theory, the primary component of desire, but a supplement to the mechanism of desire as such. Sexual desire, as opposed to sexual appetite, is desire before it is sexual.

Within the originary context, mimetic mediation by the others' desires is occulted by the sacralization of the central figure. The erotic may be defined as that which preserves the supplementary libidinal charge attributed to desire in the originary scene beyond the boundary of its original context. The erotic resembles the esthetic as a category at first attached to the sacred but in principle detachable from it.

The erotic, in other words, is whatever in the central being actively compels mimetic desire independently of the mimetic models on the periphery. In the originary scene, the central object's apparent withdrawal from our desire is the effect of mediation by the others. But what is crucial for the erotic is that this withdrawal be attributed to the object itself by the desiring subject—presumably in the course of the latter's act of representing its formal closure, as discussed in Chapter 2. The erotic exists as a category as soon as it can be intuited as an effect aroused in the self, and consequently capable of being aroused in others. Thus if I wish to imitate this effect of the central object, I will myself withdraw from the other's desire.

The erotic object is self-mediating because we can feel it deliberately resist our desire. Only a person, a subject of "free will," is truly capable of such resistance, although we like to attribute this capacity to animals like cats whose behavior contains elements of both dependence and independence. The first personhood is attributed to the sacred center as the originary desire-object and the model for the actions of human desire-objects in the life-world.

Desire for another human being, although not exclusively sexual, is given its most powerful orientation by the libido or sexual appetite. But the eroticism of objects other than sexual is not a deviation of the libido from its sexual aim; it is simply proof of the noncoincidence of the erotic with the sexual.[2]

Desire cannot emerge as a human phenomenon in the intimate sphere of sexuality. On the other hand, it cannot operate without the sexual energy that attaches us to our fellow humans. Even in the prehuman state, appetite for the other is more labile than appetite in imitation of the other. Already in the lower animals we can distinguish between the physical reality of sexual pleasure and the specificity of its object; an analogous distinction exists only marginally in the alimentary sphere in the difference between taste and nutritive value. But although the higher animals can be "perverse," their one-on-one operations of sexual competition are not yet erotic. The model of the mimetic center confers on the other an eroticism only possible in the human universe of the sign. The lability of sexual desire makes the erotic as mediated by the sign the typical human desire, one not wholly dependent on a corporeal need, yet funded by a visceral source of energy that we may call with Freud the libido. In contrast with the prehuman world, which is dominated by appetites directed to extraspecific objects of alimentary consumption, the exemplary human desire is erotic attraction to a fellow human.

The eroticism of culture supplements the zero-sum game of mimetic desire and resentment. Secular culture seduces us through the erotic, which appears to give our desire something for nothing. The erotic object as self-withholding subject lures us to construct an imaginary scene on which that other-subject can be possessed. We forget the mediation of our desire through the cultural sign in our erotic attachment to the otherness that is the content of the sign. We dream of an individual possession of the whole that denies its ancestry in the sparagmatic fragmentation of the originary event. From the communal scene to the erotic one, only the mechanism of desire is preserved—but this mechanism is everything. In high art, the structure of originary experience is reproduced in an esthetic oscillation that is foregrounded at the expense of erotic fixation. The popular arts are less embarrassed to provide the material for imaginary wish fulfillment. But when the esthetic mechanism remains wholly occulted and the erotic reigns undisturbed, we fall altogether out of the domain of "legitimate" culture into that of pornography.[3]

ROMANTIC LOVE

The phenomenon of romantic love as we know it since the feudal era extends to the erotic sphere the Christian revelation of the equivalence between divine and human personhood. In love, the object of desire is revealed as not simply a troubling otherness that attracts our desire by withdrawing from it, but as another subject. The so-called overestimation of the sexual object is not an illusion but, on the contrary, a realization that the structure of desire is essentially interpersonal rather than objectal. The erotic couple attempts to expel the mediating other from the scene of representation, to substitute a dual reciprocity, a mutual mediation, for the circulation of the mimetic triangle. Triangularity haunts erotic desire as its origin and inevitable temptation, but it is not the structure of the erotic in itself.

The increasingly self-aware formulations of love in the West since the eleventh century testify to the growing importance of the erotic couple as a cultural model. Romantic love includes the sacred source of being within the relationship itself. Just as the esthetic becomes independent of the public scene of representation by internalizing the scene's mimetic structure in the subject's oscillation between sign and referent, the object of erotic desire is the incarnate sign of his/her own being, generating in the partner a personal sacred that lasts at least the time of a sexual encounter, and perhaps a lifetime.

The fullest potential of the love relationship is in creating a model of reciprocity without an alien center. In the reciprocal erotic scene, as opposed to the perfect-except-for-the-center symmetry of the originary scene, each is a center for the other. This intimate version of the Gospel utopia, however unrealistic it may be as a model for social relations, can function in the erotic context because it is based on desire rather than "brotherly love." The erotic is both figural and intersubjective; it is attached both to the material reality of the other and to his/her status as subject.

Because the erotic creates a microcosm of the human universe that requires no external transcendent figure, it is the privileged content of secular culture, which must arouse and purge desire without the benefit of the ritual reconstitution of collective presence. This privileged status only clearly emerges in the neoclassical era, which is characterized by its thematization of the scenic.[4] Love creates a personal scene of representation homologous to the public one, with the beloved as its sacred center; this homology is thematized from the beginnings of romantic love with the troubadours and systematized as a worldview by Dante and the neo-Platonists. Throughout the neoclassical era, the private erotic scene draws away the energies that classical forms concentrated on the public scene, until the romantics finally enshrine it as the authentic scene of origin.

Yet the movement toward the intimate love scene reveals that the essential characteristic of the erotic figure is its "otherness," its possession of another self that it withholds from us. This otherness both requires figurality and conflicts with it. The selfhood of the other is only visible through the figure but, at the same time, as figure it is fixed in its frame, subordinated to the gaze of the spectator. The inherent tension between the other-subject's freedom and its fixation in the image is latent throughout the neoclassical era, which remains attached to the public scene of representation; it emerges explicitly in the idolatry of postromantic decadence, and becomes irreconcilable at the onset of modernism, the moment of divorce between high art and the erotic. The crucial moment in this history is that of realism, the first modern challenge to the esthetic legitimacy of the Platonic Idea.

REALISM AND THE EROTIC

The crisis in mimetic art that we call realism is the first moment in esthetic history in which the artist conceives it a duty to present disagreeable material to the audience, not in the context of an operation of purgation, nor as a challenge to mimetic technique, but simply because it is "real," the criterion for reality being the banishment of the erotic from the figure. Yet realist narrative material is most often, and not coincidentally, erotic in theme; the effect of realism is to induce us perversely to desire the undesirable. An exemplary case is the Goncourt brothers' early novel *Germinie Lacerteux* (1864). Following a preface that opposes the authors' self-proclaimed honesty to the meretriciousness of the audience's presumed erotic tastes ("les petites oeuvres polissonnes, . . . les saletés érotiques" [dirty little works, . . . erotic filth]), the body of the novel deals rather clinically with the life of a servant girl who turns to prostitution. The denunciation of the reader presages the modernist avant garde. Realism affirms, without ever being able altogether to effect it, an absolute separation between the antierotic, "scientific" position of narrative mastery shared by author and reader and the eroticism of the fictional world. It claims to regret and disown any contamination between the two, when in fact this contamination, so evident, for example, in Zola's sensual passages, is its principal attraction, perverse because "supplementary." Realism loses its status as high art as soon as this ambivalence itself comes to be thematized by the moderns.

What the Goncourts announced in their preface, Flaubert had already actualized in narration in *Madame Bovary* (1857). The moment of crisis in the relation of the erotic to the cultural may be summed up by the question: Is Emma Bovary sexy? Emma's desires, as we all know, come from books; but the text transmits to the reader an undeniable erotic investment in her, not simply because she attracts the desire of a number of other characters, but because it is precisely her position that provides a model for the desiring self ("Madame Bovary, c'est moi!"). To "possess" Emma and to be Emma are no longer discernible options.

Although Emma is virtually the sole object of masculine desire in the novel, we are given no exemplary masculine position to occupy with respect to her—unless it be that of the strictly medical Dr. Larivière, often referred to as the sole positive character in the novel, whose role, not uncoincidentally, is to incarnate the scientific conclusion that Emma cannot live. As the prototypical realist heroine, Emma withdraws from our desire by desiring in a new mode, that of the modern consumer, who can never be satisfied because she consumes with the goal of going beyond consumption. Realism is the disillusionment of narrative textuality: the satisfaction of desire can end a narrative, but not satisfy us forever as literary characters are supposed to be satisfied. Emma shares this disillusionment; she consumes the objects in her life as we consume her story. She is always in our sight, yet her description is vague. Emma is withdrawn from us concomitantly with her own eroticism; the author's emphasis on her awaiting of her lovers' desire expresses an emergent awareness of the seductive power of this withdrawal on the reader.

Thus realism is the moment in which the strategic withdrawal characteristic of the erotic other has begun to be a figural absence, a lack of figuration. The figure of beauty that was never other than a sign, a support for esthetic oscillation, now appears to block the circular movement of this oscillation by offering too much to the audience's desire. The driving force in this evolution is the increasing integration of desire into the market system—the emergence of "consumer society"— which reveals the dependency of the supposedly anarchic force of desire on the social order it is supposed to be contesting. In this context of the commercial circulation of desire, the esthetic oscillation between sign and referent comes into conflict with the quasi-permanent investments of the erotic.

The erotic retained the spectator's interest in the sign-cum-referent as a whole; it operated as a supplement to the esthetic, the apparent "free lunch" from which the romantics believed they could profit without penalty.[5] But now the hitherto unproblematic constancy of the image, whether conceived as a conventional figure or as an imaginative creation, is discovered to be a cultural artifact. When I invest my libido in the other as figure, it remains blocked at the level of the image and cannot return to the sign because, like Emma, it takes the image as an article of consumption.[6] The image is a fetish that hides the sign-nature of the fictional figure. In consumer society, the centralized image is no longer sacred but cynically manipulative; it is too productive of resentment to perform the cultural task of purging it. Late romantic art turns away from and problematizes the figure, not because it has lost its power—the heavily charged eroticism of the Decadents is proof of the contrary—but because this power is no longer under the artist's control. Whence the wild oscillations in this period between asceticism and pornography (and the pornography of asceticism), as exemplified by the careers of Wilde, Beardsley, Verlaine, or J.-K. Huysmans.

THE (POST)MODERN EROTIC

The emergent incapacity of high culture to maintain a direct relationship with the erotic, its evolution in the direction of a second-degree eroticism in which the oscillation between sign and image is henceforth figured in the image itself, prohibitively raises the stakes for the investment of erotic energy in high art, thereby liberating vast esthetic resources for popular or "mass" culture.

Already in the modern era and certainly in the postmodern, popular culture is more vital than high culture, more revelatory, if not of the universal structure of desire, then of the specifics of its operation in a new age. Erotic seduction continues to take place in reality and to be figured esthetically. Unlike high art, popular art takes this reality as its point of departure, but it is not bound to remain there. "Ennobled" forms of popular culture, like jazz or art cinema, construct a self-aware esthetic on the basis of the first-level eroticism that the high culture has discarded.

The submission of the figure to the gaze remains an a priori condition of this eroticism, but the erotic object can transcend rather than passively accept this condition through the self-conscious exhibition of irony, the means, as we observed in Chapter 5, by which the absolutes of form are recognized and deconstructed within the world of content. There is no real transcendence of the erotic, only the ironic sign of it. The bite of the irony comes from combining the revelation of the impossibility of avoiding the erotic with the demonstration that the erotic object as subject-other is "narcissistically" independent of the look to which she subjects herself.[7]

In the ironies of postmodern high culture, the esthetic effect loses itself in reflection on form; the figure's withdrawal deliberately avoids the immediacy of the erotic because, once provoked, erotic desire is an imaginary investment that fails to circulate. In contrast, popular art must produce a genuine erotic effect of measurable market value. The tendency of postmodern as opposed to postromantic high art not merely to take over elements from popular art but to *become* popular art supplemented by high-esthetic ironies demonstrates the centrality of the erotic in art and, by extension, the priority of popular over high culture.

It is characteristic of erotic seduction to exploit whatever level of self-reflection is effective at a given moment. Because the object of sexual desire is always another subject, even a gesture of absolute submission is an ironizing of the formal necessity of this submission. The result of the more aggressive irony of our era is only to emphasize the erotic all the more in its most blatantly sexual form. The erotic figure is precisely the one that continues to produce its effect not in spite of but as a result of the ironization of the form in which it is presented. It is present as objective figure and absent as subjective irony; this merely restates the principle of the erotic in general, which is the tantalizing withdrawal of the subject-other.

The more ironic, the more erotic; the more open the eroticism, the more the self-staging of life becomes indistinguishable from art, as a figure like Madonna makes clear. The deliberately seductive figures of popular culture are translated directly into the seductions of the life-world. Let us recall that the source of the privilege accorded the erotic element in culture is that it provides the spectator with the context-free conditions of desire that obtain in the world of intimacy. As esthetic form loses its historical innocence, this imaginary intimacy can no longer be segregated from that of everyday life. In order to be able to resist the seductions of popular culture, we would have to refashion the entire erotic imagery of our daily lives. This is not within our capacity. We can renounce active participation in the culture, but not absorption of its imagery; desire even after analysis retains its mimetic power.

It is no coincidence that our culture comes to be stigmatized as offering only the temptations of "sex and violence" at the very moment in which it is experiencing a qualitative leap in the reciprocity of sexual relations. The postmodern rejection of the naive culture of the (essentially if not exclusively feminine) image parallels the demise of the masculine warrior-ideal. The new sexual reciprocity, in personal as opposed to instrumental relationships, is anything but a sterile nondifference. A satisfactory love relationship cannot be founded on an abstract symmetry; to the extent that it refuses hierarchy, it must cultivate and generate difference rather than identity.

Postmodern popular culture helps us to understand the mechanism of the generation of difference within the erotic sphere. Erotic content is typically perverse, coquettishly designed to seduce the desiring subject through an appearance of self-containment. But the erotic figure is in fact wholly dependent on the desire of the other that it is designed to arouse. This is the reason for its irony. The cultural image that operates within the limits of esthetic form avenges itself in the erotic sphere by assuming its objectality in full awareness of its power over the spectator's desire. The same eroticization takes place in the sphere of intimate relations, where the members of the couple ironically exploit erotic figurality in acts of mutual seduction. In love relationships, as with a lesser intensity in all human relationships, ironic self-consciousness guarantees against the instrumental domination of one person by another.

Esthetic culture always operates ironically in that it deconstructs absolute formal oppositions into relative and therefore reversible ones.

It is by means of this imaginary reversibility that resentment is deferred. But in the postmodern era, irony attacks esthetic form itself. For this consciousness, the absolute differences whose function is to defer resentment have themselves become sources of resentment and must therefore be understood as reversible, although the cultural forms by means of which we acquire our ironic distance are themselves founded on these differences. What saves the situation from the sterile circularity of postmodern high art is the erotic, by means of which the attraction of formal difference is dissolved in the reciprocity of sexual relations and then regenerated anew.

A final observation on the operation of the erotic in our era: the erotic ironizes the victimary mode that dominates contemporary cultural discourse.[8] The otherness of today's minoritary culture becomes an object of erotic desire. The minoritary figure is a subject-other who in the apparent plenitude of its own local communal relations simultaneously withdraws from and is present to our gaze. In the social as in the intimate sphere, potential hierarchical differences (male-female, majority-minority) are deferred through erotic seduction.

The Unconscious

The unconscious is a necessary yet invisible category, a paradoxical candidate indeed for inclusion in the paradoxical scene of origin of human consciousness. Freud first performed a kind of originary analysis of the unconscious in *Totem and Taboo*, by tracing its origin to the repressed memory of the murder of the father who had kept all the women of the "horde" to himself.[9] But this has not been the path followed by psychoanalysis. However decentered the psychoanalytic vision of the human subject, however dependent it may be on language, the idea that the unconscious could have a collective origin has only been preserved by those who entertain the misguided notion of a "collective unconscious."

Were the unconscious merely the complement of the conscious, it would have no conceptual weight. Clearly I am unconscious of everything of which I am not conscious. But we come closer to a useful understanding of the concept when the field of potential consciousness is limited by the minimality of the originary scene. Simply to note that, in this scene, if I am conscious of the central object I am unconscious of everything else is already to give a preliminary definition of the unconscious: it remains only to specify the "everything else."

If we need a concept like the unconscious, it is because of a lack within consciousness that is constitutive rather than empirical, an incapacity not merely to contain all content but to grasp the totality of the very event it observes and retains in memory. In contrast with the originary hypothesis that postulates a minimal event of which all human history is both a forgetting and a remembering, the postulation of "forgotten" or "repressed" events in an individual's life history gives only an empirical basis for the unconscious. A theory of repression implies that had some particular event not been forgotten, consciousness would be complete, and that in order for us to forget it, it must first have been in our consciousness. On the contrary, we only need a concept of the unconscious if it designates not a stock of images forgotten yet retrievable in the memory but an inherent limitation in consciousness itself.

In what sense am I conscious of the central object in the originary event? What new element has been added to animal awareness of objects of appetitive interest? Consciousness is not the simple equivalent of mediation by the sign. The subject's re-presentation of the referent's formal closure constitutes an imaginary scene of representation that doubles the external scene of origin. To be conscious of an object is to (with)hold it in the imaginary place where it is potentially representable.

From the metaphysical standpoint, consciousness's withholding of its object from the practical sphere is a guarantee of its perfect lucidity, its transparent self-presence as revealed in the *cogito*. Sartre gave the name of *néant* or nothingness to this metaphysical clear space between me and the object that I "intend." In contrast, in metaphysics' deconstructive self-critique, an unconscious is constituted by the "repression" of the specificity of the unmarked member of the binary oppositions established by the centralizing logos—man as opposed to woman, white to colored, speech to writing. Just as Marx accused the bourgeoisie of taking its own interests for those of humanity in general, so is Western (white male) thought accused of taking its own position as neutral. This repression of the unmarked is the foundation of the oppression of the marked member of the pair. But this limited strategy of derepression is ultimately incompatible with the psychoanalytic conception of the unconscious as the historical residue of the signifiers of desire, which appears to the metaphysician—rightly perhaps, but metaphysics has no valid substitute for it—as a precritical *fourre-tout* of materials indistinguishably ontic and ontological, like the Lacanian phallus. The question for us is whether the premetaphysical notion of the unconscious does not have a legitimate anthropological function that can be disengaged from the Freudian mythology that continues to envelop it.

The desire directed to the center of the originary scene is mediated by the others, or in the triangular model, the other, on the periphery. This mediation is *our* knowledge, an element of our theoretical model; it is the basis of our analysis of the mimetic origin of language. The turning-away from the direct imitation of the other that permits the imitation/representation of the object creates an opening for this representation's own modeling by consciousness; the history of consciousness is made up of the successive stages through which representation turns back toward its mimetic origin. Consciousness of mimesis is accessible to the participants in the scene itself only through the mediation of the center, which is also to say the alienation of this consciousness to the center. The interminable process of understanding this alienation is the basis of our historicity; but concomitant with our increasing lucidity about mimesis is our growing awareness that its "unconscious" triangular structure cannot be grasped from within.

The collective mediation of the participants in the originary scene is the real cause of their resentment of the central object. The obstacle to their desire is not the object itself but the concurrent desires of their fellows. Should we then say that what we really resent is not the center itself but these other desires? But this formulation is unsatisfactory; we cannot resent anything but the object of our resentment, any more than we can desire the desire-object of the others rather than the object that in fact we desire. It is therefore preferable to say that our resentment is indeed directed to the center, but that it is determined by our *unconscious* mimetic relationship with the desiring others on the periphery.

This formulation locates the unconscious in a different place within the scene than Freud's or even Girard's model. For Girard as well as for the author of *Totem and Taboo*, what must be repressed is the relation to the center itself, conceived as an originary murder. The murder is differently motivated in the two theories. For Freud, the father is the object of a universal thematic and prescenic resentment, the result of his monopoly of the women, who are the "natural" desire-objects of the group of sons. For Girard, the originary victim is arbitrarily chosen during the scene itself rather than in advance. This difference has enormous consequences for the respective theories of desire each derives from the originary scene—Freud's "derivation" being determined a posteriori by his preexisting model of the Oedipus complex. Because of the intentional nature of the murder, Freud cannot speak of the repression of its memory in the originary context. Instead, he makes the notion of *guilt* the basis for a new internalization of the interdiction of the center, which will eventually lead to this repression, as well as to the various forms taken by the religious commemoration of the dead father, who provides the model for the transcendent divinity. Throughout his work, it is aggression against the father/center rather than the more notorious desire for the mother that is the exemplary object of repression.

Girard avoids the embarrassment of having to explain the repression of a thematic intention. In the absence of such an intention, it is indeed possible to speak of the "repression" of the emissary murder. Myth mystifies this violent event by recalling only its beneficial consequences; as many mythical and quasi-mythical texts attest, the disappearance of the central figure is presented as the effect of its own "divine" will.[10] The repressed mediation of desire that was the key to the mimetic model of *Mensonge romantique* remains at the root of Girard's theory of desire; its translation to the cultural realm changes the object and scope of repression, but not the structure of mediation.

A founding murder is a memorable event the repressed memory trace of which may easily enough be imagined as a kind of space-occupying content displaced from the conscious to the unconscious mind. But a rigorously conceived unconscious should not be a mere double of consciousness; the very ease with which we imagine the murder scene should warn us that this conception of the unconscious is as mythical as its purported content.

This problem does not arise if the originary content of the unconscious is the collective mediation of the subject's desire for the center. Mediation is not an event; it is not "visible" even when recognized. Because the originary hypothesis dispenses with the concrete figures of emissary or paternal murder, it can also dispense with the dubious notion of an already-figural unconscious content.

*

The idea of an unconscious is incompatible with the propositional universe of metaphysics. What can be "repressed" from a world of propositions can only be another proposition, and the missing proposition can always be reconstituted from its elements. What requires an unconscious is one's own situation within the universe one represents, just as the paradoxes of representation are the inevitable byproducts of self-reference. Mimesis leads to paradox because of the impossibility of definitively separating the world of the model from the world of the subject; their reunion is deferred by metaphysical language only at the cost of eventual deconstruction. No doubt paradox is formalizable only in propositional forms, but we can grasp the anthropological significance of paradox only once we realize that rather than a perversion of the declarative proposition, paradox is inherent from the beginning in the verticality of language.

The unconscious, as Lacan says, is "structured like a language." But Lacan has no idea, beyond those of Saussure, of how a language is structured. It is the paradoxical origin of language that leaves the unconscious as the unformulatable residue of the sign. Our claim that mediation by the periphery is the unconscious of our consciousness of the center functionally equates unconscious and paradox. What is paradoxical in mimesis is the entry of the model into the universe of the subject; what is unconscious in desire is the copresence of the model within the field of desire yet outside the field of vision concentrated on the center. It is fundamental to the structure of desire that the model cannot be represented, thematized, from within. The circle (or in its minimal configuration, the triangle) is constituted by the concentration of all attention on the central object. The others are present only laterally, as subjects with whom I communicate, not as objects I can point to.

But if, as this analysis suggests, there is no unconscious event or fact, there is an unconscious subject of desire—that of the other/model. The mediator is he who stands beside me so that I cannot become aware of him as significant. He is wholly human, in contrast with the sacrality of the signified object. One must stand outside the circle in order to perceive the mimetic structure of desire as a whole. For the subject to gain this perception, he must look back toward the center from which he has escaped, recentering it in a larger scene.

Metaphysics, in turning its back altogether on the circle of collective desire in order to found a purely cognitive relation with the object of consciousness, cuts off all access to the mediating other. Thus it is not surprising that the postmodern reconstruction of the circle/triangle of mimetic desire began not in philosophy but in the domain of cultural criticism.

The metaphysical philosophy of consciousness finds its minimal formulation in the lucidity of the cogito. The emergence of the conception of the unconscious in the late nineteenth century coincides with the opening phase of the deconstruction of metaphysics, the shift from a model of the subject-object relationship based on cognition to one based on desire. For metaphysics, language is a vehicle of binary, propositional knowledge. Desire can be incorporated in this model only so long as its triangular, mimetic nature remains hidden. The thematization of this hiddenness under the name of the unconscious is an opening to the exploration of the mimetic structure of desire.

The principal historical condition for this thematization is the decline of the noncirculating transcendence of religion, not so much as a practice—although this has followed—but as an epistemology. At the dawn of modern market society, Kant's antinomy of the existence of God shows that there is no longer any useful way to distinguish religion from metaphysics, the transcendence of God from the verticality of the Idea. As the revelatory, ostensive link to the originary event loses its traditional reinforcement under the pressure of the ever-accelerating bourgeois exchange system, the individual self-consciousness or Freudian ego becomes indistinguishable from the metaphysical subject. The residue of the immortal soul unrecognized by metaphysics provides the first content for the unconscious in the form of the romantic's "irrational" aspirations to centrality. The loss of divine mediation is a preparation for the understanding of human mediation.

When Descartes attempted to define the human subject, he left it to God to guarantee the relationship between this subject and the empirical world. Now that it is certain of its individual being, the self of the cogito, having put aside desire (the "passions") and even empirical knowledge, requires a transcendental mediator to reestablish what has been destroyed. In contrast, the romantic bourgeois self is no longer bound by communal mediation; he has become ostensibly self-mediating. But to absorb the mediator into the self is not to eliminate him, merely to render his domination unconscious. In its typically modern, "internal" form, mediation becomes invisible to the subject and at the same time figurable within the world of narrative; this is the theme of *Mensonge romantique*. We need not take the mediating figures in these works at face value, as though we each walked the streets of the modern city shadowed by our personal mediator. The individualized, thematized mediator or Dostoevskian double is just as usefully understood as the external projection in a unique Other of the multiple mediations installed within the self, of what we may begin to call the character's unconscious. The force of mediated desire has become visible to the subject in his moments of acute self-consciousness in the form of an inhabiting other, an alienated self.

This late romantic sense of alienation, of being possessed by a double, is the coming to consciousness of mimetic desire as an operational element in an evolving exchange system within which the deliberate mediation of desire through advertising and product diversification has become essential. This is the onset of the mature, desire-based phase of the market era that we call consumer society.

The historical significance of consumer society has been difficult to evaluate in the face of the century of diatribes with which it has been greeted by the intelligentsia from Thorstein Veblen on down, incorrigible believers in the resentment-free utopia that will satisfy all their resentments. We are perhaps still insufficiently distanced from the Marxian-socialist illusion to carry out this evaluation. Nascent consumer society is clearly the efficient cause of modernism and its associated political extremisms, as well as of the decline of traditional metaphysics. The establishment of the priority of desire over cognition is not a temporary aberration engineered by the self-serving bourgeoisie, but the revelation of a revolutionary anthropological truth, the liberation of a genie that not even the most ruthless dictatorships have been able to put back in its bottle.

The mature market system raises mediation, the long-repressed unconscious of desire, into consciousness. But nothing had really been "forgotten." The seductive model of historical progress as the remembering of the object of an originary forgetting is a naive preformism: the end was in the beginning. In this apocalyptic perspective, history is governed not by dialectical progress but by a pattern of fall and redemption, repression and the "return of the repressed." This kind of thinking evacuates the epistemological problem posed by the new revelation; if what we know now was previously known and forgotten, then we have no need to concern ourselves with the specific faculties required for this knowing.

But although the end of culture indeed consists in understanding the beginning, this understanding is not static, and in no case consists in recuperating lost knowledge. The unconscious is what the originary mechanism of signification necessarily excludes from consciousness. History then becomes not the return of the repressed, but the elaboration of indirect, mediate means to thematize the excluded figure of mediation.

*

The term "unconscious" is paradoxical on its face; if the unconscious were really unconscious, we could never talk about it. Like the other paradoxes we have discussed, the paradox of the unconscious is a "view" of the fundamental paradox of mimesis from within a particular domain of experience. The unconscious tells us both that all elements of desire are ultimately thematizable, and that this thematization is the historical working-through of a deferral. The usefulness of the term is in dramatizing our revelatory discovery of the mimetic structure of desire, which we must constantly discover anew in the mode of the already-present-but-inaccessible-to-consciousness.

To understand the originary form of desire is not suddenly to remember, as in a horror story, the figure one had not consciously noticed, but to become conscious of the alienation of desire in the present. When the hysteric is cured of her paralysis by being made to "remember" a scene of childhood trauma, she is not extracting her infantile memories from a repository named "the unconscious," but learning to bring the internal other of mediated desire to consciousness in a human figure rather than in a paralyzed limb. It is to be hoped that the producers of psychoanalytic discourse may similarly be cured of their infatuation with objectal cathexes by letting emerge within their own theoretical consciousness the basis of desire in the scene of human origin.

PART TWO

Sparagmos and Resentment

Originary Violence

The Origin of Language borrowed unchanged René Girard's model of the originary event of humanity as a lynching or "emissary murder." But from the outset, the destruction of the victim at the hands of the collectivity, the core of Girard's theory of cultural origin and renewal, has not played a major role in the development of generative anthropology. The emphasis on the origin of the linguistic sign as a form of renunciation of violence made the originary murder unnecessary, and it was abandoned in my later descriptions of the event in *The End of Culture* and elsewhere. The event was recast as a hunting scene in which killing the "victim" was subordinate to averting the potential conflict within the group inspired by its presence. The division of the victim's remains among the participants, the originary source of the human exchange system, was described as peaceful because it was undertaken under the auspices of the sacred, but little attention was paid to the process of division itself.[1] The result has been to perpetuate within generative anthropology an unspoken dualism in which the forms of representation belong to a "Gansian" domain while the more or less explicit figures of collective violence that are the typical content of cultural representations are explained in "Girardian" terms.

I was recently obliged to confront the problem raised by this dualism in reexamining the difference between high and popular culture. In the past I had interpreted this difference on the model of that between "ontic" things and "ontological" words, as opposing high culture's maintenance of the deferral of desire as mediated by the sign to popular culture's anticipation of the eventual consumption of the object designated by that sign. In this perspective, high culture, understood as preserving humanity's fundamental commitment to representation, was treated as the primary model; popular culture, which naively disregards the difference between representation and reality in its rush to satisfy the popular appetite, was a vulgar derivative of it. But this "alimentary" explanation of popular culture was not fully compatible with the other function I had attributed to it: the discharge, as opposed to the sublimation, of originary resentment toward the scenic center. Here, too, appetitive satisfaction is deferred, but this time in a movement not of renunciation but of aggression. The originary analysis of this cultural operation pointed to the violent discharge of resentment within the originary scene itself.

My attention was further drawn to originary violence by reflection on the Holocaust, to which I proposed to trace the ubiquitous victimary discourse of the postmodern era. In the historical context of this reflection, one encounters within Western culture the phenomenon of antisemitism, understood as the defense of Christian figurality against Jewish "anesthetism."[2] It is no accident that the present volume's integration of the element of originary violence—or evil—within generative anthropology is associated with a more distinctly Judaic perspective on Western civilization, in contrast with the Judeo-Christian outlook of *Science and Faith*. The *fuite en avant* of the indefinite awaiting of the Messiah more closely models the operation of the postmodern market system than the guarantee of moral closure provided by the Christian revelation. The inclusion of the Girardian scene of victimage as a moment within the originary hypothesis of generative anthropology is a reinclusion of the Christian within the Judaic that reflects the impossibility of a Christian solution (unless it be the "final solution") to the problem of originary resentment. This operation is not unrelated to the dominance of the "Jewish thought" of Marx and Freud in the modern era. This theoretical power is that of the internal Other of the Christian West; it sheds light on the cultural power of the minoritary in postmodern, post-Holocaust times.

The Sparagmos

Here is Girard's description of the founding "emissary murder":

Plus les rivalités s'exaspèrent, plus les rivaux tendent à oublier les objets qui en principe la [*sic*] causent, plus ils sont fascinés les uns par les autres. . . . Il n'y a plus d'autre terrain d'application possible pour la mimésis que les antagonistes eux-mêmes. [The more intense the rivalries become, the more the rivals tend to forget the objects that in principle are their cause, the more they become fascinated by each other. . . . There is no longer any possible field of application for mimesis other than the antagonists themselves.] (*Des choses cachées*, pp. 34–35)

Entre l'animalité proprement dite et l'humanité en devenir, il y a une rupture véritable et c'est la *rupture de meurtre collectif,* seul capable d'assurer des organisations fondées sur des interdits et des rituels, si embryonnaires soient-ils. [Between true animality and inchoate humanity, there is a veritable rupture and it is the *rupture of collective murder,* the only thing capable of guaranteeing institutions founded on interdictions and rites, however embryonic.] (Ibid., p. 106; italics mine)

For Girard, scapegoating is at the origin of the human. The first human event is defined by a change of scene: the transformation of mimetic conflict centered on an appetitive object into unanimous mimetic aggression centered on a victim more or less arbitrarily chosen in the course of the original conflict. The participants in the event abandon their mutual hostility over the object for mutual harmony mediated by the victim. Only at the end of this process, after the aggressive energy of the group has been purged through the victim's murder, can the phenomena of human culture emerge.

The most obvious weakness of this model is that, like its Freudian ancestor in *Totem and Taboo,* it generates a humanity for which language is epiphenomenal. The origin of the human is the origin of language. For violence to be part of the originary event, it must be situated *after* the emission of the sign expressing the renunciation of appropriation by individual members of the group, at the moment in which the central object is divided among them as participants in the new human community. The moment of division discharges the mimetic tension that had been redirected from their fellow participants to the central object in the form of originary resentment. This aggressive discharge is the equivalent of the scapegoating aggression of Girard's scheme, but located now subsequent to the invention/discovery of the linguistic sign, that is, within the originary event of generative anthropology.

This inclusion allows humanity to address the problem of violence within the peaceful framework provided by the sign. The sign expels violence from the group by concentrating it against the central figure. In historical phenomena such as the Dionysian sparagmos or rending of their victim by the Bacchantes, or the camel sacrifice observed by Robertson Smith—a scene that plays a central role in the argument of *Totem and Taboo*[3]—the violence of the action far exceeds that required for the rational division of the object; this excess is the measure of the specifically human phenomenon of violence.

It is to emphasize the resentful nature of this violence that I have used "sparagmos" here rather than Girard's "emissary murder." The term also connotes a subtle but fundamental difference with the Girardian interpretation of the scene. Girard speaks of the body of the victim as "the first signifier," implying its continued existence as a figure; but in the sparagmos, the figural nature of the victim, the object of originary resentment, is precisely what is destroyed. Nothing is left; the only worldly guarantee of the existence of the being that had occupied the center of the scene is the persistence of the scene itself. As Mallarmé put it in *Un coup de dés* . . . , "Rien n'aura eu lieu que le lieu"; nothing will have taken place but the place. Girard's act of violence, because it must be the direct source of both the fragility and stability of the nascent human community, is both too radical, in that it occurs outside the universe of the sign, and too limited, in that it leaves unscathed the figurality of the victim.

As with all institutions of mimetic desire, the sparagmos, the praxis that realizes the intention of originary resentment, is paradoxical: it seeks to abolish the central figure while incorporating the power that derives from its very figurality. The violence of the sparagmos is the originary example of evil, of disorder within a structure of order. It inspires doubt concerning the moral standing of the originary event, indeed, of humanity itself: has the deferral of violence led only to greater violence? But conversely, in the ethical world founded on the sacrificial violence of the sparagmos, this violence becomes the originary focus of moral reflection. This reflection has taken two directions, privileging respectively the human periphery and the sacred center of the scene. The first or "Greek" path is that of "political science": the critique of sacrificial violence by thinkers like Xenophanes and Heraclitus leads to Plato's and Aristotle's deritualized models of the organization of the human community. The second, "Hebraic," path is the iconoclastic critique of the esthetic or idolatrous element of the sacred exemplified by the Mosaic revelation.[4]

The revelation in the sparagmos of the internal violence of the originary communal order opens the political space within which higher— freer but less equalitarian—forms of organization will arise. Resentment at others' real or fancied proximity to the center provides the fuel for the motor of history, a motor that does most of its work in crises, when the accumulated resentment of a social group is released in sparagmatic rage against its object.[5]

The minimality of the originary hypothesis requires not merely that the appetite originally aroused by the central object be satisfied, but that discharge be provided for the supplementary tension contributed to the scene by the mimetic relationship among the participants. The projection of this tension onto the central figure is sufficient to make it an object not merely of appetite but of desire; its inaccessibility gives it an esthetic value as a form re-presented by the sign. Similarly, in the sparagmos, the rational appetitive operation of dividing the object is supplemented by the violent discharge of this tension in what is also a defiguration, a destruction of the very formal-esthetic closure that was imitated in the transformation of the appropriative gesture into a sign. Appetitive satisfaction, eventually conducive to reproductive fitness, is the bottom line of the evolutionary selection-value provided by the event, but the sparagmos makes indissoluble the link between the physiological reality of this satisfaction and the need to discharge the originary resentment occasioned by its deferral.

The minimal scene is thus not merely a minimal deferral of violence against the center, but a minimal mastering of the original movement toward generalized mimetic violence. In the sparagmos, where the violence of each is directed toward the object rather than the other participants, the state of prelinguistic chaos is *almost* reintroduced. But this is a violence contained within the peace brought by the center. Disorder is contained within order, evil within good.

The superiority of monist over dualist, "Manichean" theology lies in its recognition of this containment. The symmetry of good and evil,

God and Satan, is an attractive concept only from a purely worldly or "ontic" perspective—the zero-sum attitude associated with popular rather than high culture. Only when the human is accepted as a given of nature rather than a cultural self-production can the forces of good and evil be seen as symmetrical. Manicheism is oblivious to the initial triumph of good over evil without which humanity could never have come into being. The Manichean remains within culture, yet judges it as if from without, denying the monist reality that permits him to enunciate his dualism. He exemplifies, in other words, the structure of resentment.

The Esthetic and the Anesthetic

The originary sign is both the name of God and the primordial work of art. The sign institutes the sacred by pointing beyond the concrete central object of the sparagmos to the permanently subsisting center. At the same time, the sign provokes the oscillatory experience between the sign-representing-the-referent and the referent-represented-by-the-sign by which I have defined the esthetic.[6] Is there an inherent conflict between the sacred and esthetic roles of the sign as determined by these two moments of its constitution?

The originary sign produces an esthetic effect because it re-presents the central object as figure, perceptible form. It is only after the destruction of its worldly correlative in the sparagmos that the subsisting sign becomes independent of this specific referent. In earlier formulations, I spoke of the sign as designating the subsistent central locus rather than the mortal being that filled it. The more rigorous triangular derivation of the sign presented in Chapter 2 permits a more concrete analysis of the notion of the "subsistent locus" considered as the equivalent of subsistent sacred being, or God.

The mimesis of formal closure that went from the object to the sign now proceeds from the sign to the locus vacated by the object. Because the sign retains its formal closure, the mimetic nature of representation implies the closure of the locus as well, as a sacred space centered on, *formed by* the now-absent object. The form-in-the-absence-of-the-object is the originary form of what Plato will later call the Idea and Saussure the signified. The derivation referent → signifier → signified makes it clear that the signified is not simply a generalization of the referent but that it supplements the latter's absence by "imitating" the form of the signifier. In terms of Saussure's mimetic analogy of the two sides of the paper, it is the signifier side that is first divided up. This is the anthropological significance of the "primacy of the signifier" celebrated by the deconstructionist school.

The sign was always the "name of God," but it is the sparagmos that first reveals the necessary unworldliness of the sacred referent. In the postsparagmatic moment of religious revelation, as distinct from that of the originary manifestation of the sacred, sacrality is no longer attached to a present object of desire; the sign lacks a visible, concrete referent. Whether individual or collective, revelation is, as its etymology suggests, an unveiling of the hidden—hidden because destroyed as a reality in the sparagmos, but capable of renewed presence on the imaginary scene of representation. Attachment to the subsistent center of the scene is reinforced by the collective action of ritual, but the primary locus of this subsistence is the internal scene of representation of the individual participants, where the postsparagmatic signified remains as the ultimate correlate of the sign.

The sacred appears in its distinctive institutional form as religion only after the disappearance of the central object. In this it is opposed to the esthetic, which depends on the at least imaginary presence of this object. The religious imagination is not immediately aware of the radical nature of this distinction. The biblical polemic against idolatry should not lead us to believe that the idol worshiper really believes that the physical object is the divinity. The divinity incarnates itself in the object, but its being remains separate from its incarnation, as ritual sacrifice demonstrates. The relation between being and incarnation will first be satisfactorily articulated in the Christian Trinity. Until then, the direction of the guarantee between the sacred and the appetitive object is ambiguous: the divinity is ontologically prior to its image, but it is as an incarnation that the divinity is made visible to its worshipers.

Insistence on the incarnate image leads to the subordination of the religious to the esthetic, a development the locus classicus of which is the humanization of divine imagery in the *sourire grec*. This tendency is analogous to the later emergence of metaphysics in the cognitive realm; in both cases the immediate, ostensive revelation of otherness is softened and assimilated to the contemplation of an idealized version of everyday human experience. Neither Greek religion nor Greek philosophy is capable of grasping the ultimate incompatibility of the religious and the esthetic that is made explicit in the Mosaic revelation. The forms of high art realize the understanding that the enunciation of the sign is primordially a renunciation of its object, and that, as representations, artworks derive their power from this renunciation, which they reproduce in our imagination. The idolatrous moment of incarnation provides a pleasure that is continually sacrificed and renewed in the oscillatory movement of the imagination from esthetic sign to imaginary referent.

The work of high art defers or sublimates originary resentment by maintaining the paradoxical duality of mimesis, the identification with both the mediator and the object, both the periphery and the center of the scene. To identify with the central object is to condemn the sparagmos from the totalizing perspective of the sign in the process of representing its object; to participate in the sparagmos is to take the sign for granted as an already-constituted substitute for the object. The participant identifies with the central figure only in the negative sense, retained in popular art, of desiring the destruction of its formal closure, which he experiences no longer as the basis of his representational "imitation," but merely as a barrier excluding him from the center. Only if the whole is broken can the breaker possess his part. The fact that formal closure must be realized as a prerequisite of its destruction is an element of the self-consciousness of high, but not of popular art.

Yet popular culture has its answer to its rival's claims. The "end" of culture, in the Darwinian sense that explains why humanity survived in the first place, is to permit a group that mimesis has made its own potential worst enemy to obtain appetitive satisfaction. The sparagmos shows that the originary deferral of potential violence through the sign was not free of cost; the resentment generated by this deferral provokes this supplementary violent discharge of mimetically bound energy when the deferral is terminated.

High art well understands that the primary operation of secular culture is not the provision of appetitive satisfaction but the renunciation expressed by the aborted gesture. But for the bottom line of human society to be positive, what is deferred must be accomplished, and this applies not only to appetitive satisfaction, the ultimately realized pleasure of consumption, but also to the discharge of originary resentment in the sparagmos. There is no a priori reason for culture to reflect on itself; culture need only defer consumption sufficiently for it to take place without conflict, even at the additional cost of the violent discharge of resentment. To the extent that all cultural activities perform the same basic function, high culture's ascetic pretensions strike the partisan of popular culture as hypocritical. Whether or not one accepts one's individual responsibility for the violence of the sparagmos, it is the necessary evil that esthetic culture continues to reproduce on the imaginary scene of representation.

High art is the formal expression of cultural totality. The renunciation of the material referent is rewarded by the beauty of the (nearly) immaterial sign. Because religion lacks the flexibility of art in abandoning the reality of its referent, religious sacrifice can defer originary resentment toward the divine center, but not mature resentment toward a human occupant of the center. The society of the Greek city-states only evolved a secular esthetic once it had freed itself from the ritually fixed hierarchies of the archaic empires.

But if Greek religion takes second place to art, in the other birthplace of Western civilization, Hebrew religion dominates and expels the esthetic. Indifferent to the secular distinction between art and entertainment, the anesthetic divinity has no use for images of any kind. The esthetic elements of ritual that do not fall under this ban, such as song and dance, are activities of the human periphery rather than representations of the sacred center. When Chassidim dance in honor of God in imitation of their biblical ancestors, the center is left empty; none of the dancers represents God himself.

The central question of Western civilization before the postmodern era has been how to reconcile the high art of the Greeks with the uncompromising Hebraic expulsion of the esthetic, which continues to be reflected in Christian suspicion of secular art. Secular culture since the Renaissance sees its relationship to religion in terms of oppression and liberation, categories that find easy analogies in the political sphere. The originary hypothesis gives us a vantage point from which to examine this relationship anew.

Esthetic experience depends on the paradoxical oscillation between the contemplation of the sign with its referent and the contemplation of the referent without the sign. The sign assures us of the significance of the referent, but the referent cannot stand alone without losing its significance and returning us to the sign. This model describes the experience of the esthetic at a moment prior to any conceivable distinction between high and popular. The oscillation is that of ostensive signification itself, circulating between sign and referent. The subject attempting to forget the sign's reminder of triangular mediation in order to possess the thing-in-itself is continually thrown back upon this mediation when the thing-in-itself vanishes before his eyes. The object can be appropriated imaginarily only through the sign; this is the origin of the specifically human imagination.

What makes art so powerful an anthropological discovery procedure is our need to purge ourselves of the violence inherent in the centrality of the image. In the end, what justifies representation is its management of resentment in the service of appetitive satisfaction, and this management necessarily passes through the sparagmos. We may purchase a good conscience by imagining ourselves in the place of the tragic hero who is the object of our resentment rather than give this resentment free rein. But in the end, we are participants in his undoing. In the last analysis, our esthetic pleasure, whether in tragedy or in the crudest popular fantasy, derives less from taking pleasure in the details of the hero's suffering than from the experience of formal necessity that justifies our imagination of this suffering. Even the ultimate Mallarmean deconstruction of the image, "le sein brûlé d'une antique Amazone" ["the burnt breast of an ancient Amazon"—that is, the right breast, supposedly prevented from growing so that the Amazon could draw her bow], leaves just enough to the imagination to provide a focus for imaginary violence. *Hypocrite spectateur* . . .

But if the introduction of the sparagmos into our model of the originary scene problematizes the purgative operation of the esthetic, it makes clearer the crucial function of maintaining in memory the imageless sign. This operation is accomplished by religion. The originary category of the sacred cannot differentiate between the central object and the being of the locus it occupies; religion proper begins when the feast is over, the object has disappeared, and the sign remains in the memory along with the image of its referent. The subsistence of the ostensive sign as a communal cultural reality after the central locus has been emptied is guaranteed by the persistence of both this image, which no longer corresponds to anything the community can point to, and the central locus bereft of its occupant.

The "being" of the locus is the divinity. Like the content of all revelations, the dissociation imposed by the Mosaic revelation between the divinity and the image was already present from the beginning. The central object is remembered through the image, but the image masks the real source of significance, which is not the object but the total configuration of the scene, held together by the mimetic tension between center and periphery. The religious moment internalizes the founding principle of the community in its union around the originary center.

The tension inherent in the dual conception of the central locus, spatio-temporally particular but ontologically absolute, is not resolvable within religion itself. It is reproduced in our era in the tension between physical anthropologists' search for concrete paleontological evidence of human origin and the deconstructors' insistence that the representational phenomena that define the species have "always already" existed: two antithetical evacuations of the originary event. The religious remains bound to a specific locus just as the esthetic is bound to an image; the religious locus is a place of sacrifice, just as the esthetic image is a figure of the victim.

It is nevertheless the image rather than the locus that is the privileged object of intercultural dialogue. *Originary Thinking* insisted on the centrality of this dialogue to the process of historical self-understanding. We understand other cultures through their images, which can be shared, rather than through their religious loci, which retain their spatio-temporal specificity even in the highest religions—a trip to Jerusalem will convince anyone of that. But the iconoclastic religious critique of the image leads us to suspect this dialogue as ultimately a pretext for vicarious participation in other societies' sacrificial practices. Born in the Holocaust, profoundly suspicious of the centralized figure, postmodernity has moved away from the high-cultural universality of the *musée imaginaire*. The "multicultural" conversation that has taken its place is a sharing less of immortal images than of figures of victimization. The revelation of the resentment at the heart of the cultural makes the central figure a focus rather of victimary guilt than envy; but the guilt engenders in turn a backlash of envy directed at the victims themselves. The living culture of today belongs to those too young to be troubled by such contradictions.

Esthetic history, like all history, is the story of society's attempt to keep one step ahead of the resentments it generates. But the ultimate guarantee of success is not available in the esthetic domain. The sign defers resentment, but the sparagmos reveals this deferral to be only temporary. The esthetic illusion of the adequacy of the beautiful sign is secretly dependent on the religious awareness of the inadequacy of any worldly object to maintain the culture inaugurated by the sign. Esthetic form cannot rely on the original object of its imitation as its transcendental guarantee of closure. What makes possible the eventual declaration of independence of esthetic form from the ritual reproduction of the originary scene is the guarantee conferred on the sign by the sacred Being of the scene's defigured locus.

*

The sparagmos is only ex post facto a communal activity; it is the action of a community in dissolution whose members act each for himself. Only after the fact does it become clear that the group has not dissolved in chaos, that the community formed by the sign has outlasted the destruction of the object referred to by the sign. The participants who approach and dismember the object act as a community only in the minimal sense that they are bound together by the memory of the sign; this minimum of virtual solidarity, consonant with the parsimony of our hypothesis of origin, is just sufficient to permit them to survive the sparagmos.

This minimally cooperative action is the prototype of all ethical activities. In contrast with the symmetry of the originary emission of the sign, the archetype of the moral order, which is characterized by a temporary but absolute deferral of conflict, the sparagmos is not the prototype of a communal ideal. It is just cooperative enough so that the community does not dissolve in the contagion of mimetic violence.

But if the origin of the ethical is only minimally moral, then it is maximally immoral. The violence of the sparagmos makes it the origin of evil; the first collective act is the "fall of man." The criterion of parsimony would indeed be violated by any model that required a durable state of nonviolence as a consequence of the emission of the sign. The sparagmos is the originary violent act, for violence is conceivable only within the human order of representation. Viewed from the standpoint of its future repetition in ritual, it is a cultural act, a "tradition." But this only goes to show that violence is inherent in cultural traditions. The dedifferentiation of violence exceeds all differences but the difference of language. Disorder that exceeds language is no longer human; it is the horizon against which the human drama plays itself out, and which the violence of the drama continually challenges.

We must therefore avoid the temptation to reduce the violence of the sparagmos to the "discharge of aggression." What is being discharged is not some Freudian *Trieb* but originary resentment against the center, which itself derives from the mimetically induced excess of appetite for the central object. Only in hindsight does this discharge of resentment appear to have taken place safely under the control of the culture of deferral inaugurated by the sign. The violence that destroys the central figure eliminates the originary inspiration for the (esthetic) judgment that produced the sign. Religion founds the community on the subsistent being of the center. But the primal experience of Being is that of mourning; the mystical intuition of an ineffable essence recalls the loss of its originary incarnation. The central figure that originally attracted the group's appetites has been de-figured by those who henceforth depend on it all the more as their cultural model.

Religion and the Problem of Evil

The problem of evil is usually posed as follows: why does God, good and omnipotent, allow evil in the world? In the broadest treatment of the question, evil includes not just human but natural violence, so that the Lisbon earthquake of 1755 could constitute an argument against Leibniz's theodicy. But even when evil is restricted to the human sphere, the problem is generally raised in the context of a critique of divine providence. An omnipotent God could prevent our sufferings; if he does not, then we are forced to deny either his omnipotence or his benevolence toward humanity.

To engage in originary thinking is to return this theological question to its anthropological roots. We need not even abandon the vocabulary in which it is traditionally couched, provided that we interpret it in the spirit of the originary hypothesis. It is not trivial to ask why God permits evil; nor is it possible to discuss evil as a fundamental anthropological category independently of the idea of God. Only creatures who possess this idea can do evil, precisely because evil— "eating of the tree of knowledge"—is what gave us the idea of God in the first place.

In the development of generative anthropology, the question of locating evil in the originary scene had to be subordinated to the liberation of the theory from the weight of Girard's scapegoat mechanism. If the divinity is the apotheosis of the emissary victim, then clearly God must permit evil, since humanity is the product of an evil act. The difficulty in Girard's model is rather to explain the origin of good. In this model, the originary self-consciousness of the participants in the event is mediated not by the formal reality of the sign "imitating" the object, but by the de-figured remains of the sparagmos, which is taken to precede the constitution of the human community.[7] In the terminology of *The Origin of Language*, the passage from the act of collective violence to the "signifier" constituted by the victim assimilates formal representation by the sign to the institutional representation of ritual, making representation the most uneconomical of activities. Thinking then becomes impossibly difficult in the absence of divine intervention.

But on renouncing this construction to create a model of human order founded on the sign, we encounter the inverse problem of where to include within this order the disorder we call "evil." In the symmetry of the moral community of sign users, there seems to be no room for the perpetration of an evil act. Yet to exclude evil from the originary scene would be to banish it from our fundamental anthropology; evil would become an epiphenomenon.

No doubt the hypothesis that humanity is constituted symmetrically by the freely chosen arbitrary sign leaves open the possibility of "absolute evil," of not aborting the gesture of appropriation but of pursuing it to the point of communal self-destruction. But conceived in this manner, the act of absolute evil would have prevented the event from taking place at all. The right choice must be made the "first" time because previous wrong choices do not count; they are not accumulated in the collective memory of humanity. The finite concept of evil that alone is of anthropological significance is possible only once the good, the moral foundation of the human, has been established.

This foundation is the deferral, not the definitive expulsion, of human conflict. What remains of this conflict is what I have called "originary resentment," which is directed not to the others' real or imagined access to the object, but to the latter's denial of itself to the subject—the very operation that averts the danger of rivalrous conflict. Resentment of the central object accompanies recognition of its sacrality. The evil action of the sparagmos is preceded by evil intent. Each participant commits the crime of appropriation in his imagination at the very moment he renounces it in practice; the renunciation and the crime are inseparable.

The enigma of originary evil—that it must exist in a situation of human symmetry and cannot therefore involve a crime of one human against another—is solved by the insight that evil is in the first place directed against the nonhuman center. Man's first crime is against God rather than man. The human potential for evil is contained not in any relative dissymmetries among the periphery, but in the absolute dissymmetry between periphery and center, the first product of which is originary resentment. In resentment, the aggression deferred by the sign is accumulated within the new human order in preparation for its discharge in the sparagmos, which is indispensable to the successful conclusion of the event. Although evil is not the origin of the human, it is a necessary component of the universe of human virtuality created by the sign.

The sparagmos offers to the violent imaginings of originary resentment a partial but real fulfillment. The individual participates in the de-figuration, the destruction of the formal wholeness of the worshiped object. In so doing, he loses himself in the collectivity, where his violent action is "irresponsible," not observed and judged by his fellows. The techniques of ritual murder (lapidation, induced leap from the Tarpeian rock) reenact this irresponsibility by absolving any given individual of responsibility for inflicting death. But at the same time, while in this "invisible" condition, the participant acquires a portion of the victim, from which he obtains not only appetitive satisfaction but the originary notion of personal property. The sparagmos creates the private individual by effacing the public visibility of his action and its results, in contrast to that of the original (aborted) gesture of appropriation.

This *passage à l'acte* provides the model for the crucial realization of evil intent, which would otherwise remain the purely imaginary object of esthetic catharsis. There is no need to postulate an internal differentiation of the community that would violate the equalitarian morality of the sign. The sparagmos, in which the exercise of violence toward the sacred center is accompanied by the denial of individual responsibility for this violence, is the model for all acts of evil, both collective and individual.

Freedom for Good or Evil

The notion of "evil" is only meaningful in the context of the normative one of "good," which originates in the common intention to represent the central object. The model of morality derived from the originary event defines the human community by its participation in the reciprocity of linguistic communication. The point of the originary scene from the standpoint of social organization, its qualitative advance over animal social systems, is that it creates equality as a free, conscious choice, a self-limitation.

This is not the utopian dream of originary freedom as desire unfettered by the social order. On the contrary, the first experience of freedom is one of constraint; one can only thematize one's freedom to do something once one has found oneself obliged to renounce it. Like predication, freedom originates in negation, in the originary resentment of the self-withholding central figure that is the intentional basis for the "original sin" of the sparagmos. It is through the alienation of his freedom to the center that the individual participant begins to become responsible for his act before the community. The alienation of responsibility to the center that gives rise to evil is at the same time a movement toward self-understanding. The evil of originary resentment is the price man pays for a first glimmer of lucidity, for eating of the tree of knowledge.

The good community is egalitarian, its peripheral members arranged symmetrically around the central figure. The collectivity of the sparagmos too is symmetrical, but only insofar as it is a group of separate individuals engaged in mutually invisible violence. From the beginning, the desiring imagination resentfully inverts the morality of the originary scene. Although its image of satisfaction is mediated by the others' desire as "expressed" in the sign, it would deny this mediation and possess the object for itself. Rivalry among the individual members of the community is subordinated to the opposition between periphery and center; the peripheral others are insignificant in the light of the central figure illuminated by their desire, the apparent source of all being.

Because each individual acts independently, the symmetry of the sparagmos is a collection of individual asymmetries. The horizon of each remains the appropriation of the entire object, but the force that appears to emanate from the object limits the violence of the action in pursuit of this goal. The consequent "equal" division of the object is the result of this limitation rather than the intended goal of the participants. Hence although the sparagmos, like the emission of the sign, concentrates all difference in the center, it carries out in the most literal sense the deconstruction of the moral model. Instead of consecrating the central difference, it seeks to abolish it, paradoxically constructing a circle without a center. Resentment against the center is the first step toward equality with it; but for the moment, this development can only express itself through the radical asymmetry of violence.

Centrality is personhood; the first person is not the self but the other, the central object-become-mimetic-model. The notion of a willing self has its source in the central being's "voluntary" formal closure, by which it constitutes itself as a "person" withholding itself from the desires of the human group;[8] the emission of the sign is the recognition of the personhood of the center as a force superior to animal appetite. Nor is the sparagmos a simple reversal of this inequality. The personhood of the center as acknowledged by the sign is mimetically reproduced in those who resentfully destroy it. The sparagmos is in the first place an act among persons, the destruction of the originary person by the collectivity of its imitators.

The happy failure of this resentful aim becomes manifest only after the event, in the subsistence of the sign and of the central locus as the support of its significance. Interpersonal aggression has failed in its ultimate aim: the sacred person has remained intact. The universe of signification has saved the human community from returning to animality. We are justified in calling aggression against the central being "evil" even in the purely human sense of "antisocial." But our analysis also makes clear that evil in the latter sense is a derivative notion; in the absence of the central guarantee of communal unity referred to by the sign, aggression, intraspecific or otherwise, would be merely an animal phenomenon.

This analysis is not without consequence for the theory of the sign. The process of signification requires a guarantee of the signified that the sign "means," one that subsists independently of any referential context. Such a guarantee is supplied by the subsistence of the locus of signification after the elimination of the central referent. The memory of the centralized object of desire is the content of signification, but being or centralization-as-such is the ground upon which this content rests. The Saussurean grid of relative differences is composed of elements in themselves not relatively but absolutely different; the significance of each is guaranteed *à tour de rôle* by its occupation of the center, which cannot be occupied by more than one signified at the same time. The differentiation of the signifier does not defer signification as the result of a previously existing paradigm from which this particular signifier is chosen; on the contrary, paradigmatic differentiation is itself a consequence of the deferral of appropriation. It is this deferral that creates the differential space of attention within which emerges the participants' "intention," in the phenomenological sense, of the central object.

Derrida's exposition of *différance* is tantalizingly close to that of generative anthropology—so near and yet so far:

La différence inouïe entre l'apparaissant et l'apparaître (entre le "monde" et le "vécu") est la condition de toutes les autres différences, de toutes les autres traces, et *elle est déjà une trace.* . . . *La trace est en effet l'origine absolue du sens en général. Ce qui revient à dire, encore une fois, qu'il n'y a pas d'origine absolue du sens en général. La trace est la différance qui ouvre l'apparaître et la signification.* Articulant le vivant sur le non-vivant en général, origine de toute répétition, origine de l'idéalité, elle n'est pas plus idéale que réelle, pas plus intelligible que sensible. . . . Et aucun concept de la métaphysique ne peut la décrire. (*De la grammatologie*, p. 95; emphasis the author's)

The unheard-of difference between the appearing and the appearance (between the "world" and the "lived") is the condition of all other differences, of all other traces, *and it is already a trace.* . . . *The trace is in effect the absolute origin of meaning in general. Which is to say, once again, that there is no absolute origin of meaning in general. The trace is the différance* that opens appearance and signification. Articulating the living upon the nonliving in general, the origin of all repetition, the origin of ideality, it is no more ideal than real, no more intelligible than sensible. . . . And no concept of metaphysics can describe it.

"No concept of metaphysics can describe it." The trace as the source of *différance* is anterior to the plurality of signifiers, but not to the vertical difference that institutes signification. Yet Derrida can conceive of no act that could institute language because he denies the essential difference between human language and the "language of life," the genetic code as the (truly originary) institution of the trace. In the absence of an anthropological conception of language, Derrida bases his argument for the always-already on what might be called the "paradox of difference"—that the sign qua trace has no origin, since the difference between its extratemporal constitution and the temporality of life is the trace itself. But this paradox (like that of the "third man" with which it has much in common) is just a metaphysical version of the paradox of mimesis discussed in Chapter 2, expressed in a vocabulary that recalls the Heraclitean argument in the *Cratylus.*[9] For the sign of language to constitute itself as a trace of a different (or *différant*) kind from those of previous life-forms, including their "language," the recuperation of the "trace" by unconscious mimesis must be revealed to be inadequate. This revelation, the matter of the originary hypothesis, is entirely lacking in Derrida's ontology. What is missing from this philosophical exposition is the very notion of the human. This is the ultimate demonstration of metaphysics' incapacity to generate an anthropology.

*

The upshot of our analysis is that the realized resentment we call evil is indispensable to the constitution of the human community. In order that the center be constituted as a being independent of the material object that occupies it, this object must be destroyed. But the revolt against God must end in failure. The participants in the sparagmos, in seeking to destroy the center itself, attain only its material occupant; their intent is frustrated by the persistence of the sign and the significant memory that guarantees it. The sparagmos is the *felix culpa* by which alone humanity could come into being bearing the "knowledge of good and evil" imparted in the originary event.

The postmodern era has is a "problem of good" rather than a "problem of evil." Positive social science finds it harder to understand altruism than selfishness, order than disorder. Scientists seek to explain human as well as animal selflessness by the presence of an "altruism gene" that would contribute to reproductive fitness. In this modern equivalent of phrenology, a material equivalent is sought for "dispositions" that are simple consequences of human mimesis. Evil behavior, on the contrary, seems to require no explanation, as though the success of human societies could be measured by the reproductive fitness of its individual members taken separately. This cynicism reflects the widespread resentment of the social order as such in the age of "the end of culture." In these circumstances, it is useful to recall that the originary form of moral good is preserved and reproduced in the virtual scene of representation that is actualized in our everyday use of language. The inalienably reciprocal structure of linguistic communication lies at the core of our humanity; it is a model of good that precedes any possible model of evil.

The sparagmos introduces into our model of the originary scene a moment of apparently unbounded selfishness that anticipates Nietzsche's movement "beyond good and evil," while at the same time debunking through its mimetic symmetry his resentful dream of the superior "overman." The individual participant in the sparagmos is able to act without concern for his fellows' actions because his act, however violent, cannot lead out of the community defined a priori by the sign; but this implies that, by the same token, all his fellow participants act in exactly the same manner.

The guarantee provided to the social order by representation as such, independently of the ritual repetition of the originary scene, is a resource first tapped by the bourgeois market system—and by the romantics whose ostensibly antimarket individualism was in fact an adaptation to this system. In the first stage of this process of "secularization," the selfish desires of the participants in market exchange are recuperated for the benefit of the whole, as in Mandeville's eighteenth-century "Fable of the Bees." But a second crucial moment comes with the recognition of the mimetic nature of these "individualistic" desires, and the birth of the institutions of consumer society that generate as well as exploit them. This is the cultural era of modernism. The romantics continued to respect the traditional opposition between good and evil, which they saw being sacrificed to the immorality of the free market. The modernists followed Nietzsche in their rejection of this opposition. In their case as well as his, the ultimate and unexpressed article of faith was the universality of the originary scene. But the Holocaust, the ultimate political expression of modernism, forces us to rethink this universality in the postmodern era: to what extent can the unity of the scene innocently be *imagined*?

In ending the deferral initiated by the sign, in lifting the moral inhibition on the aim of the originary appropriative gesture, the sparagmos opens the space of the ethical. In this collective rather than communal action, the symmetrical concern for one's fellows that characterized the moment of signification has been replaced by a violent concentration on the object in an undifferentiated context of resentment and appetite.[10] The communal peace, instigated by the sign, that is the ultimate guarantee of the sparagmos is for the moment no longer a matter of concern. In the sparagmos, the sign, as the expression of renunciation, is "forgotten"; with the destruction of its original referent, it passes out of consciousness into the unconscious of collective mediation wherein its guarantee resides. The forgetting of the sign defers the moral model with respect to which the participants in the sparagmos would be condemned for their act. Although the individual members of the community remain within the moral context established by the sign, they are not for the moment guided by the renunciation of desire imposed by this context.

The possibility of crime, that is, of deviation from ethical as opposed to moral behavior, is prefigured in the originary evil or immoral act of violence toward the center. Just as the criminal typically satisfies his resentment in isolation, the sparagmos already isolates its participants from each other by suspending the communal reciprocity created by the sign.

The criminal's isolation is that of the individual usurper of the center. The origin of social differentiation is the act of such a usurper (the "big-man" referred to in *The End of Culture*), and this breach of originary equality, socialist utopias to the contrary, can never be healed. This human usurpation of the center—and the "mature" form of resentment that follows from it—had already been anticipated in the unconsciously controlled anarchy of the sparagmos.

The "Jewish Question"

The purest expression of the fundamental religious intuition that the sacred being of the scene subsists independently of its central figure is found in the revelation to Moses at the "burning bush" in Exodus 3.[1] The foregrounding of the sparagmos sheds new light on this scene, while giving particular urgency to the "Jewish question" that the Holocaust was intended to foreclose: Is the anthropological truth of the Mosaic revelation indeed transcended by the Pauline revelation that founds Christianity?

The Hebrew and Christian Revelations

The burning bush is a locus of ritual sacrifice. Its nonconsumption is the sign that the sacrificial violence of the sparagmos has been overcome. The Hebrew God is the first radically afigural deity; rather than show himself, he sends his messenger/angel in the de-figuring flame. Here religion is liberated from the esthetic; the religious intuition has understood that what guarantees the human community formed around the sign is not the figure that inspires violence but the subsistence of the central being of the scene as the eternal source of significance. God withdraws from the figural, which is also the sacrificial. The sacrifices that continue to be carried out within Hebrew religious practice are acts of worship rather than actualizations of divine presence.

Whence the sentence-name *ehyeh asher ehyeh* (I am what/that I am), which cannot be used as a vocative-imperative.

The Mosaic revelation effects a transcendental separation between God and humanity, one that excludes from the outset the possibility of esthetic mediation. This is the religious in its purest form. The worldly designatum of the sign is necessarily figural; because the sign re-presents the formal closure of its object, the act of representation transforms even its empty locus into a figure. The Mosaic revelation sacrifices the figural to the religious in order that the ground of being may be revealed in the sign alone. The expulsion of iconicity effects an absolute separation between the world of signs and the world of things, the divine and the human.

The withdrawal into a "declarative" name that prevents human manipulation of the divine is analogous to the displacement of ostensive-imperative language by the proposition in Greek metaphysics. But in the Mosaic revelation, religious scenicity is not eliminated but reinforced. Thus where metaphysics reduces language to the declarative sentence and the scene to a tabula rasa, Hebrew religion reduces man to the declarative but leaves the imperative with God. The ostensive no longer designates the divinity, who has become unexperienceable; but when God calls to Moses, he ostensively re-presents himself: "Here I am."

In this intuition of pure religious transcendence, God and man share the use of language. The dialogue between center and periphery is unequal: God enunciates the law, man can only interpret it. But once enunciated, the divine imperative is inherently no different from a human law (it *is* in fact a human law). Divine or human, language is devoid of intrinsic hierarchy, inherently dialogic. The impossible necessity of dialogue provides the particular tension of Hebrew religion, which is decanted in the Christian era to an ineffable Jewish irony.

Christianity provides what appears to be the definitive resolution of this tension in the Trinity, which is the closest theology has come to grasping the paradoxical structure of the scene of representation.[2] The subsistent but invisible being of the Father engenders the worldly incarnation of the esthetically visible and vulnerable Son; the Christian God is both present at the origin and historically contemporary. The Holy Spirit, as the agent of the sign-system that links the originary and the contemporary, the being of the subsistent locus and the victim that temporarily occupies it, presides over the unity of trinitary theology. The promotion of the victim as the incarnate sign to an equal part in divinity revalorizes the esthetic while respecting its inapplicability to the Father who alone was revealed by Hebrew religion. God is subsistent, yet he is also worldly. Presumably there is nothing in the Old Testament that has not been transposed into the New.

The historical moment of Christianity is that in which the human community understands that its very existence has hitherto been dependent on victimage, that even in the absence of a figure, the scene as such is the locus of the sparagmos. The establishment in the ultimate clarity of the Spirit of the oscillatory identity of Father and Son, deity and victim, is intended to abolish the resentment of the human periphery. But because the revelation of the identity of God and victim cannot eliminate the scene of representation, it cannot abolish the originary resentment of the center on which victimage depends. The mimetic structure of the originary event remains that of human culture as a whole.

That we have become aware of the analogy between the scene of divine violence and that of human desire only makes the occupancy of the scenic center all the more onerous. In the postmodern era, as we seek to assuage our guilty figurality by identifying with the victim, we are forced to admit that we have sinned from the beginning in coveting the victim's central position. The end of the age of sacrifice is the beginning of the age of publicity; the victim's figurality, coveted as a guarantee of central Being, becomes the object of a new kind of desire.

Nietzsche was the first to grasp the power conferred by the victimary position on its occupant, the "man of resentment." In the postmodern era, victimary credentials have become passports to fame and fortune. The immediate result is to drive up the price for these credentials, which then falls as they are reproduced for the mass market. The equation between the central and the victimary is no sooner made than discounted in the economic and political marketplace.

Messianic Awaiting

The structure of awaiting is always vulnerable to attempts to close the circle; awaiting must be satisfiable in principle. But in the Mosaic revelation, not only is awaiting thematized in what Martin Buber emphasizes as the future sense of *ehyeh* (I shall be), its permanence is implicit in God's reply of a declarative sentence to the request for his name.[3] To await the divine in the world is to accept its ontological separation from the world (which is not to forgo the ironic questioning or deconstruction of this as of any formal separation). Because the awaited arrival of the Messiah, even were it eventually to take place, can never be anticipated, the Jew is defined by his thematization of awaiting rather than by his expectation of what he awaits. This thematization has come to dominate postmodern thought in its secular translation as *différance*, or deferral. To await the Messiah is to inhabit a worldly scene defined by the deferral of his arrival. This awaiting has the same structure as the impossible desire of the man of resentment to abolish the scene of representation on which alone his desire is defined.

The Passion demonstrates that the enunciation of the moral model of absolute reciprocity as an ethic sufficient for the conduct of everyday life, far from providing an "ontological proof" that the moral Kingdom is realizable on earth, is destined to reanimate the originary resentment that led to the sparagmos. Unlike the self-perpetuating thematization of awaiting in the Mosaic revelation, making explicit the implicit moral configuration of the originary event undermines its original deferring effect.

At the origin, the sparagmos occurs once the sign has appropriated for its peripheral enunciators the formal closure of the central figure, so that it is no longer necessary for this closure to subsist in itself. As it comes to appear superfluous, the figure's figurality becomes vulnerable to the resentment it generates and open to the disfiguration of the sparagmos.

But what this central figure "says" to the periphery in the originary event is the substance of what Jesus would articulate as morality: "You are all equal, because you all imitate me." This message of peace is in effect a call to war; the central figure affirms its difference from its peripheral imitators in the act of denying it. There is no escaping from this impasse any more than from any other variant of the foundational human paradox.

Those who bewail the perversity of the Jews' rejection of Jesus's message tend to forget the Gospels' insistence on the unanimity of this rejection at the moment of the crucifixion. The utopian Kingdom of Jesus's preaching could not be convincing in itself. The light that shone in the darkness and that the darkness knew not is a metaphor for the sparagmatic extinction of the one who would usurp the center. The first real Christians were the Gentiles converted by Paul's centralization of the Christ, not the Jews convinced by Jesus's moral omnicentrism.

The success of Christianity is founded on the failure of Jesus's moral revelation because this revelation is part of a whole that includes the worship of the victimized divine enunciator, the Word made flesh. For Christians, God's promise of deferred but eternal presence was fulfilled in Jesus because the crucifixion demonstrates the eternity of this presence in the *logos*—in language as the ultimate guarantee of human reciprocity. Those who remained Jews claimed, on the contrary, that if this guarantee indeed exists, there is no particular reason to value either Jesus's enunciation or its enunciator. All were already aware of the moral imperative of reciprocity; but they also knew that it could not become the ethic of a real human community. The difference, ultimately, would be a matter of esthetics.

Jesus, whose moral doctrine was devoid of, or in any case independent of, any personal pretension of divinity, did not disturb the anestheticism of Hebrew religion. Only the crucifixion revealed the equivalence between the enunciation of the moral utopia and the assumption of the victimary role of the Son, in contradistinction to the withdrawal of the Mosaic Father-God as a precondition of his enunciation of the ethical Law. It is not in the moral configuration of linguistic communication but in the sparagmos-crucifixion that Christianity finds the trinitary structure that models the originary constitution of the sacred.

The opening in Christianity within which Judaism would survive is figured by the difference between Christianity's figural center, the scene on the cross, and its historical point of departure, Saul/Paul's revelation on the road to Damascus. The surprising if not scandalous absence of the cross from the imagery of Saul's exemplary conversion demonstrates that the esthetic is necessary to Christianity only as a means of access to the Gentiles: the very origin of institutional Christianity enacts the Jewish denial of the figure. If Saul's persecution of the early Christians was a superficial attempt to enforce traditional

Jewish anestheticism, his revelatory blinding suggests that, at its deepest roots, Christianity is as anesthetic as Judaism. Nor does Paul make his conversion scene an example for the Jews; he chooses rather to preach to the Gentiles the esthetic centrality of the Crucified.[4]

What appears to Saul is not the esthetically centralized figure on the cross but a blinding light that, like the burning bush, obliterates the figural, but without a concrete reminder of ritual sacrifice to connect it with the chain of commemoration that leads back to the origin. Jesus's presence to Saul as the victim of his persecution is independent of any imaginary sacrificial scene; it takes place within the soul of the persecutor, who cannot therefore avoid it by fleeing public space. The Christian revelation is Western civilization's last world-historical revelation; it signals religion's abandonment of the public for the private scene of representation.

One who can be converted by the voice of the persecuted Jesus must already be obsessed by his persecution. Such an obsession is a likely characteristic of an aggressive Judaism that will stop at nothing to maintain control over an embattled but well-defined religious community; it is in this light that the persecutions of Saul the Pharisee are presented in the book of Acts. Yet the fundamental movement of Judaism is *exodus*, withdrawal. Persecution of the Christians is a falling-away from the exilic, a movement toward compactness, mimetically inspired by the Roman occupiers. It is Saul's falling-away, not his Judaism itself, that is revealed to him on the road to Damascus as already tantamount to belief in Christianity. Judaism is not meant to be an established church. The eternal exile who commemorates each year the Exodus from Egypt should permit the Christians to withdraw in their turn from an Israel defined by the eternal awaiting of God's presence. Such a one would not have been visited by a revelation of the centralized victim.

The First Minority

Why does the movement toward the universal God of monotheism occur in a minority culture within a larger society whose Gods are particular and figural? The answer given by Freud in *Moses and Monotheism* is simply that no independent Hebrew culture existed, that Moses was an Egyptian, a follower of the "henotheistic" pharaoh Akhenaton.[5]

In this view, a universal religion can emerge only in the "universal" society of empire.

But the dialectic of history is more subtle. The universal God of the Hebrews is a defense against worldly imperium; religious universality trumps any earthly universality. This is a strategy conceived in the resentment of a minority that would claim to be the chosen people of the one true God and the superior of the larger society. Its lowly worldly status was proof not of their God's weakness but of their own sinfulness toward him. The privileged relationship posited by Hebrew monotheism between the universal God and a small ritual community is an exodus in the spiritual sphere that prefigures the material Exodus, a return from the hierarchical complexity of empire to the equalitarianism of the originary scene. Humility has taught the Hebrews that the most powerful imperial religion cannot possess Being in a figure. Their relationship to God is mediated only by the figureless voice of the center. The first gesture of a purely religious understanding of the scene of representation must be to reject the esthetic; its future reintegration into religion is grounded on this prior rejection.

The exodic community never developed a stable relationship with other peoples; it existed only in the process of departure and provisional arrival in a new land, where it could do no better than to establish its own short-lived idolatrous kingdoms. But with the advent of the Christian era, the Jewish minority comes to be surrounded not by pagans but by the followers of an "ecumenical" version of Hebrew universalism that restores figurality to the divine center.

In Christianity, the return of the central figure in human form denies the absolute center-periphery difference that had guaranteed the tribal universality of the Hebrews. All potential conflict is to be purged by the passion story, in which the sparagmos is exposed as a lynching for which everyone is responsible. Everyone; yet the chief actors in the story are the Jews, who refused to accept the reevaluation of the figural as a guarantee rather than an obstacle to universal religion. The particularist interpretation of the Passion, which puts the blame on the Jews rather than on mankind in general, is no doubt a sacrificial misreading of the Christian message. But it is not only suggested by the Gospels, it is historically inevitable. Just as Jesus's omnicentric moral message is overshadowed by the centrality of its enunciator, so mankind's universal guilt for the crucifixion is eclipsed by that of his local adversaries.

Persecution of the Jews was never altogether successful, nor really intended to be so. What constitutes them as the first Western minority in the sense of realizing an articulated cultural interaction with the surrounding majoritary world is the paradoxical necessity of their survival in their guilt-bearing scapegoat role. The mimetic behavior required by the *imitatio Christi* is accompanied by the resentment of those who refuse to imitate, who follow God's Law rather than a divine-human mediator. The position of the Jews as a stigmatized minority in Christian society articulates the tension between the figural and the religious, or, in other terms, between incarnation and abstraction, that is the source of the West's peculiar strength.

The anesthetic universality of the Hebrew God was a reaction to the Hebrews' dependent status in the Egyptian empire, but the relationship it established was exodic rather than minoritary. The Hebrews could borrow from the "wisdom literature" of their masters, but their theology—their originary anthropology—belonged to a different world. In contrast, in the Christian imperium, the underlying theology was the same. The "chosen people" were no longer the unique witnesses of the true God; they became the original witnesses of his promise, now renewed and once again deferred. The "ecumenical" Gentiles accepted Christ's guarantee of the fulfillment of the promise; only the Jews could accept the horizon of endless awaiting.

The all-too-familiar figure of the Jewish moneylender is a caricature of the minority's function within the majority: the agent of exchange value as opposed to use value, deferred as opposed to immediate satisfaction. The alien minority's anesthetic ease with exchange and circulation and the majority's world of figural stability stand in a relation of mutual resentment.

As the self-abolishing goal of Christian resentment, the elimination of the Jews, by conversion or "final solution," has been throughout history the touchstone of Christian universality.[6] The success of Christianity as a universal religion requires in principle the conversion of all humanity, but the measure of this success is the conversion of the group from which Christianity recruited its original membership. Yet the Pauline epistles offer no specific model of Jewish conversion. Paul's preaching, whether to the Romans or the Hebrews, consistently demands mimetic adherence to the scene of the crucifixion.[7] His establishment of the centrality of the crucified Christ makes further conversions on the model of his own inconceivable.

The birth of organized antisemitism in medieval Europe coincides with the Crusades, whose participants, bearing the sign of Christ, were incited to impose stigmatizing signs on those not of their number. This differential stigmatization was precisely what the anesthetic imperative of the Mosaic revelation had been meant to prevent. To stigmatize the Jews with a figure only demonstrates the superiority of their afigurality, whereas the centralization of the figure of Christ as the mediator of the omnicentric community reinforces the center as a locus of sacrifice.

The Jews' anesthetic faith kept them—or at least a "saving remnant"—from succumbing to the seduction of Christian figurality at a time when there was as yet no ethical ground on which to condemn the particularism of this figurality. Today the prudential advantage of the anesthetic position is clearer. In spite of the Bible's paternalistic language, the unfigurability of the Hebrew God evacuates polemics about such things as God's gender. The attribution of gender to God is ultimately a matter not of theology but of figuration; but figuration unsupported by image is merely heuristic. We think of God in something like a human form because the human is our only model of a person, but there is no objective support for our image. Thus, in a patriarchal society, we imagine the "typical" human language user and the God who created him in his image as male; when gender roles become more equal, our imaginary figure of God may be modified accordingly.

The postmodern era is well aware of the strategic role of the scenic center in the mimetic exchange of resentments. Even if the figure of Christ cannot legitimately be called a figure of resentment, it remains a potential focus of concentration for the resentful, like the grain of sand that brings about crystallization in a solution at the saturation point. Pure water remains unaffected; but how many can apply this metaphor to their souls? The historical revelation of the single son of God cannot but provoke the envy of those not so honored, whatever assurance we are given of his infinite imitability. Today one might ask, for example, why not the daughter of God? No figure can be general enough to include the entire human community; as soon as attention is concentrated on it, someone is bound to see in it a sign of exclusion. One lesson of the postmodern era is the essential plurality of the human, its inexhaustibility by any single figure.

By rejecting the Trinity's integration of religion with history and God with man, Judaism maintains a clear separation between the sacred and the profane, or in other terms, between words and things. Whereas the Jewish pseudoeschatology of the Messiah is no more than an ironic commentary on the paradoxical unliveability of indefinite deferral, the Christian eschatology guarantees to its believers the closure of worldly history.

The Christian apocalypse defines human self-knowledge as finite, where the less ambitious Mosaic epistemology of deferral can accommodate the unbounded knowledge that accumulates throughout history. The awaiting of the Messiah is a learning process, a time of ethical evolution, whereas Christ's return or "second coming," although similarly deferred, reveals only what had already been revealed on his first appearance. The canonical account of this return in the book of Revelation presents the historical time of awaiting not as a process of the acquisition of ever greater degrees of freedom, but as the societal derepression of violence. To the Christian preconception of the "apocalyptic" state of the world at the second coming, we may oppose the quizzical dicta of rabbis and secular Jews alike on the coming of the Messiah, which is not unlike that of the "unexpected examination" discussed in Chapter 3.[8]

The Holocaust and the Victimary

The product of an antisemitism that has thrown off the religious trappings of the Crusades and the Inquisition, the Holocaust reveals both the historical dependence of Christian society on antisemitism and the importance that this dependence never be understood clearly enough to provoke the desire to eliminate it. Hitler's final solution discredits Christian eschatology, along with its counterpart, the secular eschatology of utopia-directed progress. The Holocaust is the primary precipitating event of the postmodern era, the age that can no longer believe in historical destiny.

Modernism rejected what it conceived as the closed historical objectives of bourgeois progressivism—a closure caricatured by Marx in his apocalyptic (and more than marginally antisemitic) vision of capitalism as concentrating the means of production in the hands of an ever-diminishing oligarchy of monopolists. Each modernist manifesto, and there were many, was a profession of faith in infinite experiential openness. Yet all this insistence on the new betrayed a linear historicism uncannily similar to that of the despised bourgeois. No doubt the moderns were expected to do violence to the very forms of cultural apperception, in contrast with the milder, content-oriented revolution of their romantic predecessors. But whatever the ostensible project behind modernist frontiersmanship, a linear progression founded on primary experience must inevitably exhaust itself. The primitivism of the moderns, who saw themselves as returning to a state of the self prior to civilization, to forms of desire and expression anterior to language, was only superficially compatible with an open-ended philosophy of history. Indeed, its very submission to a "philosophy of history" marks modernism as but another avatar of Christianity.

The postmodern age is another story. Rather than seek primitive authenticity, it appears to reject the very notion of authenticity. But what it really rejects is the linear closure of the eschatology that has dominated the Christian era from the beginning. It suddenly appears that history has no well-defined end, that the rhythm of conflict and deferral are endemic to the human condition. Postmodernity defines itself more by the disavowal of modernism than as a new era. Indeed, it cannot define itself as an era at all; it is our liberation from eras. But there was a price to pay for this liberation, the first installment of which was the Holocaust, carried out in fulfillment of a barbarous but not unrecognizable redefinition of the eschatological project of the Christian West.

Hiroshima and Auschwitz epitomize the excesses of violence that make World War II the last full-scale war that humanity can survive. The role of Hiroshima is that of the victim of a human violence too technologically enhanced to be ever again tolerated, a violence so massive as to efface the difference between guilt and innocence, aggression and self-defense. The main currents of contemporary thought operate as though this were the essential lesson of Auschwitz as well: the industrial world has just too much capacity for violence. But the Holocaust was more than unprecedented violence. It was primarily directed, not at killing so many million people (or Gypsies, homosexuals, communists, dissenters, etc.), but at eliminating the Jews. *Mein Kampf* and the Nazi propaganda it inspired make no secret of this fact. An effective analysis of postmodernity cannot fail to explain the central importance of the "Jewish question" to the overall project of both Nazism and Western civilization.

Both Hiroshima and Auschwitz put into question the scenic configuration that has been from the outset the distinctive form of human interaction. The locus-victim of the Bomb, Hiroshima becomes the exemplary placeless place of Duras-Resnais's prescient masterpiece, in which a new postmodern esthetic transforms the failed aggressors of World War II into its victims.[9] Technological violence has exploded the boundaries of the scene, destroyed its closure. The world has become omnicentric *par la force des choses*; self and other can no longer defer their mutual recognition. What is missing from this apocalyptic vision is a concept of how the scene is to function in a postscenic era. Culture, and cultures, go on after the Bomb; the "Hiroshimists" only repeat the impatience of the first Christians in thinking that deferral has been abolished and culture returned to a state of nature.

In contrast to this emphasis on physical destruction, the Holocaust is about a human violence that exceeds and discredits the scene of culture. So long as the scene of representation wholly contains the violence that is perpetrated upon it, we remain within the domain of the esthetic. Evil, as we have seen in the preceding chapter, follows the model of the sparagmos in its destruction of the worldly correlate of the scene of representation; it is the irreversible de-figuration of the figure. We may then understand absolute evil as an evil so great that it has no figure whatsoever.

Evil can be recuperated by culture, but only a posteriori. Its intent is to destroy the scene of culture; the failure of its intent is the failure of resentment, since it depends on what it seeks to annihilate, but its failure in reality is the result not of internal logic but of insufficient means. The postmodern era begins at the moment in which we realize that the means are indeed available.

The originary violence of the sparagmos intends not merely the de-figuration of the central figure but the obliteration of its very being. Its failure to do so is due to the religious preservation of the being of the scene, not to any lack of intention on the part of the participants— to conscience, we might say, rather than consciousness, this being the moment at which they are distinguished. In the derived mode of sacrificial ritual, the radical nature of this de-figuration is mitigated by the force of religious commemoration.

With the decline of the religious under the pressure of modern resentment, radical evil is rediscovered in the form of a transsacrificial
purgation, a de-figuration that exceeds and denies the scenic in de-
memorializing its victim(s), obliterating every trace of them from the
internal scene of representation of those who are to "benefit" from their
elimination. Those who actually carried out this work, as their leaders
told them in the horribly perverted but still recognizable terms of the
Judeo-Christian civilization they were attempting to transcend, were
obliged to steel themselves "heroically" to the task of denying the sacral-
izing effect of the figures of death they were obliged to witness. The
mission of the final solution was to cleanse the esthetic scene once and
for all of those whose anesthetism made them the living reminders of
the sparagmatic origin of the figure, whose existence was therefore incompatible with tribal compactness.

The horror of the camps is their scenelessness; for the first time in
history, a central policy of violence is deliberately excluded from the
scenic structure of culture. The rationalized, industrial slaughter carried out far from the German heartland was meant to avoid attracting
public attention, to permit not only denial but ignorance. This destruction was not intended to be exemplary, to play out a sacrificial
drama in which the executioner is in complicity with his victim, but
simply to be effective, to remove a certain figure from the scene.

Thus, what makes the Holocaust exemplary of a newly radical category of evil is not the multiplicity of its victims, but their lack of esthetic exemplarity. The victim of the sparagmos is a figure; the victims
of the Holocaust were *chiffres*, abstractions. The antisemitic rage that
had fueled the Nazi movement and that had been vented in moments
like the *Kristallnacht* had to give way to an industrially rationalized ex-
termination; it was no longer a matter of discharging this rage, but of
purging it once and for all. Like a carnivore killing off the species it
feeds on, the Nazi model was not meant to express antisemitism but
to abolish the need for it. The more Nazi society revealed its mimetic
obsessions with "ugly" images, whether of Jews or of "decadent" art,
the more desperately it sought the final expulsion of these images, after which its obsessions would presumably be lifted.[10] This was history's most radical attempt to expunge the Pauline revelation of the
centrality of the victim in the cause of reserving the center for the positive figure of Aryan exemplarity. It nevertheless remains within the

Pauline-Christian context by the very fact of this attempted abolition. Paul's problem is that he cannot forget the figure of the other he has persecuted. But if that is the sole difficulty, then it should suffice to remove the figure of the persecuted other from the scene so as to leave nothing but the celebratory image of the self.

The failure of this repetition of the Pauline experience of persecution in Christian Europe after nearly two millennia revealed the ultimate inadequacy of a recuperative, which is to say, a political, esthetic. The final solution, the culmination of this esthetic, is also the first act of the postmodern transcendence of the esthetic.

For resentment cannot be abolished any more by sating it than by ignoring it. As a result of the Holocaust, the victimary figure, rejecting esthetic catharsis, returns with a vengeance. Rather than dwell on the paradoxical nature of the Nazi project as a scenic hatred that would abolish the scene of its hate—a structure it shares with so many lesser projects—we would do better to regard its apocalyptic accomplishment as a revelatory antidote to future utopias of all kinds.

It took some time for the Holocaust to enter the general consciousness as the largely successful realization of a model of absolute evil. It offers a powerful and easily exploited model of human conflict—one in which there can be no doubt on whom to place the blame—as opposing a powerful state to the unarmed, unorganized members of a stigmatized group, in short, the "majority" to a "minority." The effect of this one-sided model of persecution has been to precipitate a postmodern victimary revolution in which stigmatized ethnic, sexual, and social groups of all kinds have denounced their victimization at the hands of the dominant majority. Colonial peoples and American blacks have been followed by women, homosexuals, the handicapped, even the "angry white male." Groups are granted victimary status to the extent that they can plausibly claim to have served as discriminatory *figures*, generally speaking as representatives of visible and unchangeable (ascriptive) traits. The poor, for example, are not included as such in the victimary list; even the homeless have only marginal status.[11] The Holocaust marks the moment of the transmission of the radical suspicion of figurality, characteristic of Judaism, to Western society in general.

Postmodern victimary discourse interprets the social order by the figure of the sparagmos, as though it were the only moment of the originary event. The imposition of this radically dichotomous model obliterates the historical nuances of social differentiation and interaction, reducing all social roles to those of persecutor and victim. It sacrifices to the power of its resentful rhetoric the means to understand the very movement toward social equality that it is ostensibly promoting. But as our own originary model suggests, discourse has more vital functions than theoretical understanding. The reinforcement of the victimary self and the consequent power of intimidation it exercises in the postmodern political environment are first-order dividends that explain the immense success of this discursive mode.

Antisemitism is the archetype of Western utopianism. The ideal society described in the Gospels is within our reach; only one final obstacle remains, the continued existence of the Jews. The lesson of the Holocaust is not simply that we must abolish antisemitism or even "prejudice" in general; what must be abandoned are all variants, including the Marxian-socialist variant, of the utopian model of total reconciliation, of universal harmony. This abandonment does not imply that it is no longer possible to hold out goals for the social order. But these goals must be dynamically conceived to admit the eternal persistence of difference and conflict.

Girard accounts for the persistence of the sacrificial in the Christian world by its (necessarily) imperfect understanding of the Gospel message, which he reformulates in explicitly victimary terms. But Girard's reinterpretation of the Christian revelation is the historical product of another revelation, that of the Holocaust. Following the Hiroshima rather than the Auschwitz model of postmodernity, Girard sets out our historical crux in the apocalyptic terms of nascent Christianity, which believed the last judgment to be imminent: we must abolish sacrificial violence or perish; utopia now or annihilation.[12] But were this the case, we would indeed be doomed. In the nonviolent utopia of universal love, there would be no means available to carry out the essential cultural operation of *différance*: deferral through differentiation.

Conflict is inevitable within society as an open system. It was deferred and controlled but not simply eliminated at the origin, and we cannot conceive that this will change in the future. Resentment cannot be abolished; on the contrary, it will only continue to proliferate as society acquires additional degrees of freedom. What limits conflict is not abstract uniformity but social differentiation, no longer ritual-based but professional and consumerist. The ever-proliferating resentment generated by the social order can only be contained by the *fuite en avant* of ever-increasing differentiation. This model puts a premium on our growing knowledge of the natural world and the uses to which we may put it—including maintaining and restoring the ecological equilibrium.

The mere renunciation of utopianism is sterile. If it was important to provide an originary justification for the market system at a time when socialism still appeared to offer a functional alternative, antiutopianism has no clear political purpose in the postsocialist era. But perhaps just this is its virtue. In a world that has drawn back from the esthetic politics of modernism, that is beginning at last to understand that the socialist and fascist utopias are cut from the same poisoned cloth, no millennial image of the good society can have any but harmful effects. The only figure we need is the figure of the origin, the only scene absolutely necessary for the constitution of a single human race. This scene is not utopian; it is the locus of an interminable agon.

*

In the postmodern era, the ultimate effort, and ultimate failure, of the most resentful forces in Western civilization to destroy the memory of its anesthetic Mosaic basis have transmitted the specifically Judaic suspicion of the figural to the rest of Western and world civilization. All postmodern modes of thought, from existentialism to deconstruction, and in its own way, even "multiculturalism," have been characterized by the demystification of the figure-centered scene.[13] Nor is it a coincidence that Girard's pioneering attempt to found an anthropology on the mimetic theory of desire takes as the fundamental mode of human interaction not conflict-deferring language but spragmatic violence. Perhaps only one inured to eternal awaiting can afford to be more optimistic.

Originary and Victimary Rhetoric

Rhetoric, the *frère ennemi* of philosophy, has had a bad name in Western thought since Plato. But without rhetoric, ethical revolutions would never take place. *Force majeure*, military conquest explain nothing; what force made the soldiers march? Historically better causes only replace inferior ones when people are persuaded of their superiority. Originary thinking must clarify our understanding of the sources and consequences of these revolutions.

Like originary resentment, of which it is the expression, originary rhetoric is an "immature" form the full development of which awaits the possibility, realized with the declarative sentence, of thematizing the latent symmetry between the peripheral human subject and the sacred center. In the originary scene, the loci of being and language are incompatible; the sign exists only to represent—to imitate—the center that its user cannot possess. In the "early" phenomenon of thought described in Chapter 7, the "first" participant discovers the necessity of converting the gesture of appropriation into a sign. In contrast, originary rhetoric is the mimetic appeal of the visibly already-constituted community to the "late," isolated individual who for fear of exclusion from this community is induced to renounce his attempt to appropriate the central object. (Needless to say, what are distinguished are not different individuals but different moments of the founding relationship between the human individual and the community.) From the beginning, rhetoric attacks not the other's utterance but his *position*, vulnerable through its excessive claim on the center.

The originary event allows for no neutral vantage point from which the instrumental force of its rhetoric can be perceived. The persuader is as moved by this force as the interlocutor whose difference from himself he seeks to abolish; the former's priority in the use of the sign leaves him with no residual superiority over the latter in the face of the absolute difference accorded by the sign to its central referent. To persuade one's fellows—and oneself—to defer conflict precludes the language of individual desire.

At the origin, it is the (free, symmetrical) form of language that liberates humanity from the animal world, not its content. If we examine this content alone, we see only the alienation of human freedom to the center in something like a Hobbesian social contract. (Hence a superficial understanding of the originary hypothesis has led some to consider the scene of origin as nothing but a staging of the social contract.) The originary rhetoric that persuades the participants to avert conflict by renouncing their appropriative movement toward the center is effective only because its dynamic is symmetrical. Had the signal for renunciation been given by a single dominant individual, it would by definition have failed. For this is the pattern of prehuman conflict avoidance, where each subordinate animal recoils before the "alpha"'s threat rather than conceiving itself—through the necessary mediation of the center—as a member of a community capable of enforcing general equality.

The sacralization of the center is the "better cause," not by virtue of any quality inherent in the central being itself, but because it defers conflict within the group. The model of originary rhetoric is not that of the lawyer persuading a neutral jury, but that of the disputant who is able to persuade his adversary—inspire him to linguistic mimesis—because his language bears the force of the community. Powerful rhetorics need no third parties; they undermine the presuppositions that sustain their adversary's dialectical capacity.

The operation of linguistic persuasion for which we use the term "rhetoric" is associated with the law court because it is there that the linguistic transcendence of potential conflict was first thematized. But the thematization of persuasion is already resistance to it; to speak of "persuasion" rather than logical demonstration implies that one is not oneself persuaded, and even that to persuade others requires that one not be oneself persuaded. The study of rhetoric is the beginning of its demystification—of demystification in general. To teach rhetoric is to step back from the scene of its originary use, to declare oneself sufficiently far from crisis to be able to resist its persuasive force. Persuasion can only be reduced to a repeatable technique once the rhetorical power of the community, as manifested in ritual, has become an object of reflection drained of its sacred aura, no longer revelatory but instrumental.

Although the Greeks taught other agonistic arts, rhetoric is the only one that depends on the deliberate reproduction of the critical tension of the originary scene. To teach racing or wrestling, one steps back from the phenomena to observe them, but one does not "demystify" them; in learning to anticipate the moves of my adversary, I do not concentrate my effort on resisting their mimetic force. Reflection on persuasive language, on the contrary, is a conquest of a new freedom from the clutches of communal belief; I learn to resist the persuasion of the scene in order better to produce it in others. Rhetoric exemplifies the secularization of the institutions of human interaction that will become the driving force of market society; the market gains efficiency and dynamism from the continual discounting of reflection on its operations. What is bought and sold at the nerve centers of the market—stock markets, currency exchanges—are the products of the ever-changing anticipation of others' knowledge and intentions.

The paradox of originary rhetoric is that persuasion, indifferent to truth, is accomplished by means of an utterance the signified of which is the absolute truth on which humanity is founded. From the beginning, the relation between the rhetorical and the representational use of language is one of mutual dependency; we are persuaded to represent the central object because of its significance, but the object is significant only because we are persuaded to represent it. At a later stage, this relation will evolve into the opposition between rhetoric and metaphysics. The scene of metaphysics requires no persuasion, only logical demonstration of a truth indifferent to person and place. Plato/Socrates' scorn for Gorgias and his ilk is founded on the rhetor's indifference to truth as he ups the ante of the oratorical agon. Since the typical civil case involves roughly symmetrical arguments, the winner may well be the one whose skill "makes the worse cause appear the better." But really powerful arguments overwhelm their adversary without need for judge or jury; these are never understood as merely "persuasive."

Just as the symmetrical oppositions of Saussurean linguistics cannot exist within originary language, which represents the uniquely significant, so the rhetorical duel of the law courts cannot exist within originary rhetoric, which begins with communal unanimity. Like all symmetries, that of the rhetorical agon derives from a unique difference. In the courtroom reproduction of the originary pattern of crisis and persuasion, each of the opposing advocates attempts to reproduce in his hearers a crisis state of isolation from the community that only his language is "originary" enough to resolve. Each speaker in the debate persuades us in turn. The ultimate measure of rhetorical persuasiveness is not logical conviction but transrational unanimity—the unanimity of deferral that later becomes, and may therefore be claimed to anticipate, the unanimity of the sparagmos.

The rhetorical legacy of the originary event is language that cannot be contradicted for fear of failing to reconstitute the community of discourse within which it is spoken, language that is therefore ethically necessary. New rhetorics, such as the current rhetoric of victimization, spread irreversible ethical revolutions throughout the discursive practices of a society. The speaker of the older discourse suddenly discovers that it can no longer be spoken, that the new language is henceforth the only one acceptable. This is the pattern of mass religious conversions. One day, one speaks the language of paganism, the next, that of Christianity. These changes are not vagaries of fashion; they correspond to reconstitutions of the fundamental ethical relations of the community.

Resentment fixes on the other's central position as the object of a necessary but impossible mimesis. Rhetoric gives voice to resentment by attacking the other's position as asymmetrically "self-centered." The rhetorical challenge to an opponent's discursive position is *ad locum*, an attack on where the speaker "speaks from" rather than on what he says. By making untenable the naive attitude toward the center exemplified by the prehuman gesture of appropriation (and expressed in predeclarative language by the imperative), rhetoric contributes to the enhanced awareness of human symmetry that is the touchstone of ethical progress.

Mature Rhetoric and Resentment

Mature rhetoric originates as counterrhetoric; the nascent declarative sentence is a rhetorical device that persuades the speaker of the preceding imperative to abandon his position. The passage from imperative to declarative is effected not simply by the creation of a new form and a concomitant new set of expectations, but by the overthrow of the preceding set, those of the imperative speaker. The declarative is not an appropriate response to the imperative, which is a request for nonverbal performance; it is a metaresponse that denies the first speaker's expectation, and consequently transforms that of the second as well. Here rhetoric is no longer a communal act that forces the abandonment of all nonconforming positions, but an interpersonal one that redefines the positions of the speakers.

Similarly, resentment is "immature" in the originary scene, where it can be directed only to the sacred center. Resentment against other humans is incompatible with the order established in the event; it can only emerge once the human has been admitted into the sacred precinct. *The End of Culture* associated mature resentment with the birth of hierarchical society and the observable reality of the occupation of the communal center by another human being. But it is not necessary to posit so rigid a connection between models of interaction and social structures. Centralization is relative to the scene on which it occurs; it need not await realization in the most visible forms of social practice before being thematized in everyday human interaction. Just as we may take the inauguration of the imperative-declarative dialogue to be the beginning of mature rhetoric, so we may take it to be the first act of mature resentment.

In the terms of the linguistic universe obtaining when he speaks, the speaker of the imperative need have no thematic sense of superiority to his interlocutor, any more than a baby calling for a toy or its mother considers itself superior to those it expects to obey it. The linguistic structure of the imperative provides the sole necessary asymmetry. But the declarative reply, by bringing to light the difference between the locutor and locutee of the imperative, provides the occasion for the scandalized thematization of the other's centrality that we call resentment. The imperative speaker is now shown to have usurped the center in attempting to speak with its authoritative voice. The declarative is no doubt the constative form that lends metaphysics its objectivity, but in its subversion of the imperative intentional structure it is in the first place the formal expression of mature resentment, which is to say, of rhetoric. Metaphysics and polemical rhetoric, the *frères ennemis* of Western thought, are the *fils jumeaux* of the declarative response to the imperative.

In the declarative versus imperative model of mature rhetoric, the agon is decided by position on the scene of representation, not position in the world. The declarative reply denounces the naïveté of the imperative's assumption that language has power over reality. In place of the immediate presence defined by the originary community and invoked by the user of the imperative, the declarative offers the purely imaginary presence of a linguistic model.

The offer of a sign instead of a thing is an objectively unfriendly gesture toward the original speaker. We all know the joke about the man who asks his valet to go see if he left his hat on the bed; the valet returns, saying that yes, he did leave his hat on the bed. We suspect the declarative speaker, like the valet, of playing dumb in resentful revolt against his master. But whatever the intention or ability of the declarative speaker to carry out the command, the metadiscourse of the declarative, as opposed to the normal nondiscursive response to the imperative, opens up a new linguistic possibility within which resentment can insert itself.

The declarative reply functions as an objective expression of resentment in denying the central discursive position of its interlocutor. Yet it is also the linguistic nonviolence of the declarative form that guarantees the conceptual utopia of metaphysics. The movement from the elementary linguistic forms to the declarative is the exemplary nonviolent revolt. The declarative sentence turns its back on the immediate referentiality of these forms. In its repositioning of the object demanded by the imperative from a worldly to a linguistic model, the declarative carries out an implicit critique of the imperative position while avoiding the conflict that would follow upon a direct refusal.

The declarative speaker claims a more objective position than his interlocutor, one farther from the mimetic tensions of the center where reality is distorted by desire. But this claim has two possible emphases, depending on whether it is focused on the reality of the object of desire or on the interlocutor's proximity to it. In the first case, if the declarative turns away from the correspondence between desire and reality assumed by the imperative speaker toward the reality that resists this correspondence, it takes the path of metaphysics, defined by the "forgetting" of the imperative other and of the ostensive, situational basis of language. Conversely, the rhetorical use of the declarative subordinates the objective representation of the object—which it may use for its own purposes—to an interpersonal attack on the imperative speaker. If the latter had entertained the delusion of absolute power implicit in imperative language, his adversary's response reveals the vulnerability of his position without itself making a similarly refutable claim on the center.

What are the ethical consequences of this analysis of rhetoric? The rhetorical deconstruction of the naive imperative position is a movement toward symmetry—the symmetry that is the horizon if not the actual aim of resentment. But, precisely, it is only at the horizon that symmetry is the measure of ethical progress. Because interaction in concrete situations requires the speakers to occupy stable positions, rhetoric interferes with dialogue. In the worst case, its resentful denunciation of centrality engenders the deadly configuration of the sparagmos.

In a state of crisis such as that brought about by plague or war, we abandon our differential roles and fall prey to the indefinite proliferation of the mimetic. The threat of disorder, real or imaginary, encourages the rhetorical denunciation of the other's supposed proximity to the sacred center. The ultimate rhetorical achievement is the panic sown in the resentful crowd by the orator skillful in augmenting its indifferentiation as against the designated adversary's central specificity. The comfort of our previous discursive position is destroyed; we become part of an undifferentiated periphery surrounding the resented center. This structure is that of scapegoating.

The Rhetoric of Mastery

Both originary and mature rhetoric are products of an equalitarian society in which centrality confers not privilege but danger. Our originary analysis defines rhetoric as the denunciation of the other's unjustified proximity to the center. But we cannot ignore the prevalence in the hierarchical society of premodern—one is tempted to say, pre-

Nietzschean—times, of a rhetoric in which the speaker boasts of his own centrality and implicitly or explicitly warns the interlocutor not to challenge it. The ultimate form of such rhetoric is the language attributed in myth to the gods.

The rhetoric of mastery is an inverted form of the rhetoric of resentment. Whether sacred king or tyrant, the human occupant of the center is always a usurper of its originary being. From Shakespeare's Richard III to Corneille's "clement" Augustus, rulers must deal with their own resentment of a scene in which their politically central position can never guarantee their centrality in the imaginations of their subjects, or in their own.

Like equalitarian rhetoric, the rhetoric of mastery attacks the adversary's position as being too close to the center, but in this case, the rhetoric is claimed to emanate from the center itself as the source of language. The master of hierarchical society is not afraid to speak from the place of the central being, just as the original "big-man" was not afraid to usurp the central role in distributive ritual.[1]

The rhetoric of mastery reminds us that the central divinity, as the originary person, is also understood to be the originary source of language. The participant's shift from imitating the other's appropriative gesture to representing the central object makes him conscious of his act of representation but not of his agency in creating the new gesture or sign, which is attributed to the central object as the new mediator. Originary rhetoric is meant to force the "late" individual to use the sign; it does not proclaim its own "earliness."

Because the divine center is understood as an extra-anthropological source of language, the discourse attributed to it in ritual texts typically extrapolates from the anthropological domain to the cosmological. It is not by chance that the archetypal example of God's word in the Western tradition is the series of absolute imperatives that manifest God's cosmic power in the Genesis creation scene. Theological cosmology is a dubious extrapolation from anthropology. God has power over man, not over light and darkness. In contrast, in the most theologically significant speech attributed to God in the Bible, the revelation to Moses, the biblical text, which elsewhere simply indicates that "God spoke," is careful to insist on God's invisibility as speaker; the language of the center emanates from it, but is not enunciated by it.

The Genesis creation speech is exemplary of the overreaching nature of the rhetoric of mastery. The language does not persuade by itself, but as a supplement to a power relationship, the vulnerability of which it thereby reveals. Feminist cultural analysis has promoted a model of human interaction that defines male privilege by the use of language, and more generally by the occupation of the spectator's peripheral position on the scene of representation. But this model only reflects the increased circulation of desire and its discourses in nineteenth-century bourgeois society and the concomitant decline of the rhetoric of mastery observed in its early stages by Nietzsche. As a general rule, the use of signs is not an attribute of mastery but its opposite. The master *is* the sign, he need not emit it. The iconography of majesty, as practiced, say, by Louis XIV in the early modern era, consists in concentrating maximal expressive power in a minimal sign, a vanishingly slight gesture—which nevertheless remains an ever-so-small indication of weakness. The only authentic rhetoric of mastery is silence.

Victimary Rhetoric

In our analysis, the rhetoric of mastery is derivative of the primary form of rhetoric, which emerges from the periphery as a denunciation of those who usurp the center: the outsider, or the collectivity of outsiders, undermines the position of the insider. By the basic geometry of the center-periphery opposition, rhetoric is a "majoritary" phenomenon; the peripheral denouncers are more numerous than their central targets. But the essential features of the circle are derived from those of the mimetic triangle, where numbers are irrelevant. The success of the declarative rhetoric that persuades the original mediator/imperative speaker to renounce his claim to the center is independent of the threat of many against one. The rhetoric of mastery retains the fundamental geometry of the mimetic triangle/circle while inverting the direction of communication. But modern victimary rhetoric performs a geometric inversion of the mimetic configuration itself.[2]

This is not a simple switching of positions. "Victim" is a central, not a peripheral category. Victimary rhetoric attacks the majoritary periphery by positing the equivalence of the eccentric position of the persecuted minority with the sacrificial center. Thus victimary rhetoric is not simply the dialectical antithesis of the rhetoric of mastery. In defining a new peripherality as the result of exile from the center, victimary rhetoric temporalizes the static geometric structure; the postmodern victim is a victim of history.

The violence of the sparagmos demonstrates that, in the minds of the participants, it is they rather than the central figure who are the original victims. The victimary is not the unequivocal category it may appear to be from a cursory reading of Girard. The distinction between persecutor and victim is an etic, not an emic one; the use of these categories destabilizes the human center versus periphery configuration. Once they are thematized and become weapons in the rhetorical agon, the respective positions are revealed to have been reversible from the beginning. The sparagmos is the revenge of the "victims" of the object's withdrawal from the arena of mimetic desire, and the object's revenge for its defiguration in the sparagmos is the constitution of subsistent divine Being in its place. This originary series of reversals is the foundation of the institutions that preserve the cultural order.

The historical emergence of the category of the victimary corresponds to the cultural articulation of the reversibility that resentment has reflected from the outset. Originary resentment already makes an inarticulate victimary claim. Exclusion from the center is always felt as victimage, however ethically justified this exclusion may be and however dependent the resenter may be on the center he attacks.

Explicit victimary rhetoric is an innovation of Christianity. How indeed can Saul answer the complaint, "Why do you persecute me?" But the exemplarity of Christ as the victimary model maintains the emphasis on the center.[3] In contrast, today's victimary rhetorics emerge from and remain on the periphery of the circle; indeed, they put the very idea of a circular scenic structure into question.

Rhetoric is the voice of resentment against centrality, whether the speaker seeks to confound an opponent or to urge his own partisans to action. Traditionally, this resentment is not expressed directly in noncritical situations. Following the model of the imperative-declarative dialogue, traditional rhetoric opposes the objectivity of the subject's position to the subjective illusion of the opponent's. The rhetoric of explicit invidious comparison belongs to the context of social revolution, where it functions to encourage the slaves to throw off their chains. In contrast, the persuasive force of victimary rhetoric is directed essentially to the majority rather than the minority. Victimary rhetoric insistently thematizes positional difference. It makes explicit the critique of centrality that has always been the motivation of rhetoric, a revelation that can only be made with impunity from the inverted victimary position—the position of internal exile created by Rousseau in his *Rêveries du promeneur solitaire.*[4]

Jesus appears to Saul on the road to Damascus as the accusing representative of a persecuted minority. But the revelatory force of the scene depends on Jesus's transcendent position; he is invulnerable to persecution at the very moment when he protests against it because his accusation has already been internalized by the one he accuses. Supernatural explanations of Jesus's status in this scene explain nothing. On the contrary, this status is itself a generative model of the supernatural. The worldly persecution of a supernatural figure is futile by definition. The real relationship is the reverse: the figure begins to appear supernatural because, rather than driving it from consciousness, persecution reenacts the concentric violence of the sparagmos.

The unique supernatural status of the sacrificial victim is transformed in postmodern victimary rhetoric into a worldly collective one. The minoritary collectivity takes the place of the crucified savior. Its accusation is not neglect nor even mistreatment but persecution, as terms such as "sexism" and "racism" strongly imply. Neglect or avoidance of the victim only give proof of an unconscious mimetic obsession. This claim is no doubt best exemplified by the term "homophobia," which denotes not merely obsessive fear of homosexuals, but fear of them as bearers of one's own secret homosexuality. The minority's marginalization becomes the equivalent of victimary centralization. Victimary rhetoric radically binarizes all social value distinctions: unconscious differences in attitudes or statistical differences in income level are taken as prima facie evidence for persecution. Once the victimary status of a distinction has been confirmed, the role of persecutor is then extended to all those who do not suffer from it.

The Jesus of Paul's vision could not have hoped for a more successful generalization of his revelatory accusation. Victimary rhetoric attacks all identifiable majority attributes. It turns every defeat into victory by permitting the weaker party to take its adversary's superiority as itself a proof of victimage. The radicalization of the victimary makes it ultimately impossible even to argue against it, for the power of argument is just one more form of victimizing superiority.

Rhetoric Versus Metaphysics, Again

The contemporary emphasis on the positional—the insistence on the place from where one speaks—signals a rebirth of rhetoric, which has entered a new, radical stage of its rivalry with metaphysics. Plato's doctrine of Ideas is founded on the rejection of rhetorical ostensivity. But this rejection involves a contradiction that is only now clearly revealed. Metaphysics is the world of the context-free declarative sentence, inhabited by the transcendental Ideas/signifieds. Yet rhetoric knows that the declarative was not originally a bearer of impersonal truth but the denial of another subject's desire. In an age where centrality is profoundly suspect, the revelation of the positional nature of all language unmasks metaphysics' pretension of objectivity.

The founding argument of Platonic metaphysics, as discussed in Chapter 6, is that the terms of value that rhetors use for persuasion, such as "courageous" or "beautiful," are derived from the universally held concepts/signifieds "courage" and "beauty." Because these concepts provide all with the same mimetic models beyond any possibility of worldly conflict—this is the ultimate, if implicit, justification for the doctrine of Ideas—they guarantee the peace of the social order. The rhetor, on the contrary, turning his back on the universal concept of the Good, would persuade us to differentiate among unclear instances of goodness in order to promote a particular course of action. That the situational language of rhetoric is parasitic on the transtemporal constitution of concepts is the cornerstone of post-Socratic philosophy.

The metaphysical doctrine of the concept gives it the atemporality of the declarative sentence or proposition. By the same token, the postmodern attack on metaphysics affirms the nonoriginarity of the declarative proposition—in other terms, its rhetoricity. Witness Austin's theory of speech-acts, or Derrida's deconstruction of "logocentrism." But the former remains narrowly empirical, whereas the paradoxical insights of the latter never lead beyond a metaphysical conception of mimesis.[5] Victimary rhetoric, which has by now largely subsumed the discourse of deconstruction (reduced in the popular intellectual mind to a technique for contesting "hegemony") provides, as a result of its explicit worldly agenda, a more trenchant and ultimately more revelatory critique of metaphysics. There can be no final victory of the rhetorical over the metaphysical any more than the other way around, but postmodern victimary rhetoric appears to put an end to the naively nonsituational discourse of traditional metaphysics.

Marxism and Victimary Rhetoric

After Rousseau, Karl Marx is the greatest contributor to the arsenal of modern victimary rhetoric. The classic example is Marx's denunciation of the universalist anthropologies of the Enlightenment as ideological instruments of the bourgeoisie, which he presents as naively and self-servingly equating itself with humanity in general. Today the Marxist technique of demystification is applied to anthropological discourses in which race, gender, and sexual orientation have become the chief rubrics of what used to be "class analysis." This is a vulgarization of Marxism only in the sense that it is its generalization. And just as, in their heyday, Marxists were able to find political content in discourses on matters ostensibly indifferent to human interaction, so today's victimary critics claim to find hegemonic content even in the discourses of physics and mathematics.[6]

The kernel of Marx's argument against the bourgeoisie is his definition of the ostensibly reciprocal exchange of the worker's labor for the capitalist's wage as "exploitation," which is really no more than a scientific-sounding term for victimization. The hidden premise of Marxian analysis—one more congenial to generative anthropology than to Marxism—is that economic structures ("production relations") are in the last analysis ethical structures, and therefore ultimately answerable to the moral model of the originary scene. That the economic model with which Marx sought to underpin this argument is secondary to the moral one is made clear by the ease with which his argument has been shorn of its economic basis in the theory of surplus labor and adapted to victimary critique in every area of the social order. Whenever an apparently free exchange exceeds the originary reciprocity of signs—whenever, in other words, human interaction has any kind of socioeconomic function—it is suspected of being a disguised form of domination.

As a form of victimary rhetoric, the Marxian critique of the bourgeoisie cannot be refuted directly, because it contests the ground of discourse itself. The bourgeois who tries to defend himself by appealing to objective rationality suddenly discovers that it is this very appeal that condemns him as a bourgeois. This technique is all the more effective when the trait separating the dominant majority from the dominated minority is ascriptive, like race or sex.[7] Because a bourgeois can become a proletarian, he is in principle able to be "reeducated" to think as a proletarian, which is to say, as a universal human being. In contrast, the logical goal of minoritary discourse, however political compromise may mitigate the directness of its pursuit, is the silencing of the universalist discourse of the majority, redefined as majoritary or hegemonic. The only appropriate role in dialogue for one without a minority affiliation is to proclaim his inability to participate any further—to abdicate. Anyone in the academic world has been witness to acts of this kind. But the lesson learned by the majoritary witness is not continued abdication, but self-redefinition as a member of a victimized minority of a different kind. This may not lead to victory for the "victims," but it is clearly a victory for victimary rhetoric.

Victimary rhetoric reaffirms the reciprocity of the Christian moral utopia, not as universal love, but in the resentful mode of "the last shall be the first," the "last" being defined as the collective victims of historic injustice. To occupy the victimary position absolves one of the narrowness of one's own worldly interests; the place of the victim is the sole locus of human truth and the sole human truth is that of victimization. But the victimary critique of universal anthropology is circularly self-fulfilling. It is an anthropological hypothesis only in the tautological sense that its denial of universality makes it the only universal statement conceivable in its own terms.

Victimary rhetoric is able to blackmail traditional liberalism because it hides its ontology behind an empirical mask. The universalist opponent is ostensibly denied his discursive position only until such time as the victimary difference has been abolished. What is not generally recognized is that the basis of this rhetoric is the denial of the universal as such, that is, of any discursive position not implicated in victimization on one side or the other. The claim to take such a neutral position is ipso facto proof that one is on the side of the victimizers.

The victimary position is historically associated with the Left. But

the very distinction between Right and Left, born with the French Revolution, is one that emphasizes the symmetry of resentments on which
modern politics is founded. As a complement to the age-old grievances
of the have-nots is opposed the defining feature of the modern political configuration: the grievances of their former masters deposed by
the Revolution. What defines the resentment of the Right in opposition to that of the Left is the "sacrificial" death of Louis XVI in which
de Maistre saw the inaugural moment of a "redemptive" era of history.[8]

   The symmetry of Right and Left is not mechanical, but it is more
fundamental than their differences. The Left's use of victimary rhetoric
is "classical," referring as it does to the long-term effects of broad-based
social distinctions, whereas that of the Right is "romantic," directed at
the usurpation of power by an illegitimate demotic elite. The pre-
dominance of the Left in postmodern victimology—a phenomenon
that would have been impossible to anticipate in the 1930s, and one
that may not continue indefinitely—is the result of the demonstration
given by the Holocaust that whatever the evils of minority resentment,
the resentment of the majority holds ultimately the greater danger. But
the long-term promise of postmodern victimary politics is to defuse
the old, simplistic resentments by creating new means for the marketplace to arbitrate between the competing claims of "disadvantaged"
categories.

*

   The great debate of the postmodern era is whether there can be a
debate at all; whether human society in the era of the universal market can tolerate universal dialogue. The principle of the free market,
broadly conceived, is that the exchange process is a positive-sum game
from which all parties benefit in the long run. Victimary rhetoric directly contradicts this principle by reducing to the binary opposition
of persecutor and victim the differentiation of positions on which any
exchange is based.

   The traditional defense of difference has not been made from the
dynamic standpoint of exchange, but from the static one of the struc-
tural-metaphysical opposition of ideas. Derrida's identification of the
operation of differentiating deferral or *différance* is a major turning
point in postmodern understanding. But the victimary accusation of
nonreciprocity can never be satisfactorily answered within the universalism of metaphysical discourse, since the accuser simply relabels

the universal as the majoritary. The response in which we may seek the—always provisional but no less real—ethical solution to the postmodern dilemma can come only from within a way of thinking grounded in the moment of human history in which the universal and the particular are (still) the same: the moment of origin. The ultimate offensive of rhetoric against metaphysics reveals our need for an originary anthropology that understands better than either the mimetic origin of human truth.

The End of Culture

Culture in its most inclusive sense may be defined as any exploitation of the material, "horizontal" elements of the signifier. Culture is found wherever we do not adhere rigorously to the *arbitraire du signifiant*. The sign itself is the minimal constituent of the human, and the binding force of the human community, but it is everywhere supplemented by the material specificity of culture.

If we claim to be able to put in question our attachment to this supplement, it is surely not through naive reliance on the intuition of presence that exemplifies for Derrida the universalism of classical metaphysics. We are surrounded by culture, our lives are suffused with it. It is only in the midst of cultural plethora that we can have the luxury of belonging to no culture in particular. Postmodernity is "the end" of culture because postmodern culture is such that the pretense of belonging to it knows itself to be an illusion.

"Double-minority" Culture

The essence of all culture is the deferral of resentment. Popular culture expresses and offers imaginary satisfaction to "the people," those who define themselves by their collective rather than individual resentment of the social order. In traditional societies, this self-definition was a given; in modern ones, it is, regardless of economic circumstances, essentially voluntary. The social configuration of postmodern popular culture reproduces the structure of esthetic paradox: the "people" expresses its resentment through the mediation of internal minorities who define themselves by their resentment of the people themselves.

The exemplary source of the phenomenon of minoritary culture is America's black minority, which has provided the dominant models of American popular culture since before the Civil War. The white-black interaction resembles more the archaic majority-minority relationship between Greeks and "barbarians" than that between Christian culture and the Jews. "The" Jew is hated because he refuses to humble himself to the *imitatio Christi,* whereas the blacks have been stigmatized as a mass whose very human capacity for the *imitatio* is put in question. In keeping with this distinction, the Jewish cultural contribution to the West has been made by individuals idiosyncratically integrating their "anesthetic" Jewishness into the esthetic culture of their time, whereas American blacks have evolved a distinctive communal culture of their own that has served as a mimetic model for the white majority. The really distinctive Jewish element in modernity is not the contribution of Marx, Freud, Einstein, Proust, or Derrida, but, as we saw in the preceding chapter, the suspicion of esthetic centrality put on the world-historical agenda by the Holocaust. The black element, on the other hand, is central to modern popular culture, because the stigmatized position of the blacks makes their community a model for the deindividualized "people" in general.

The worldwide popularity of American mass culture, which gives it a near-monopoly over what is fast becoming a frontierless market, is no doubt to be attributed to the peculiar intensity of this black-white relationship, which has undergone a significant shift in the postmodern era. Until that time, the majority culture assimilated minority contributions by absorbing toned-down versions of them into its own less parochial universe. Nor was black culture itself overtly hostile to the white majority. Today minority resentment is no longer merely the underlying source of American popular culture; it has become its principal theme. The more violently this resentment is expressed, for example in rap lyrics, the greater the sales among the very whites against whom the resentment is directed.

This suggests a model of postmodern culture in which the status of persecuted minority has become the sole source of cultural legitimacy.

The majority participates in this culture only passively, by consuming the creations of appropriate minorities, thereby purging itself of its "white guilt."[1] But the particular success of postmodern minoritary culture depends on an additional articulation. Minority status is not confined to racial or ethnic difference. The most culturally significant American minority is not African Americans but *youth.*

The consumerism, expanded affluence, and prolonged schooling of the postwar years made of youth an open-ended cultural minority capable of standing in for those minorities that exemplify victimization. In the postmodern era, the youth culture has become so dominant in the popular sphere that the peculiarity of its dominance is overlooked. Cultural awareness now belongs to those with the least historical awareness; the only persons who can create a living culture are those too young to have roots in its past. The youthful minority subsumes and subverts all the others. It is by now virtually all-inclusive, since even the middle-aged can identify with the youth culture of their own time (witness the strength of baby-boomer nostalgia for the Beatles). Present or retrospective resentment against adult society is the only membership requirement. In America's unique "double-minority" configuration, youth as the open minority provides a vehicle for near-universal mass identification, while its model of resentment is borrowed from the closed, ascriptive minority exemplified by the blacks.

The postmodern era is a turning point in cultural evolution. The worldwide triumph of American popular culture based on the double-minority configuration suggests that culture is produced by and for victims; victimage is the prior guarantee of its appeal to the general population. The high culture invented by the Greeks now appears to have been but a temporary deferral of this victimary structure, one that ultimately remains governed by it.

The typical participant in contemporary popular culture is obliged to assume attitudes specific to the open minority (youth) within which he may be included, attitudes which in turn have their source in the closed minority (blacks) from which he is in the general case excluded. Hence the attitudes expressed by the youth culture are uncharacteristic of the middle-class youth—white or other—who are its chief customers. Their assumption is an exercise in role playing. For their part, its producers must be able to demonstrate their minoritary-victimary status concretely. These persons, however financially successful, however reflexively self-ironic, must serve the majority as incarnations of "their" culture. Because they must renounce, whether naively or ironically, their essential freedom with respect to this culture, they are supremely inauthentic at the very moment when cultural authenticity becomes their source of fame and fortune. Their performances, however ostensibly inner-directed, are as mediated by the eyes of the majority as ritual dances performed by Indians for tourists.

Role playing has always been a sine qua non of cultural performance, but now for the first time the performer must in addition to his performance role play the existential role of an "authentic minority representative," hostile or, at the very least, indifferent to the majority that provides him with the greater part of his income. This role may be assumed in the most outrageously ironic fashion, and, indeed, the success of the violent hyperboles of rap attests to its consciousness of this irony and even to the sharing in it by its consumers. One should not underestimate the postmodern sophistication of our minoritary popular culture. But the bottom-line selling point of this culture is that it bears an indubitable, irreversible guarantee, a mark of "nonwhiteness"—whence the cultural exemplarity of American blacks.

Postwar/Postmodern

Nazism attempted to resist the centrifugal tendencies of market society through a return to esthetically centered social compactness—to precisely the archaic sacrificial universe from which the Mosaic revelation had turned away. In reaction, postmodern culture is hostile to majoritary solidarity and suspicious of its imagery. Unlike postmodern high culture, which operates in an ironic, citational mode, mass culture cannot function without figures on which desire and resentment can focus. The necessary esthetic closure that postmodernism rejects becomes permissible in the interest of affirming the cultural closure of the minority, which can presumably never victimize the majority.

The current, historically unique experience of reverse discrimination deconstructs anew the absolute difference between persecutor and victim that the Holocaust seemed to have established once and for all. In the light of the Holocaust, the scenic opposition between center and periphery, hitherto the hidden basis of all cultural structures including language, takes on an unambiguous victimary aspect; our ideal moral certainties are regrounded in the opposition between (Nazi) persecutor and (Jewish) victim. But the descent of the absolute into the empirical world is the moment of its undoing. As soon as we posit an absolute difference between victim and persecutor, the underlying symmetry of their relation reasserts itself. When the SS torturer becomes the villain of the war film, he is turned into a sacrificial figure, a scapegoat, the structural equivalent of the Jew Süss in Nazi cinema. In the already tiresome clarity of this symmetry, culture has been abandoned to youth; adults are too world-weary to participate wholeheartedly in the eternal and now transparent structure of victimary resentment.

The minority experience, which is fast becoming the universal model of experience in a multicultural society, follows two contrasting models. On the one hand, the minority forms a relatively autonomous community modeled on the society as a whole; on the other, it plays the role of the isolated, "late" subject who is reconciled to the originary community on the basis of originary resentment of the central figure. The "double-minority" configuration of popular culture is founded on the tension between these models of inclusion and exclusion.

The "late" individual in the originary event is both (weakly) a part of the community and (strongly) excluded from it. The dynamic of the emission of the sign carries him from the first position to the second, from fear of exclusion and its potentially violent consequences to participation in reciprocal communication. Contemporary popular culture repeats this configuration in an esthetic mode. Its typical participant is strongly excluded by the black community and weakly included in the youth community. The emphasis on the cohesion of the minority group in opposition to the noncommunal larger society leads members of the majority to identify with and participate in the minority community's victimary status by the very fact of their exclusion from this minority. In listening to his rap record, the white youth experiences the hostility of the black community as a means of identifying with the black experience of the hostility of the white community. The white guilt that motivates this paradoxical identification is ultimately indistinguishable from the desire to participate in the cultural privilege conferred on blacks by their victimary status.

Nietzsche thought that the "weak," the "slaves," were sterile, that creativity, especially artistic creativity, was the privilege of the masters alone. This antidemocratic inversion of the Hegelian master-slave dialectic—in which enforced contact with reality makes the slave, not the master, the creator—was to have terrible consequences. Its real target is not the slave at all, nor even his proletarian counterpart, but his bourgeois employer—the "freed slave" in Alexandre Kojève's Hegelian construction of political history.[2] The violence latent in this inversion does not come from the underestimation of the creativity of the oppressed, in whom Nietzsche had little interest, but from the hyperromantic condemnation of the market system as one in which all parties are equally enslaved, and against which whatever the master-artist-superman does is consequently justified.

Nietzsche failed to realize that the same resentment he discerned at the root of Judeo-Christian religion was equally at the heart of the high-cultural works he admired.[3] The twentieth century reveals the bankruptcy of this most radical of all attempts to differentiate popular from high culture. Today culture has become ever more clearly the property and the occupation of the "weak." Group resentment has replaced individual resentment—the point of essential difference between the high and the popular—as the primary object of cultural deferral. The "strong"—but who today would be willing to be called by that name?—are at best capable of theory.

The revelations of minority culture are of two kinds. On the one hand, there is the resentful myth of an inaccessible majority paradise, which serves to mask the underlying unity of the human that the high culture, faithful to the lesson of the originary sign, always held out to its audience. But on the other, minority culture, more vital because less implicated in the social order than that of the majority, provides an object-lesson in the everyday deferral of resentment. A long-lost Dionysian frenzy reappears in the ecstatic forms of postwar popular culture, in its music and dance, the audience of which more than that of any other popular form incarnates the "people." These central genres of the youth culture are not coincidentally those most subject to black and other minority influences. The rhythms and chord progressions of popular music dissolve individuality in a real or imaginary group movement that is the historical heir to sacrificial ritual. They create, in an imaginary context, the resentful unanimity of the sparagmos.

The internal tension of popular music—melody/rhythm and lyrics—

parallels and reinforces that generated by the double-minority structure of its audience. Even before the advent of the youth culture, African rhythms in their American distillation had become the driving force in Western popular music. In contrast to the lyrics, these rhythms can be participated in directly. On the one hand, one is drawn to a cultural universe from which one will always be excluded—the pseudosadistic world of rap lyrics, for example, but in an earlier era, the world of idealized romantic love was sufficiently exotic. But on the other, by giving oneself over to the rhythms of the music, one renounces one's individual identity for the sake of maximal participation in what is now experienced as a minority community.

Unlike high culture, with its unlimited resources of self-construction, popular culture cannot function on the basis of a commitment to vicarious martyrdom. The effectiveness of popular culture depends on deindividuation, on the assimilation of the individual to the community. Popular culture protects us from the rigor of the centerless, victimless marketplace. That it can only be participated in through this very marketplace is the paradox that makes bourgeois culture the instrument for the revelation of the paradoxical foundation of all culture.

Since the romantic era, the cultural sphere has been obsessed by a resentful denial of the bourgeois exchange system, but today the cultural world can no longer pretend to be separate from the world of the market. The market's universality depends on its ability to sell particularity, all the more so when minority particularity expresses an internally generated resentment against this very universality. To turn away from the nonuniversal is then to reject cultural content in general, to experience the end of culture. Is such a rejection an "antilife" gesture? We should not be too quick to give our answer in a world whose artists are functionaries of the marketplace.

The Unesthetic Universal

The following letter appeared in the January 1993 issue of *Consumer Reports* magazine under the heading "Opposites Detract":

I never would have guessed that *Consumer Reports* would be frightened by the religious right into supporting its view of the proper "family values." I guess

I was wrong. There it is on page 725 of your November issue. You suggest that someone trying out a sleep sofa "have someone of the *opposite sex* take part in the shopping." I guess that leaves out all of those lesbian and gay couples without the proper gender mix for buying sleep sofas.

WEST HOLLYWOOD, CALIF.   F.G.

The rhetoric of this text, which reveals its inherent assumptions, is striking in its historical specificity. I doubt if a similar tone would have been taken even a year earlier. The writer misinterprets, "naively" if one likes, but with a blindness that has become all but obligatory, the magazine's offhand reference to the "opposite sex," which not long ago he (she?) would most likely not have remarked at all, as a product of deliberate censorship. The traditional stereotype of the heterosexual couple has now become so offensive that the only conceivable explanation for its evocation by decent people is fear of "the religious right"—a demonized group whose members presumably do not read *CR*.

There is another point to be made about the specificity of the offense of which *CR* is accused. The author is offended by the exclusion of "lesbian and gay couples." Presumably someone whose tastes extended to sleeping with animals or with more than one partner would not have a similar right to feel excluded. The stereotype has been expanded to include homosexual couples, but it remains a stereotype. Yet we shall see that despite this comforting appearance, the stereotype has definitely changed its character, to such an extent that the term "stereotype" is no longer altogether appropriate.

The point of the letter is that the presupposition of a heterosexual norm is offensive because it implicitly excludes persons of other sexual orientations. The heaviness of the sarcasm suggests that although the offensiveness of this norm is something less than universally acknowledged, its author feels he has history on his side. Such convictions are not to be taken lightly; they signal sea changes in the social order. This letter illustrates what has come to be known as "political correctness" or the "PC" phenomenon, far from the university setting to which some not long ago thought it confined. The magazine published it without comment; it is difficult to imagine that its editorial staff has not been "sensitized" on this matter for future sleep-related reviews.

It would seem that a minor change in language would obviate the accusation of exclusion. Instead of "bring someone of the opposite sex," "bring your significant other" would suffice. (We aren't yet ready for "others.") Since the buyer's sex is indeterminate, there would be little loss in the vividness of the expression. The difference is nevertheless of historic importance. The image of a couple, a man and a woman, is replaced by an abstract association of two indeterminate individuals. This raises the question of the cultural function of such stereotypical images.

The current preoccupation with nonexclusion concerns many groups of greater numerical importance than the homosexual community. But it is in this particular case—which not coincidentally puts in question the fundamental biological purpose of the sexual associations that "sleep sofas" cater to—that the problematization of the stereotype, the universal image, extends from the pictorial into the verbal.

The category of the stereotypical is halfway between the semantic and the grammatical; it refers to the imaginary content of a minimally described human situation. The figure of the heterosexual couple as imagined from the CR text does not require us to consider, for example, its racial or religious composition; minimal descriptions of humanity do not generally force their users to make such distinctions. Sexes are another matter. Most languages have a concept of gender that makes it difficult to avoid identifying a given individual's sexual identity. The change from "opposite sex" to "significant other" imposes a clear loss of semantic information. Expressions like "significant other" are justifiably perceived as euphemisms that reflect the political tensions of our era with regard to the legitimacy of couplings other than traditional marriage. The elimination of the expectation that couples be heterosexual, let alone married, forces us to decrease the semantic content of our language, and thereby to face, in the kind of minimal situation where stereotypes are in order, a *de-esthetization* that deprives the figure of the social universal of imaginary presence. The de-esthetization of language is crucial because it affects our most fundamental means of communication. The image is supplementary to the word. If we have to restrain our words, the restraint cannot be eluded by an image; it has become integral to human communication.

Not long ago, the "typical" American was a white male, most probably a WASP. Today any group intended as typical will include members of several races and both genders. The least problematic solution for a single individual is abstraction—a figure belonging to no race or gender in particular. A single white male may still be acceptable, but such a figure sets up a tension that demands the presence of members of other groups—in the next advertisement, for example. Abstraction is the unmarked, and therefore safer, solution. The esthetically visible specification of the white figure as opposed to the neutral one is felt as *de trop*, as an excess that must be counterbalanced, or in the simplest case, eliminated.

But a more effective remedy is available that avoids the loss of esthetic effect. Particularly in cases where one seeks exemplarity and not just typicality, for example in children's books, which are expected to convey to their readers a figure of what the world should, rather than does, look like, the process of de-esthetization comes full circle: the formerly typical image is re-esthetized in nontypical form. In such books, for example, doctors—who, in the real United States, are overwhelmingly white and male—are more often than not female, nonwhite, or both. A children's book that depicted more or less as it really is the racial and gender composition of the professional world—or, conversely, the world of crime and homelessness—would almost certainly be labeled sexist and racist. This is even becoming true of less sensitive forms of popular imagery such as television shows.

These problems of universal imagery contrast sharply with the relative simplicity of minoritary ethnic imagery. A magazine for blacks will use black models in its advertising, and would lose customers if it did otherwise. The same would be true for a white ethnic publication, provided ethnicity be emphasized over whiteness. Within the local community, there is no need for de-esthetization. On the contrary, our newly aroused ethnic consciousness (the point of departure for which is often said to be the mid-1970s TV series *Roots*, which conveyed the victimary specificity of the African-American experience to the American public at large) makes for an increased esthetization of local groups that in the past did their best to acquire the appearance of the majority. It is these local images that have taken over the higher reaches of popular culture. There is no longer a typical majoritary cultural figure; the universal has been de-esthetized, and in its place are presented the diverse figures of various subcultures.

All this has taken place in a very short historical time span; but the irresistible and apparently irreversible nature of this change, the power it gives to the rhetoric of such documents as the letter to *CR*, demonstrates that it is of far more significance than the derisive label "PC" suggests. PC is the extension via victimary rhetoric of the postmodern esthetic into the ethical sphere. But this "multicultural" ethic offers no coherent model of human relations. Every visible sign of difference is both a laudable example of "diversity" and prima facie proof of victimage. Victimary rhetoric is esthetic-driven, founded on images rather than concepts. It is too early to know whether this is ultimately a weakness or a strength. This rhetoric may well reflect an unconscious anthropological sophistication, a greater appreciation, however naively expressed, of the tension between morality and ethics than earlier, more concept-driven ethical movements, up to and including the American civil rights movement.

What has occurred is that the figure of the universal is experienced as exclusive rather than inclusive. An image is a mimetic object, something one conforms to. In the past, the exemplary figure, typically the WASP, provided a model for the aspirations of other groups; henceforth, such a figure is experienced rather as excluding these groups. It is not the message but the image of the messenger that is rejected. In its place, we put figures of the nonmajority, the nonuniversal, the diverse, which are acceptable because they are not meant to occupy a social center but to exemplify marginality.[4] We can all identify with them as images precisely because they cannot become universal mimetic models. Ultimately there are no universal images, only minority images, including WASP minority images. However passionately we cultivate them and play at imitating them, their naive or cynical esthetic coherence marks them as reflecting, within our complex social order, not a lost simplicity but a resentful critique of inevitable complexity.

For the first time, the esthetic of society-as-a-whole (the *Gesellschaft*) no longer pretends to be that of a community (*Gemeinschaft*). Any compactness in collective imagery is experienced as inauthentic and dangerous, potentially "fascistic." This is as yet a largely American phenomenon, but as ever in the recent history of popular culture, the United States stands in the avant garde. Not only is there a worldwide clientele increasingly aware of the American scene and impatient to reproduce it for its local market, but majority cultures in the economically advanced countries cannot help feeling the breath of this multiculturalist iconoclasm. PC is, or soon will be, a worldwide phenomenon.

The decline of the traditional forms of universalism is proof only of their inadaptability to the postmodern world. Esthetics that unreflectively posit the exemplarity of a majority group cannot indefinitely resist minoritary rhetoric. The new universal culture of the cosmopolitan media minoritizes all of its participants, including the members of the traditional majority. Like all esthetic phenomena, the creations of the media operate mimetically, but without coercion. Nor is anyone forced to support them—it is rather the surviving forms of high culture that must be subsidized.

The multicultural scene abounds in local color; the more local the imagery, the more concrete. Yet this imagery too suffers from de-esthetization. However complacently patronized by the larger society, it is nonetheless a reminder of the minority's eccentricity; its images cannot perform the same unifying function as the unmarked figures of the majority. The result is a delicate combination of folklore and modern resentment, the fragility of which is revealed when "multicultural" university courses convert culture into politics by extracting the resentment from its esthetic envelope.

De-esthetization is one with the refusal of compactness. The esthetic depends on closure, but because closure is no longer possible save from the victimary position of the minority, the image presented as that of a world is really only that of a fragment. The scene of esthetic representation must pretend to completeness and at the same time display its incompleteness, indirectly but unambiguously. It is because one must be able to grasp this disparity at a glance that the visible traits of racial and other minorities have become sources of esthetic privilege.

Judaism began as an exodus from the esthetic scene, which the Greeks preferred to liberate from its ritual origins. The triumph of Christianity in the West was founded on the synthesis of these complementary liberations. But postmodernity forces a revision of this synthesis. The esthetic remains, indeed, thrives as never before, but as a cult of personality rather than of representativity. The expelled victim recentralizes himself on stage; the dreams of participation that drive our "double-minority" culture never allow us to forget that the ultimate minority is that of those whose talent and good fortune have made them figures of the media. Since the romantic era, Jesus's central martyr role has been coveted rather than feared; in a world where "there is no such thing as bad publicity," where the average person can only dream of "being famous for fifteen minutes," the sufferings of the crucified are as nothing compared with the joys of universal recognition. Under such conditions, the universal recentering promised by Christianity cannot take place: the "stone rejected by the builders [that] has become the keystone" can no longer be an agent of transvaluation.[5]

Minoritary Esthetics and Victimary Ideology

High secular esthetic culture appears to be going the way of ritual as a transcended stage of cultural evolution. In the dialectic of ever-accelerating exchange, centralized figures of beauty are unable to keep the pace and are withdrawn from circulation to be replaced by more fungible objects. What is left to hold society together is language, proliferating but always translatable. Language is our minimal human possession. No doubt we cannot help but imagine a referent in association with the sign; but since the beginning of consumer society, and unambiguously in the postmodern "age of information," the signifying imagination has lost the initiative to the world of scientific and commercial production.

Hence the reesthetization of the minoritary is anything but a genuine restoration of the esthetic. These implicitly victimary figures easily become illustrations of an explicitly victimary ideology, as, for example, in the current trend of testimonial literature (which like the other victimary aspects of postmodernism would appear to have originated with the Holocaust). As in all propaganda art, the figure becomes a mere guarantee of the word that transcends it; the most visible case of victimage is the purest source of victimary discourse. As minoritary rhetoric becomes a kind of "theory," it comes in common practice to declare that the theoretical understanding of minority cultures is only possible from within the minorities themselves.

This last tendency is the most dangerous aspect of PC. The esthetic terrain may arguably be conceded; the greater society can and perhaps should live without figures of communal solidarity, and those which have been lost cannot well be restored. We have plenty of inoffensive imagery to put in their place, beginning with the "soft" particularity of the Disney figures, which derive ultimately from sacrificial ritual distilled through fable, and whose audience is age-based rather than ethnic. But anthropological theory is the privileged terrain of thought itself.

Universal anthropology cannot abdicate in favor of a set of regional systems. The human universal remains the horizon of all thought; local ideologies only choose to deny this for tactical reasons because their protection against neighboring ideologies is more political than intellectual. Language has no way of limiting its truth according to the group affiliation of its speaker. On the contrary, the postmodern de-esthetization of the center gives us the opportunity to replace discredited images by rigorous theoretical constructs.

PC engages us in a debate over the place of the esthetic in anthropological discourse. The traditional view is that the esthetic element of any theory is merely a contingent aid to its comprehension. Like the natural scientist, the anthropological thinker needs no images to demonstrate the truth of his affirmations. The minoritary suspicion is that, on the contrary, because anthropological discourse always operates with a particular model of the human, it can never eliminate the esthetic element, and with it, a prerational preference for the unmarked majority over those marked with minority status.

What inflamed the *CR* letter writer was an image. *Consumer Reports'* reviewer had referred to a heterosexual rather than a "gender-free" couple because he had in mind the image of such a couple. This image can be de-esthetized. But the crucial question is whether there is implicit in anthropological discourse a degree of esthetic specificity incompatible with genuine human universality. Because de-esthetization is not an all-or-nothing process, will there not always remain a figural residue that at a later historical moment may come to be denounced in the same terms that our letter writer uses today?

Following this line of reasoning, if we cannot help using images, then unless these images are specifically those of a minority, that is, marked as nonuniversal, they will turn out to be those of the unmarked "white" majority. Consequently, only minoritary discourse, because it accepts the specificity of the esthetic, can be authentically human; there can be no universal anthropological discourse because there is no way to figure the human-in-general. To give an all-too-familiar example: since "he/she" or "he or she" creates two images rather than one, whereas "he" falsely hides its unmarked status, the only authentic option becomes "she." In this case, the "minority" member does not claim universality; on the contrary, she rejects a priori the validity of such a claim, while claiming that maximal human truth comes from openly accepting one's dependency on the particularity of the image, as only the "marked" are ready or able to do.

Different groups have always had their own readings of history as well as their own religious and secular eschatologies. But each thought of itself as universal, and their relative power was measured by the ability of each to integrate the others' gods into its pantheon. What is new in our era is the promotion of nonintegrative local theories, the ideas of the survivors rather than the winners of history, as though they were the only theories conceivable and it were no longer possible for the human community to think itself as a whole. Feminism and other minoritary approaches, which maintain their link with universal thought only through the unacknowledged mediation of the Christian centralization of the victim, are fast driving out other forms of cultural interpretation.[6]

The de-esthetization of the center is the latest stage of the long-term human liberation from mimetic compactness that began with the origin of language. The silencing of the center as a source of discourse is another matter. In its haste to rewrite history from the perspective of its victims, the new ideology denies its own source in the historical dialectic. PC's radical rejection of human temporality reflects the prophetic excesses of the Judeo-Christian ancestry that it rejects. Where metaphysics flees the world of human conflict to that of the concept, the timeless and placeless abstraction of the Ideas or the First Mover, PC proposes to leap back beyond the violence of history to the originary moral configuration of perfect reciprocity. On the model of Christian morality, it asks us to reject worldly success and reserve our sympathy for failure. This is a more radical position than mere cultural relativism. For the relativist, there is no hierarchy of cultural beliefs, but the anthropological dialogue in which he participates is exempted from this refusal of evaluation. What is now proposed makes no exemptions because it proposes no dialogue; it substitutes the absolutism of ideology for the universalism of truth.

The origin of metaphysics lies in Socrates' intuition that because human harmony is founded on the "other scene" of language, this scene must be guaranteed from the violence of human action. By attributing the concepts of human language to an ahistorical, transcendental source, Plato laid the groundwork for the first universal cultural discourse, the first theoretical anthropology. PC, on the contrary, in an era disabused of this ahistorical transcendence, considers itself obliged to sacrifice the universality of its discourse to the originary aim of deferring the resentment it expresses. But how can the peace be kept without a universal dialogue in which all may participate with the common aim of self-knowledge?

The problems of grammatical gender can be muddled through, along with those of the imagery of everyday discourse. Despite the polemical rhetoric that accompanies these adjustments, they contribute to the long-term pacification of the cultural sphere. After the divisiveness of the sacred, that of the esthetic too is now, at least in principle, laid to rest. The imagery consumed by a cosmopolitan society is henceforth to be produced by its constituent minorities, not by the society as a whole. The center is not empty but filled with figures of peripherality. This is an equilibrium state of esthetic culture, henceforth no doubt its permanent state.

*

Our language will never cease revealing to its postmodern demystifiers its dependence on hegemonic figures. In what metalanguage then can we as members of a single species discuss this revelation? In the very same language—we have no choice—but understood as the witness to our common origin. As the romantics and their disciples the existentialists liked to remind us, we are all late with respect to the origin, speaking a language already constituted before our arrival and whose implicit figurality excludes us. But the inherent reciprocity of language dissolves our lateness and integrates us into the community.

When all are included in the dialogue, the problems of hegemonic priority, of domination and victimhood, will have been reduced to *querelles de mots*. But by then the conversation will have moved on to new resentments, new real and imaginary exclusions. To perpetuate this conversation is the end of culture, the end of history. It is also the end of originary thinking.

Reference Matter

Notes

Chapter 1

1. The principal sources for the originary scene are *La violence et le sacré* (Paris: Grasset, 1973); in English, *Violence and the Sacred* (Baltimore: Johns Hopkins University Press, 1977); and *Des choses cachées depuis la fondation du monde* (Paris: Grasset, 1978); in English, *Things Hidden Since the Foundation of the World* (Stanford, Calif.: Stanford University Press, 1987).

2. My previous works on generative anthropology, which will be referred to throughout, are *The Origin of Language* (Berkeley: University of California Press, 1981); *The End of Culture* (Berkeley: University of California Press, 1985); *Science and Faith* (Savage, Md.: Rowman & Littlefield, 1990); and *Originary Thinking* (Stanford, Calif.: Stanford University Press, 1993).

3. *Mensonge romantique et vérité romanesque* (Paris: Grasset, 1961); in English, *Deceit, Desire, and the Novel* (Baltimore: Johns Hopkins University Press, 1965).

Chapter 2

1. The complete definition, given in his letter to Lady Welby of December 23, 1908, is as follows: "I define a Sign as anything which is so determined by something else, called its Object, and so determines an effect upon a person, which effect I call its Interpretant, that the latter [person] is thereby mediately determined by the former [object]. My insertion of 'upon a person' is a sop to Cerberus, because I despair of making my own broader conception under-

204 · *Notes to Pages 5–29*

stood." See Charles S. Peirce, *Values in a Universe of Chance* (Garden City, N.Y.: Doubleday Anchor Books, 1958), p. 404.

2. This suggests an originary analysis of Roman Jakobson's familiar metonymy-metaphor dichotomy as homologous to the opposition between the horizontal and vertical components of the original mimetic paradox.

3. Freud's "originary hypothesis" will be discussed in greater detail in Chapter 9.

4. To this mimetic predisposition corresponds the cognitive evolution toward the formation of prelinguistic "concepts" referred to by Derek Bickerton and others as the necessary preliminary to human language. See Bickerton's *Roots of Language* (Ann Arbor, Mich.: Karoma Publishers, 1981) and his later synthesis, *Language and Species* (Chicago: University of Chicago Press, 1990), which is even less concerned than the earlier work to hypothesize an originary scene of language. Imitation is "always already" protolinguistic, not merely in the abstract sense that *après coup* we can recognize an unthematized version of concentration around the center, but in the very concrete sense that neurons are becoming devoted to differentiating among categories of objects as a result of this concentration. This having been said, because Bickerton's conception of early linguistic evolution, although a considerable advance over purely linguistically oriented theories, does not recognize the centrality of mimesis, it fails to take issue with what is after all the fundamental question of the origin of language: the crossing of what Bickerton calls the "Rubicon" of interactive speech.

5. See my "The Unique Source of Religion and Morality," *Anthropoetics* 1, no. 1 (June 1995; URL: http://www.humnet.ucla.edu/humnet/anthropoetics/), and *Contagion* 3 (Spring 1996): 51–65.

6. The game of "Simon Says" is a practical demonstration that in matters of simple mimesis, language only gets in the way. The ironic point of the game is the difficulty of listening for the words when it is so natural "simply" to repeat the gesture.

7. The slippage from anthropological to positive thought is notable in the following passage: "*La trace, archi-phénomène de la 'mémoire,' qu'il faut penser avant l'opposition entre nature et culture, animalité et humanité,* etc. . . . Archi-écriture, première possibilité de la parole, puis de la 'graphie' au sens étroit, lieu natal de l''usurpation' dénoncée depuis Platon jusqu'à Saussure, *cette trace est l'ouverture de la première extériorité en général, l'énigmatique rapport du vivant à son autre* et d'un dedans à un dehors: l'espacement" [*The trace, archi-phenomenon of "memory," that must be thought before the opposition between nature and culture, animality and humanity,* etc. . . . Archi-écriture, first possibility of speech, then of the "graph" in the narrow sense of the term, birthplace of the "usurpation" denounced from Plato to Saussure, *this trace is the opening*

of the first exteriority in general, the enigmatic relationship of the living to its other and of an inside to an outside: spacing]. De la grammatologie (Paris: Editions de Minuit, 1968), p. 103; translation and emphasis mine. In this passage as elsewhere, Derrida is not really tempted by positivism; he simply has no means within his metaphysical vocabulary to describe the emergence of the human (the "trace") as an *event.*

8. This nondistinction is characteristic of the formal signs of language, the "types" of which our utterances are the "tokens." It is their signifying intention that distinguishes the formal equivalence classes of language from the empirical classes of animal signals.

9. Girard distinguishes these terms in *Mensonge romantique* by the coexistence or noncoexistence of the mediator in the universe of the subject. Don Quixote does not live in the same universe as Amadis, whom he is therefore able to emulate openly; in contrast, Dostoevsky's "eternal husband" does not realize that his desire for his wife is mediated by that of the lovers he in effect procures for her, who are in turn secretly influenced by his own desire.

10. See *Originary Thinking*, chap. 7 ("Originary Esthetics").

Chapter 3

1. The formulation of Russell's theory is itself paradoxical, as Alexandre Koyré points out in *Epiménide le menteur* (Paris: Herrmann, 1947). Koyré refutes Russell's theory of types by showing through the transfinite technique of "triangulation" that the statement of the theory itself can be of no possible type.

2. The term "pragmatic paradox" was given currency by Watzlawick and Beavan's *The Pragmatics of Human Communication* (New York: Norton, 1967); like "double bind," it has its origin in the thought of Gregory Bateson. See the latter's *Steps to an Ecology of Mind* (New York: Ballantine Books, 1972), especially pp. 271–78.

3. Let us recall our definition of esthetic experience from *Originary Thinking*: the oscillation between the contemplation of the referent as formally designated by the sign (the movement from sign to referent) and the imaginary contemplation of the referent alone as content. To this worldly content, in turn, significance, the effect of the mediating obstacle between subject and object, is restored by the return to the sign.

4. The ostensive → imperative → declarative progression is discussed at length in *The Origin of Language*; see also *Originary Thinking*, chap. 4 ("A Generative Taxonomy of Speech-Acts").

5. This incompatibility holds even for a system that includes a formalized temporal dimension; the term "oscillation" as used here is not a wave func-

tion defined over time, but an indeterminate movement between two poles within which no points in time can be isolated. It is impossible to define the status of the esthetic imagination at a given time t_0 as opposed to t_1.

6. Here we reach one of the frontiers between the anthropological and the "natural" sciences. No doubt mathematics is a product of human thought that reflects the needs and interests of the creatures who invented/discovered language in a context of potential mimetic conflict. But, in contrast to the cultural forms whose structure can be illuminated by the originary hypothesis, the thematization of the scene and what derives from it can tell us only one thing about mathematics: its incompleteness. Gödel's proof, which makes arithmetic into a self-representation *malgré elle*, demonstrates that mathematical truth cannot be fully formalized; this is as close as mathematics can come to being formulated as a system of signs. But this proof does not involve paradox, which is only inevitable in sign-systems that refer, like human language, to a world that they are not.

7. There is a clear homology between these paradoxes. Just as the barber cannot shave himself, the sentence cannot affirm its own falsity. The difference is that, in the case of the barber, the paradoxicality of shaving himself is the result of a rule enunciated by the sentence itself—there being nothing inherently paradoxical in shaving oneself—whereas in the other it is intrinsic to the declarative sentence—which cannot be true and false at the same time.

8. An analogous extension procedure may be applied to the Barber paradox: instead of the man who shaves every man who doesn't shave himself, we may seek, for example, the wife of the man who cuts every woman's hair whose husband doesn't cut her hair.

9. For a mathematical discussion, see William Feller, *An Introduction to Probability Theory and Its Applications* (New York: John Wiley and Sons, 1950), pp. 199–201. Despite the player's infinite expectation per game, the author shows that a "fair" price per session, in the sense that the ratio of expected gain to entrance fees tends to 1, is $\log_2 n$, where n is the number of games. Thus a player intending to play 8 games should pay $3 per game, for a total of $24. This analysis eliminates the paradox from a mathematical standpoint at the price of complicating the theoretical model by adding the concept of variance to the simple one of expectation. (It should also be remarked that it is not typical, or practical, for gambling establishments to inquire as to how many games will be played before setting their price.) But even were this solution unknown, the paradox would remain pragmatic, not mathematical. There are no mathematical paradoxes because mathematical elements are not representations but pure *representata*; that is the most fundamental definition of mathematics.

10. Leaving time aside, if the bank has $1 million, the payoff series chokes

off after about 21 terms (10^{20} is just over 1 million), and so the game is worth about \$21—which means that a series of 5 heads, paying \$32, would already provide the player with a profit.

11. It is nevertheless the case that, in a simple mathematical model using expectation only, the paradoxical effect can only be removed by reducing the coin-flipping time to an infinitesimal. Which is to say that at the level of mathematical theory that obtained when the "Petersburg paradox" was proposed, the game poses a pragmatic paradox that holds under any conceivable worldly conditions.

Chapter 4

1. This term was originally applied to the experience of revelation. See *Science and Faith*, chap. 3.

2. This is the case for all proper names; as soon as we know what they designate, they begin to designate it generically. When I know Achilles, I can call someone else "an Achilles." The historical is always in the process of becoming conceptual; or seen from the other side, the conceptual is eternally in the process of shedding its historicity.

3. This process is discussed in more detail in *The Origin of Language* with no specific reference to truth and falsity.

4. One recalls especially the heavy-handed irony of *Limited inc.* (Baltimore: Johns Hopkins University Press, 1977), Derrida's response to John Searle's "Reiterating the Differences: A Reply to Derrida," in *Glyph* no. 1 (1977). Searle's article responds to Derrida's critique of Austin's conception of the "speech-act" in the 1971 article "Signature Evénement Contexte," an English version of which was published in the same issue of *Glyph*.

5. This has been increasingly evident since *Le bouc émissaire* (Paris: Grasset, 1982); in his most recent book, *Quand ces choses commenceront* (Paris: Arléa, 1994), Girard insists on the dependency of his theory of desire on the Christian revelation.

6. This is, of course, a simplification, since ostensive or "deictic" elements are not absent from declarative language. It is remarkable how large a proportion of the ground-breaking insights in theoretical linguistics, from Jakobson's discussion of "shifters" to Benveniste's dichotomy between *discours* and *histoire*—not to speak of the theory of speech-acts that grew out of Austin's "performatives"—make reference to this still insufficiently theorized ostensive element.

7. We need not distinguish at this point between untruths and lies. The possibility of lying is inherent in the thematization of (un)truth, since all use of language is intentional, and known to be intentional. It is because of the

thematic intentionality of language that only a sophisticated mind can distinguish between believing your predication to be false and accusing you of lying.

8. The culturally late phenomenon of fiction proper makes use of this separation between meaning and truth to construct an imaginary world. But fiction too has its truth functions, which we learn from the literary text rather than know in advance; if I say "Hamlet is the son of Claudius," I am making a statement just as false as if I say "Franklin Roosevelt was the son of Theodore Roosevelt."

Chapter 5

1. Pierre Fontanier, *Figures du discours* (Paris: Flammarion, 1968 [1827]), pp. 145–46.

2. The questioning of the absolute difference that constitutes the linguistic sign might be called "originary deconstruction." The binary oppositions such as speech/writing, male/female, etc., on which deconstruction typically operates are metaphysical derivatives of the originary dichotomy between the ostensive sign and its object. By taking this into account theoretically, we effectively merge deconstruction into generative anthropology.

3. But one could indeed say "[Oh no! Tell me] it's not raining!" in a tone of incredulity; or even in a deadpan tone: "It's not raining [again]." The interactive nature of language makes it impossible to define the limits of the ironic once and for all. My objection to the straightforward "It's not raining!" as an example of irony is rather that its mechanical negation of "It's raining" fails to reveal the wish that has been denied by the rain.

4. "You know him, reader, this delicate monster / Hypocritical reader, my fellow, my brother!" These are the last lines of "Au lecteur," the liminal poem of Baudelaire's *Les fleurs du mal.*

Chapter 6

1. The reader will recall that in Chapter 4 and previously in *Originary Thinking*, I defined metaphysics as the way of thinking founded on the principle that the declarative sentence—the "proposition"—is the fundamental linguistic form.

2. Our intuitive comprehension of this term is the simplest indication of the persistence of our attachment to the originary scene. We could not conceive the existence of God, even in order to deny it, without basing our conception on an experience of the sacred, an experience of which the name-of-God is the crystallization. (For further elaboration of this idea, see *Science and Faith*, and, particularly, *Originary Thinking*, chap. 2, "The Anthropological

Idea of God.") In contrast, the construction of a concept of God that needs no name is the task of metaphysics.

3. As the original target of deconstruction, the phenomenological notion of the "self-presence" of speech refers to the speaker's presumed relation to his utterance rather than to its specificity; for all the notion of "self-presence" tells us, he could be engaged in glossolalia. Only the context of philosophical discourse suggests that the referent of the utterance is situated on the "other scene" of the declarative. Where is self-presence in, for example, an imperative utterance that specifically designates what is experienced-as-absent? Only in the fact that (assuming I am not deaf) I hear myself speak, that is, my heard speech supplies me with feedback while I speak, not in anything relating to the specifics of human language. Only in the case of the metaphysical proposition, entirely contained within the imaginary scene of representation, can the *content* of the utterance be characterized either as absolutely present (to itself) or as absolutely absent (to the empirical world).

4. See *Science and Faith*, chap. 3.

5. As I have pointed out elsewhere (see "The Unique Source of Religion and Morality," *Anthropoetics* 1, no. 1 [June 1995; URL: http://www.humnet.ucla.edu/humnet/anthropoetics/] and *Contagion* 3 [Spring 1996]: 51–65), in the original revelation in Exodus 3.14, God already distinguishes between the full sentence by which he names himself to Moses and his instruction to tell the people "I am/will be (*ehyeh*) has sent me to you."

6. See Henry Teloh, *The Development of Plato's Metaphysics* (University Park: Pennsylvania State University Press, 1981): "The date of composition of the *Cratylus*, unfortunately, is in dispute. I do believe, however, that separate Forms appear at the end of the dialogue (439c–440d), but in a very rough and rudimentary manner, which indicates that Plato has just started to think about them" (p. 83). The fact that Teloh's arguments are taken from the metaphysical tradition only adds strength to my own very different ones.

On another point, it can hardly be a simple coincidence that the name of Euthyphro reappears in the *Cratylus* (and nowhere else in Plato), in an ironically marked fashion: "That [this onomastic 'science'] fell upon me, the one whom I consider responsible for this, Hermogenes, is above all Euthyphro" (396d). Is this not a sign of the progression of Plato's reflection on the *eidos*? It is Euthyphro who is said to have inspired Socrates with his divine etymologies; we shall see that it is precisely these which lead the Platonic Socrates from Heraclitean Cratylism to the notion of the Idea-signified.

7. In contrast, Plato is familiar enough with the plurality of "barbarian" languages to recognize the instability of the *signifier*; it is precisely for this reason that he denies the usefulness of the empirical search for "primitive" names.

8. In contrast, Parmenides, the thinker of the One, of absolute permanence,

is not a semiotician. The dialogue that bears his name and which is faithful to what we know of his thought shows that the One, far from being, like the Platonic Idea-signified, a fixed point between the contrary mobilities of signifier and referent, is as mobile as the world of Heraclitus. The word "One" designates an absolute totality that is unnameable—"One" is not a name but an attribute—and indeed, like the "set of all sets," properly inconceivable. As such it stands at the moment just prior to the emergence of metaphysics at which the sacred-ostensive component of Being has not yet been replaced by the abstract presence of the Ideas.

9. But Lacan himself has no illusions concerning the freedom of the imaginary, which he describes on the contrary as enslaved to the desire of the Other.

10. After the famous fragment 60, "War is the father, the king of all things," the last Heraclitean passage Benoist quotes is: "Denizens of the night: magicians, bacchants, lenai, myths; one is initiated sacrilegiously into the mysteries practiced among men." He then concludes, "Voici venir encore ces ombres et ces masques, ces figures de mauvais augure que l'on cache" [Here they come again, those shadows and those masks, those hidden figures of evil portent] (p. 181). Benoist would have done well to read Girard's remark on Heraclitus in *La violence et le sacré*, "N'est-ce pas la genèse même du mythe, l'engendrement des dieux et de la différence sous l'action de la violence . . . qui se trouve résumé dans le fragment 60?" [Is it not the very genesis of myth, the creation of the gods and of difference through the action of violence . . . that is summed up in fragment 60?] (p. 129).

11. See especially Bataille's *La part maudite* (Paris: Editions de Minuit, 1967).

Chapter 7

1. See Husserl's *Logische Untersuchungen* (1913), vol. 1, chap. 3, where he attacks Mill's conception of logic as a branch of psychology.

2. This is the notion that our theories of cosmogenesis should privilege the fact that such theories could only be invented in a universe that produces theory-generating creatures like ourselves. The result of this "profound" idea is to use the latest cosmogenic equations to conjure up myriads of nonanthropic universes among which ours is a "miraculous" exception. The theoretical hubris of this sort of reasoning is all too typical of originary thinking in a postreligious age. Instead of concentrating their mental energy on the genesis of the human on this planet, which alone is a fitting subject for self-inclusive, or, in other words, paradoxical, reasoning of this sort, our cosmic philosophers expend their ingenuity in finding sophisticated disguises for naive assurances of our "universal" importance.

3. See Chapter 12 for further discussion of this subject.

Chapter 8

1. See Chapter 10 for a fuller discussion of the place of the sparagmos in the originary scene.

2. On this point, Derek Bickerton's views, as expressed in *Roots of Language* (Ann Arbor, Mich.: Karoma Publishers, 1981), seem fully justified: cognitive distinctions among categories of beings must preexist their manifestation in speech. But as Bickerton is very much aware, these distinctions can be elicited from chimpanzees; the real mystery of the origin of human speech is what function it came into being to serve ("What selective advantage did the species gain?" [p. 225]), and on this score, Bickerton's hypotheses offer no improvement over common sense.

3. This resistance to appropriation is an absolute resistance that manifests itself as inherent in the sacred object, as opposed to a relative, situational resistance that the members of the group could either attempt to overcome or accept as a practical deterrent to action. The resistance of the sacred object retains our attention without permitting the generation of a praxis by means of which to overcome it.

4. We should assume the image of the object that enters into this new form of mental association to share the common tendency of perceptual traces to differentiate themselves at the generic level, broadly defined. Psycholinguistic research has established that all people regardless of language share the same basic level of perceptual selectivity; they see "dog" before either "Pomeranian" or "mammal."

5. In particular reference to music, see my "The Beginning and End of Esthetic Form," *Perspectives of New Music* 29, no. 2 (Summer 1991): 8–21.

6. The oscillatory tension characteristically provoked by esthetic form is an intentional version of the same process. But unlike the signified, which exists wholly in the imagination and has no "objective correlative," the esthetic object occupies the communal presence that precedes, and prepares, the sparagmos.

7. The phonetic system too is subject to historical change through the selection of more attractive or prestigious "supplementary" elements. The classic discussion is that of William Labov, *Sociolinguistic Patterns* (Philadelphia: University of Pennsylvania Press, 1972).

Chapter 9

1. I will not rehearse here my reasons for assuming the originary event to be an essentially masculine operation. In today's gender-conscious environment, it might be taken as a deliberate provocation to draw even so obvious a parallel as that between ithyphallicity and aggression. (I can mention as sug-

gestive evidence the ithyphallic hunter in a famous mural from Lascaux. Nowhere has anyone seen a cave drawing of a female hunter, let alone a sexually excited one.) But this parallel is of marginal importance to my argument. The erotic as conceived here does not depend on any specific genital configuration.

2. This is the valid point of Deleuze and Guattari's "anti-oedipal" theory of desire, developed in their *L'anti-Oedipe* (Paris: Editions de Minuit, 1972).

3. The disreputability of pornography strictly as an esthetic genre results from the incompleteness of the oscillatory relationship established between sign and imagined referent: at a certain point, the spectator of pornography does not return from the imagined reality to the sign, since his desire seeks real satisfaction. This distinguishes the pornographic from the erotic, in which this mediation is the operative force. This is not to deny the prevalence of erotic themes (seduction, "narcissism," etc.) in pornography. A given erotic-pornographic image or text may be situated on the scale established by this polarity.

4. In the "esthetic history" elaborated in *Originary Thinking*, the neoclassical period extends from the beginning of scenic self-consciousness in nascent Christianity down to the radical self-centering of the romantic era. Chapter 9 of that work discusses the neoclassical esthetic.

5. The theoretical source of this *mensonge romantique* is the classical Aristotelian doctrine of mimesis, which the romantics (with some exceptions) believed they could apply unchanged to the expression of their new, personal content. The first-generation romantics failed to realize that their free lunch was in reality a sacrificial meal. Alfred de Musset's famously lurid image in "La nuit de Mai" of the poet as a pelican feeding its own flesh to its children reflects the naive beginnings of this realization.

6. As Flaubert puts it, "il fallait qu'elle pût retirer des choses une sorte de profit personnel; et elle rejetait comme inutile tout ce qui ne contribuait pas à la consommation immédiate de son coeur" [She had to be able to derive from things a kind of personal profit; and she rejected as useless everything that failed to contribute to her heart's immediate consumption] (I, 6).

7. The "narcissistic" figure combines the roles of the subject-other and the object of desire; she seduces the other by the example of her apparent self-idolatry. Although the specifics of sexual identity are secondary to the structure of "narcissistic" seduction, for both cultural and biological reasons, this has typically been the woman's role. For Girard's discussion of "narcissism" from the perspective of the mimetic theory of desire, see *Des choses cachées*, pp. 391–405.

8. The reader is referred to the discussion in the second part of this volume, particularly Chapter 13.

9. *Totem and Taboo*, trans. James Strachey (New York: Norton, 1952); the original, *Totem und Tabu*, was published in 1920 with the almost caricaturally self-limiting subtitle *einige Übereinstimmungen im Seelenleben der Wilder und der Neurotiker* ("some correspondences between the mental lives of savages and neurotics"). Freud's "originary scene" is built up to throughout the book; it occurs in chap. 4, sec. 5 (on page 176 of a 200-page text): "One day the brothers who had been driven out came together, killed and devoured their father and so made an end of the patriarchal horde. . . . The violent primal father had doubtless been the feared and envied model of each one of the company of brothers: and in the act of devouring him they accomplished their identification with him, and each one of them acquired a portion of his strength. . . . They hated their father . . . but they loved and admired him too. After they had got rid of him, had satisfied their hatred and had put into effect their wish to identify themselves with him, the affection which had all this time been pushed under was bound to make itself felt. It did so in the form of remorse. A sense of guilt made its appearance, which in this instance coincided with the remorse felt by the whole group. The dead father became stronger than the living one had been" (pp. 176–78).

10. The classical example in the Girardian corpus is the Tikopia myth discussed in *Des choses cachées*, pp. 115–22. After providing the Tikopia with the basics of their culture, the hero Tikarau is said to climb to the top of a cliff and fly off into the air. To lend credence to this myth is to experience a quite literal "suspension of disbelief."

Chapter 10

1. See *Originary Thinking*, chap. 3.

2. The reader is referred to the discussion in the following chapter.

3. Smith's camel scene is found in his *Lectures on the Religion of the Semites* (s.l.: Ktav Publishing House, 1969 [1889]): "The camel chosen as victim is bound upon a rude altar of stones piled together, . . . The leader of the band . . . inflicts the first wound, . . . and in all haste drinks of the blood that gushes forth. Forthwith the whole company fall on the victim with their swords, hacking off pieces of the quivering flesh and devouring them raw with such wild haste, that in the short interval between the rise of the day star . . . and the disappearance of its rays before the rising sun, the entire camel, body and bones, skin, blood and entrails, is wholly devoured" (p. 338).

4. The reader is referred to *Science and Faith*, chap. 3, as well as to the discussion in the following chapter of the present volume.

5. The object of resentment is the heir of the originary central figure. But as the exchange system evolves, the directness of this connection is lost. The

Western era of revolutions ended when their potential targets ceased to occupy the ritual center by "divine right." Many changes of government have occurred in Europe since 1917, but the overthrow of the Tsar is the last event generally honored with the term "revolution."

6. See *Originary Thinking*, chap. 7.

7. For Girard, the sparagmos is not only the origin of evil, but of otherness; the victim is a member of the community arbitrarily chosen for exclusion from it. Since Girard's world lacks the sign, it must generate the new, "vertical" difference of signification within the real world as the becoming-ab-
solute of the relative otherness of the originary victim. But once we locate the
vertical otherness of signification in the sign where it belongs, we have no need
to generate it from within a wholly undifferentiated world. The otherness of
eater and eaten is part of life from the beginning. The truly minimal source
of the otherness of the sign is not prehuman dedifferentiation but mimetic
desire operating on the most fundamental of differences.

8. This is also the source of its eroticism, as discussed in Chapter 9. We
should recall in this context that the root meaning of "person" is "mask."

9. For the latter, see Chapter 6. The "third man" paradox is an argument
by regression: if A is a man, and B is the Idea of a man, then their resemblance
requires they have something in common that neither of them is; call it C (for
example, "human appearance"). But then A, B, and C all have something in
common that can only be named by D, and so on ad infinitum. Aristotle refers
to this argument by name in *Metaphysics* XIII, 4 (1079a) as a *reductio ad absurdum* of Plato's doctrine of Ideas; it is used (but not named) by Parmenides
in Plato's eponymous dialogue (132a–133a)—the one dialogue where Socrates
listens respectfully and does not attempt to refute his interlocutor.

10. This sharpens the definition of the moral-ethical dichotomy discussed
in chap. 3 of *Originary Thinking*; the contrast is not merely between the (moral)
exchange of signs and the (ethical) exchange of things, but between the moral
concern with reciprocal communication and the ethical abandonment of this
concern in the interest of preserving the community as a practical, worldly
entity.

Chapter 11

1. The reader is referred to the detailed analysis of this scene in *Science and
Faith*, chap. 3.

2. See *Science and Faith*, chap. 4.

3. See Buber's *Moses* (Oxford: East and West Library, 1946), and the discussion in *Science and Faith*, chap. 3.

4. In his account in Galatians 1.11–17, Paul emphasizes both the special cir-

cumstances of his conversion—"For I did not receive [the gospel] from man, nor was I taught it, but it came through a revelation of Jesus Christ" (1.12)— and his mission to the Gentiles—"But when [God] . . . was pleased to reveal his Son to me, in order that I might preach him among the Gentiles, I did not confer with flesh and blood, nor did I go up to Jerusalem to those who were apostles before me" (1.15–17; Revised Standard Version).

5. *Moses and Monotheism* (New York: Alfred A. Knopf, 1939); originally published as *Der Mann Moses und die Monotheistische Religion* (Amsterdam: A. de Lange, 1939).

6. The rise of Islam is the most visible evidence that the Pauline synthesis is insufficient to make Christianity a truly universal religion; the historical outsiders of Mediterranean civilization reject the central God-man for a human-mediated scriptural reiteration of Hebrew monotheism. But Islam is not, as is Judaism, a religion of deferral; the unfigured God mediated through the Prophet's word is more a sacrificer than a deliverer. Islam takes from the Mosaic revelation rather the promise of future conquest than the deferral of present satisfaction. Its rejection of the divine image functions less to thematize renunciation than to concentrate figural attention on the demonized enemy. This definitive separation of the figure of sparagmos from the unfigured divinity inverts the movement toward religious humanization effected by the Christian Trinity.

7. For example, Romans 6.3–4: "Do you not know that all of us who have been baptized into Christ Jesus were baptized into his death? We were buried therefore with him by baptism into death, so that as Christ was raised from the dead by the glory of the Father, we too might walk in newness of life"; Galatians 2.20: "I have been crucified with Christ; it is no longer I who live, but Christ who lives in me."

8. See Gershon Scholem, *The Messianic Idea in Judaism* (New York: Schocken Books, 1971), and Kafka's formulation: "Der Messias wird erst kommen, wenn er nicht mehr nötig sein wird, er wird erst einen Tag nach seiner Ankunft kommen, er wird nicht am letzten Tag kommen, sondern am allerletzten" [The Messiah will first come when he is no longer needed, he will first come on the day after his arrival, he will not come on the last day, but on the last of all]. *Hochzeitsvorbereitungen auf dem Lande* (Frankfurt a.M., 1966), p. 90, quoted in John Milfull, "The Messiah and the Direction of History: Walter Benjamin, Isaac Bashevis Singer and Franz Kafka," in *Festschrift for E. W. Herd* (Dunedin, N.Z.: Department of German, University of Otago, 1980), p. 187.

9. *Hiroshima mon amour* (1959). The film sets up a provocative contrast between a modernized, consumerist Hiroshima and a monumentally lifeless Europe epitomized by the somber and hauntingly named French city of Never(s).

10. The futility of this operation is most remarkable in the countries where the final solution was most effective; today in Poland, for example, there flourishes the phenomenon known as "antisemitism without Jews."

11. One should contrast the nineteenth-century vision of social victimage centered around the sentimental figure of *le pauvre*. But this figure was drawn from Christian iconography; what it provoked was pity, not guilt for discrimination. Thus it was compatible and even complementary with the contrasting discriminatory figure of the "exploiting" Jew.

12. See especially the section "Science et Apocalypse" in *Des choses cachées* (pp. 276–85), where Girard develops the idea that the Bomb imposes on us the "apocalyptic" necessity of accepting once and for all the Gospel critique of the sparagmatic-sacrificial.

In a more recent, more discursive work, *Quand ces choses commenceront* (Paris: Arléa, 1994), Girard insists rather on the openness and undecidability of history in the context of the always present, always deferred truth of Christian revelation; his refutation of Francis Fukuyama's idea of "the end of history" leads him, curiously enough, to the Holocaust: "L'Holocauste est bien un échec terrible . . . mais, espérons-le, un échec temporaire qui ne signifie pas que l'Histoire tout entière ne vaille plus la peine d'être vécue" [The Holocaust is certainly a terrible failure . . . but, let us hope, a temporary one that does not signify that History as a whole is not worth living] (p. 125).

13. See Chapter 13.

Chapter 12

1. See the discussion of the birth of hierarchical society in *The End of Culture*, chap. 6.

2. In geometric terms, a triangle has no center; but the common object of the subject and the other-mediator is clearly the equivalent of the center of the circle. The triangular model makes it clearer, in fact, that the victim's "exile" is not a movement from one closer peripheral position to one farther away, but expulsion from the very center.

3. Similarly, Jesus's premodern emulators, among the most illustrious of whom are Hamlet and Rousseau (see my "Littérature et ressentiment," in *Poésie* 29 [1984]: 115–25), are always quick to centralize their marginality, to oppose their authentic uniqueness to the false uniqueness of the conventional ritual center.

4. See my "The Victim as Subject: The Esthetico-Ethical System of Rousseau's *Rêveries*," in *Studies in Romanticism* 21, no. 1 (Spring 1982): 3–32, as well as Chapter 5 of the present volume.

5. Exemplary of this is a characteristic inversion of the gradient of defer-

ral that attributes to language a supplement of violence over the worldly act it replaces. See Tobin Siebers, *The Ethics of Criticism* (Ithaca, N.Y.: Cornell University Press, 1988), chap. 4 ("Ethics in the Age of Rousseau: From Lévi-Strauss to Derrida").

6. See Paul R. Gross and Norman Levitt, "The Natural Sciences: Trouble Ahead? Yes," in *Academic Questions 7*, no. 2 (Spring 1994): 13–29. The authors cite a number of relevant writings.

7. Whence the homosexual movement's insistence on finding a hereditary basis for "sexual orientation," although in a pre-Holocaust context this is precisely what would have constituted—and did, in Nazi Germany—grounds for its members' victimization. We may recall that Jewishness, not strictly speaking an ascriptive trait either, was defined in racial terms by Nazi law.

8. See in particular de Maistre's *Les soirées de Saint-Pétersbourg* (Paris: La Colombe, 1960), Neuvième Entretien, and my "Maistre and Chateaubriand: Counter-Revolution and Anthropology," in *Studies in Romanticism* 28, no. 4 (Winter 1989): 559–76.

Chapter 13

1. "White guilt" is a felicitous expression because it expresses not merely guilt for belonging to the (white) majority, but guilt for whiteness in the more abstract sense in which the French word *blanc* also means "blank." The white is the unmarked, only visible in contrast to the marked "other." "White guilt" is the guilt of those who lack the victimary trace of these others, those who have by default profited from the sacrificial past of civilization that culminated in the Holocaust.

The first historical manifestation of this essentially post-Rousseauian phenomenon of which I am aware may be found in Chateaubriand's *Essai sur les révolutions*. Describing an encounter with an Indian family near the Niagara Falls, the author singles out a young warrior for detailed description: "Le jeune homme seul gardait un silence obstiné; il tenait constamment les yeux attachés sur moi. . . . *Combien je lui savais gré de ne pas m'aimer!* Il me semblait lire dans son coeur l'histoire de tous les maux dont les Européens ont accablé sa patrie" [The young man alone maintained an obstinate silence; he kept his eyes constantly fixed on me. . . . *How grateful was I to him for not liking me!* I seemed to read in his heart the history of all the ills with which the Europeans have burdened his fatherland] (I, 624; emphasis mine). I discuss this text in my article "Maistre and Chateaubriand: Counter-Revolution and Anthropology" (see above, n. 8 to Chapter 12).

2. See Kojève's *Esquisse d'une phénoménologie du droit* (Paris: Gallimard, 1981).

3. See *The End of Culture*, chap. 10.

4. In popular figures of unusual appeal, marginality is not simply minority identity but the implicit or explicit transgression of boundaries; whence the success of the implicit black-white boundary-crosser Elvis Presley and, at a later stage, the explicit black-white man-boy-girl Michael Jackson.

5. Psalm 118.22–23, quoted in Matthew 21.42.

6. In *Quand ces choses commenceront*, Girard takes a critical view of contemporary victimary thought as the permeation of society by the Christian revelation, despite the failure or refusal of its practitioners to acknowledge this filiation. He defines PC as "la religion de la victime détachée de toute transcendance . . . qui vient du christianisme mais qui le subvertit plus insidieusement encore que l'opposition ouverte" [the religion of the victim detached from all transcendence . . . which comes from Christianity but which undermines it even more insidiously than open opposition] (p. 65).

Index

In this index "f" after a number indicates a separate reference on the next page, and "ff" indicates separate references on the next two pages. A continuous discussion over two or more pages is indicated by a span of page numbers. *Passim* is used for a cluster of references in close but not consecutive sequence.

Messianism, 154–55, 161, 215
Metaphysics, 7, 57–59, 75–91 *passim*, 124–25, 151, 153, 173–74, 179–80, 198
Methodology, 4
Mill, John Stuart, 106
Mimesis, 14, 16–36, 45, 93–94, 99–100, 212
Mimetic crisis, 15
Minimality, 6, 18ff, 135
Minority culture, 157–59, 165, 181, 184–87, 193–99
Moses, 81, 85, 152–53, 157, 175, 209
Music, 189–90
Musset, Alfred de, 212

Name-of-God, 53, 79f, 102–3
Narcissism, 118, 212
Nazism, 161–65, 187–88
Negation, 42–43
Nietzsche, Friedrich, 59, 150, 154, 176, 188f

Oedipus, 22, 44, 59, 72
Ontology, 94–95
Orestes, 84
Originary hypothesis, 5–6, 14, 17, 33, 131–39
Originary Thinking (Gans), 6, 24, 27, 81, 141, 205, 208, 212, 214
The Origin of Language (Gans), 5, 14, 40, 42, 67, 105, 131, 144, 207
Ostensive mode, 28, 51, 54–55, 60ff, 79–82, 85, 88, 90, 93, 97

Paradox, 4, 9, 13, 35f, 37–50, 54, 63, 101, 124, 127, 170, 205ff; pragmatic, 20, 38f, 41, 44; logical, 39, 41–45, 48
Parmenides, 209–10, 214
Passion, 73, 155, 158
Paul / Saul, 108, 155ff, 159, 164, 177–78, 214–15
Pavlov, Ivan, 20, 37
Peirce, Charles S., 13–14
Personhood, 103, 147

Plato, 44, 59, 75–91, 101, 136, 149, 179, 199, 209
Political correctness, 191, 194–99 *passim*, 218
Popular culture, 184–87, 188ff, 193f; vs. high culture, 117–19, 131–32, 136, 138–40, 189–90
Pornography, 113, 212
Postmodern(ism), 74, 117–20, 141, 162, 165–67, 184–90
Predication, 59–63

Realism, 115–17
Religion, 2–3, 83–85, 88, 101
Resentment, 67–68, 96, 144–45, 146f, 154, 166–77 *passim*, 189
Rhetoric, 34, 98, 168–83, 194
Right / Left opposition, 182
Ritual, 94, 145, 152
Romanticism, 69
Roots (television series), 193
Rousseau, Jean-Jacques, 69, 178
Russell, Bertrand, 37, 44

Sacrality, 40, 92–93, 109, 137, 140–41
Sartre, Jean-Paul, 94, 121
Saussure, Ferdinand de, 14, 30, 88, 107f, 110, 124, 136, 148
Scapegoating, 133–34, 174
Scene, originary, 5, 13, 24, 39, 79, 100–101, 106, 163
Science and Faith (Gans), 132, 207ff, 214
Searle, John, 207
Seduction, 118–20
Semiotics, 87
Sexuality, 112–13
Shakespeare, William, 175
Siebers, Tobin, 217
Sign, 13, 16, 23–24, 26–27, 30, 52f, 65, 87, 96, 99, 102–10 *passim*, 144, 203
Signification, 102–10, 136–37, 147ff
Smith, W. Robertson, 134, 213
Social contract, 168
Social sciences, 1–2